THE PLAY
BEHIND
THE PLAY

Hamlet and Quarto One

THE PLAY BEHIND THE PLAY

Hamlet and Quarto One

Maxwell E. Foster
edited by
Anne Shiras

FOSTER EXECUTORS
Pittsburgh, Pennsylvania

Davis and Warde, Inc.
Pittsburgh, PA
1991

This Book is for the Players

ABOUT THE AUTHOR

Maxwell E. Foster (1901-1983) was born in Manchester, Massachusetts; he graduated from Yale University with the class of 1923. He was a gifted actor; his mentor in drama at Yale, the actor-director Monty Woolley, thought he would make the stage his career. His co-workers on the *Yale Literary Magazine,* and the poets who published as he did in the *London Mercury,* saw him as a writer. Instead he followed the family tradition, took up the practice of law, and in due course became a partner in the Boston firm of Choate, Hall and Stewart. During the war and its aftermath he worked in Washington, first in the Office of Price Administration and later in the Bureau of Economic Warfare. Not long after he left Washington he retired, and so began to have time for the interests that had remained his avocations throughout—literature and the theatre.

The Shakespeare library he had collected led him to a study of the varying texts of *Hamlet.* He was aware that the 1603 First Quarto was considered by many to be a piracy, imperfectly printed, brief, and obviously deficient in the poetry that later versions made famous. But it was a play, and he read it as such, seeing the scenes develop and hearing the lines spoken. What he found led him to consider it further not only in relation to the sources known to have furnished the plot but also to the longer Second Quarto printed in 1604. He could not be sure the First Quarto was entirely the work of Shakespeare but he became convinced Shakespeare had had a hand in it, and had founded his concept of *Hamlet* upon it. In that case the play we know today is a revision, a rewriting that Foster felt vastly improved—but in some way also impaired—the original. Ambiguities that directors and actors must face in staging a production are more easily resolved, it seemed to him, if considered in the light of the shorter, less literary version. This book presents Quarto One as he saw it.

TABLE OF CONTENTS

INTRODUCTION

No matter how hard we endeavor to reconstruct a play written some three hundred and eighty years ago, with misprints frequent, and with hardly any stage directions other than entrances and exits and a few trumpets sounded and pieces fired, we necessarily grope and fumble. Particularly as for more than half that period of three hundred and eighty years, one of the essential texts was lost, so that many of the most distinguished critics (among whom are the lexicographer Samuel Johnson and the poet Samuel Coleridge) judged the play with relevant evidence missing.

Max Foster, 1983

The play that has posed problems for nearly four centuries is Shakespeare's *Hamlet.* And the essential text that was missing for more than half that period is the text now known as the First Quarto, written in the late 1500s and published in 1603. It is the first printed *Hamlet* to bear the name of Shakespeare on the title page. That page reads:

T H E
Tragicall Historie of
H A M L E T
Prince of Denmarke
by William Shake-speare.

As it hath been diverse times acted by his Highnesse servants in the Cittie of London: as also in the two Universities of Cambridge and Oxford, and else-where

At London printed for N.L. and John Trundell.
1603.

We do not know how the printer obtained the manuscript nor who bought the printed copies. The *Hamlet* it presents is short, full of errors, and devoid of much of the poetry so widely quoted today. There is no specific mention of it in contemporary records. It seems to have appeared only to disappear. Nothing was known about it until, two hundred and twenty years later, in 1823, a copy was found in a closet in Barton, England. Thirty-three years later another copy resurfaced when, in 1856, a student at Trinity College sold it to a Dublin bookseller for a shilling. The Barton copy is now in the Huntington Library in California, the Dublin copy in the British Museum. These are the only two copies known to be extant.[1]

Most practitioners of the theatre never see the text of Quarto One. They are perhaps aware of its existence because the editor of whatever Shakespeare edition they are using will have mentioned it in passing. These references are apt to be brief and rarely encourage the reader to pursue that Quarto further. The following are examples of judgments that have been passed:

> ...an imperfect, surreptitious and garbled version...in all probability shorthand notes taken by an incompetent stenographer during the performance of the play....[2]

> ...a bad copy of an abridged version...probably of a version cobbled up by some literary hack for provincial acting.[3]

---

[1]For an account of the discovery and subsequent history of each of these copies, see *A New Variorum Edition of Shakespeare,* ed. H. H. Furness, vol. 2 of *Hamlet,* p. 13.

[2]I. Gollancz, preface to *The Tragedy of Hamlet, Prince of Denmark,* vol. 5 of *The Works of William Shakespeare,* De Luxe ed., J. E. Burdick, ix-x.

[3]G. L. Kittredge, introduction to *The Tragedy of Hamlet Prince of Denmark,* x.

Quarto One is a very garbled version of Shakespeare's play and obviously was a piracy.[1]

Although "probably" and "obviously" are easily said, it must be admitted that there have been strong reasons for discounting the importance of Quarto One (Q1). Apparently hastily printed, its rapid descent into oblivion meant that early Shakespearean scholars had no knowledge of it when they wrote their studies of *Hamlet*. Its reappearance, more than two centuries later, came when the 19th-century idolatry of Shakespeare was rising to a pitch in England and Germany. Hamlet was becoming a hero the world over. This upstart version was obviously imperfect. It moved too fast and much of it sounded unlike the Shakespearean *Hamlet* we know. The logical inference was that Shakespeare had never sanctioned it.

In 1931, the Huntington Library published a facsimile of Q1 under the title *Shakespeare's Hamlet, The First Quarto, 1603*. At the time Max Foster acquired a copy of this facsimile, he had no predisposed theories about its authorship. What interested him was the contrast it presented to another Huntington facsimile published in 1938, *Shakespeare's Hamlet, The Second Quarto, 1604*. Here then were two versions that had originally been printed within a year of each other, 1603 and 1604. They had the same plot and basically the same cast of characters. Yet the first was, in comparison, the bare bones of a play, while the other (basically the *Hamlet* we have today) is one of the world's enduring masterpieces. Foster thought it would be interesting to trace the added imagery and philosophic thought which effected this transformation.

---

[1] G. B. Harrison, introduction to *The Harbinger Shakespeare: Hamlet Prince of Denmark*, xxiii.

The 1604 Quarto (Q2) is lengthy: 99 quarto pages as compared to 63 pages in Q1. Its title page reads:

THE
Tragicall Historie of
H A M L E T,
Prince of Denmarke.
By William Shakespeare.

Newly imprinted and enlarged to almost as much
againe as it was, according to the true and perfect
Coppie.
AT LONDON,
Printed by I.R. for N.L. and are to be sold at his
shoppe under Saint Dunstons Church in
Fleetstreet. 1604.

Although this Second Quarto abounds in errors, it is generally regarded as a "good Quarto," representing an authentic version, perhaps printed from the playhouse prompt-copy or from the author's manuscript. Another slightly different text was published nineteen years later and is also considered authentic. This is the *Hamlet* of the volume now known as the First Folio, brought out in 1623, seven years after Shakespeare's death, containing thirty-six of his plays. It was edited by Heminge and Condell, two surviving members of the King's Men, Shakespeare's troop. Although the *Hamlet* of the Folio is basically the same play as Q2, the Folio omits more than 200 lines which appear in Q2, but adds new passages amounting to some 60 lines. It is thought to represent the acting version. Most modern editions of *Hamlet* print everything considered authentic; that is, all of Q2 plus the added lines of the Folio.[1]

[1]The Second Quarto was probably printed toward the end of the year, for of the six known copies, three are dated 1604 and three, 1605. A Third Quarto was published in 1611 and it is possible that the Fourth (undated) also appeared before Shakespeare's death in 1616. These later Quartos contain a few variants in words and spelling, but do not significantly alter the text of the Second Quarto.

The First Folio was followed by three more folio editions during the seventeenth century, but again, their variants are limited to a few details of printing or wording.

Foster undertook a word-for-word study of the three texts: the First and Second Quartos and the Folio.[1] Besides this literary analysis he studied the plays as dramas, comparing them scene by scene. And he decided that when Quarto One was thus patiently examined, there were things to be said in its favor. "It moves fast," he noted, "it could use some filler. But this is no crude travesty of a play."

He found that the plot of Q1 moves in a straighter line than it does in the longer versions, and that the motivation behind the key scenes is clearer. The passage which begins with "To be, or not to be" and continues with the overheard encounter between Hamlet and Ofelia comes early (act II, scene ii). This passage serves both as exposition (alerting Hamlet to the fact that he is being watched) and as motivation (putting him on his guard against the interrogations that will follow immediately). In Q2, the planning which prepares for this passage occurs in the same place, but the passage itself is postponed to act III, scene i. By that time the action has changed direction. The Players have arrived, and Hamlet has gone on the offensive with a probe of his own. He is preparing the play-within-a-play as a trap for the King, but in Q2, because of the interpolation of the soliloquy and the overheard dialogue with Ophelia in this act, he must revert to his former tactics of parrying the probes of his adversaries. Many devotees of the play defend this Q2 sequence; they maintain that the overheard encounter (beginning with "To be, or not to be") is too important to come early in the play, and that its third-act placement in Q2 gives it the needed significance. It is true that this is a compelling passage, but there is also no denying that, in terms of the dramaturgy, it deflects the action from the line which the act was developing and to which it will revert when the passage is over. Foster was of the opinion that this deviation dilutes our interest in the impending play-within-a-play; and furthermore, that it raises doubts about

---

[1] The folio version which Foster studied was a facsimile printing of the First Folio prepared by H. Kokeritz and issued by the Yale University Press and the Oxford University Press in 1954.

Hamlet's constancy in moving toward his revenge. There are other commentators who agree. Below are excerpts of critiques by a 19th-century Shakespearean scholar, a 20th-century dramatic critic, and a 20th-century playwright, respectively.

JOSEPH HUNTER, 1845[1]

This soliloquy ["To be, or not to be"] is placed in Q1 at the beginning of what is now Act II. It stands there most appropriately....It prepares for all the succeeding action in which the natural and the artificial Hamlet are so wildly combined. Why there was a change in the arrangement, or by whom it was made, I can no more explain than I can account for many other things connected with the publication of these dramas. But that the play is greatly injured by the change I feel a confident conviction; for not only is this soliloquy wanting in the place most appropriate to it, but it is now found in a place not suitable to it.

KENNETH TYNAN, 1961[2]

With imperious intelligence Mr. Benthal has brought off a minor Shakespeare revolution. He has taken the scene order not from the Folio but from the first Quarto of 1603....The improvement in dramatic logic as well as sheer actability is enormous. Hamlet's progressive disillusionment with humanity ...is presented as an uninterrupted whole, leading up to the arrival of the players and the switch from inertia to action. ...Compare this logical sequence with the incoherent Folio text, wherein "the play's the thing" is immediately followed by "To be, or not to be," an inexplicable volte-face that halts the actor just when the movement of the play demands swiftly unfolding action....This ludicrous blockage, hitherto regarded as part of a grand incalculable design, has now been removed to its proper functional place.

[1]Quoted in *A New Variorum Edition of Shakespeare,* ed. H. H. Furness, vol. 1 of *Hamlet,* p. 206.

[2]Review of Michael Benthal's London production of *Hamlet* in Tynan's *Curtains,* pp. 185-187.

WILLIAM GIBSON, 1978[1]

Much of what remains enigmatic in Hamlet's character is born of a mishap with the text and a resultant inconsecutivity of his moves.... What? In the fever of laying a trap for the King he is debating is life worth living?... Two noted actors, meeting after separate disappointments in the role, agreed it was ungraspable. Of course it is; the character can't remember from scene to scene what he is doing. And since we cannot follow, we take it for profundity.

After the play-within-a-play, there is a scene that remains ambiguous in Q2, though quite explicit in Q1: Hamlet's interview with his mother (III.iv in both Quartos). The plot requires that the eavesdropping Lord Chamberlain be stabbed to death, and in both Quartos, his death is achieved early in the scene.

In Quarto One, the following definite occurrences then take place: Hamlet tells the Queen outright that her husband murdered his father; when he sees that he has touched her conscience by contrasting her former honorable marriage with her present incestuous union, he reveals that he is, in fact, sane, and that he intends to avenge his father's death. In return he receives her vow that she never knew of the murder and that she will assist in his revenge. "It is enough, mother good night," he says as they part. It would seem that the way is now clear for Hamlet to fulfill his mission. With the Queen as ally, his motive for regicide can be made credible. Only the unfortunate stabbing of the Lord Chamberlain stands between him and his revenge; it means he will be shipped to England before he has an opportunity to kill the King. However, the theme of the Queen's allegiance is stressed again while he is away. In a scene alone with Horatio (IV.iv) she explicitly learns of the King's treasonous designs against her son. Through Horatio, she sends a mother's blessing and a warning to Hamlet to be careful.

This is forthright exposition. Compare it with the aftermath of the play-within-a-play in Quarto Two. Hamlet goes to his mother's

[1] In *Shakespeare's Game,* pp. 138, 144.

chamber and mistakenly kills the Lord Chamberlain, just as he does in Q1, but in the ensuing interview with his mother he only hints at the murder of his father and never mentions revenge. His main purpose appears to be different; he now seems mainly to want to shame his mother into leaving the incestuous bed. For all its emotional intensity, the scene in Q2 does little to promote any lasting understanding between mother and son. It does give Hamlet an opportunity to declare he is sane, and to receive the Queen's promise not to reveal what he has said, but we cannot be sure she believes him. We cannot, in fact, be sure where the Queen stands in relation to the King and her son. With explicit mention of the murder excised, she is given no chance to declare her innocence; and since Horatio's revelation of her husband's plot against Hamlet is also excised, we never see her receive proof of her husband's crimes until, in the end, she drinks from the poisoned cup. What she has done, or known, or guessed along the way is not made clear. This uncertainty also throws doubt on Hamlet's motivation. We do not know what, if anything, he purposes.

Hamlet's state of mind becomes even more impenetrable when, on his way to England, he meets the army of Fortenbrasse on its way to war—a meeting which takes place only in Q2 (IV.iv)—and in the soliloquy "How all occasions doe informe against me" berates himself for being less brave than these warriors and for not doing a deed which he has had the "cause and will, and strength and meanes" to do. Are we prepared to believe that he is giving us a clue to his inaction, and that he has indeed a fatal flaw, a "vicious mole of nature," which has prevented him from carrying out his mission?

Thus Quarto Two is a different play from Quarto One in spite of the action and the characters they have in common. The added verse in Q2 unquestionably achieves a depth and beauty not found in Q1. At the same time this added verse, combined with structural differences in Q2, introduces a new element of ambiguity. The dialogue is memorable but the motives behind it are more difficult to determine.

Ambiguity has not proved fatal; it is, in fact, one reason for the enduring hold the play has upon us. *Hamlet* is perennially adaptable. Productions yet to come may rest upon interpretations that are unimaginable to us. But if it is Shakespeare's interpretation that is being updated, then everything the modern interpreter can discover about how the author saw the play is helpful. Max Foster was convinced that the way to find Shakespeare's *Hamlet* did not lie in delving ever deeper into the received script. That script, he felt, was the cause of the uncertainties, not their solution. The best course was to know the material the author worked with and to find out what he did with it as he went along. As usual, Shakespeare was partly borrowing and partly inventing; and, as usual, he was surprisingly faithful to the action and characterization in the borrowed sections.

This book discusses the *Hamlet*s that lie behind the canon version. Chapter One recounts the prose stories that furnish the basic plot. One is a medieval Latin "history" which contains chapters about a legendary Danish Prince named Amleth who "would have surpassed the labors of Hercules in his deeds of prowess" if "Fortune had been as kind to him as nature."[1] Fortune has been harsh however, and in the early pages (the ones Shakespeare borrowed) this hero-prince is doomed to spend his childhood and early manhood feigning idiocy, until he can find a way to kill a usurping uncle in retaliation for his father's murder and his mother's infamy. Three centuries later Amleth's story was repeated and expanded as one of the tales narrated in a French "novel," well known in England.

Both the Danish and the French were rambling stories, and ingenuity was required to compress them into the framework of a five-act drama. Even here, Shakespeare had the way prepared for him. There was a play about Hamlet on the London stage in the late 1580s, at about the time Shakespeare was arriving from

---

[1]*"Hamlet,* From the Historia Danica of Saxo Grammaticus," trans. O. Elton, in *The Sources of "Hamlet": With Essay on the Legend by Sir Israel Gollancz,* ed. I. Gollancz, p. 163.

Stratford. The script is lost but allusions in the contemporary literature refer to a ghost that cried "Hamlet, revenge!" and a hero that made "tragical speaches."[1] Now sometimes known as the "Ur-Hamlet," it is thought to be by Thomas Kyd or an imitator of Kyd. Shakespeare obviously drew from it the idea of deferring, until manhood, the hero's knowledge of his father's murder, and of having the crime revealed by the victim's ghost. There is also reason to believe that he was indebted to the old play for the Counsellor's family (i.e., the relationship of the Lord Chamberlain to Laertes, a son, and Ophelia, a daughter); for Horatio as an important addition to the Prince's household; for a re-enactment of the murder in a dumb show; and for a duel during which Hamlet and other principal characters lose their lives.

We deduce the early existence of these plot developments because they appear in another revenge-play, *Der Bestrafte Brudermord, oder Prinz Hamlet aus Dänemarck.* We know it only from a German play dated 1710. By that late date some of it may have been taken from Shakespeare's *Hamlet;* and, obviously, elements were added to suit German actors, particularly German comedians. But it contains allusions that seem to link it to a much earlier period, and in many ways it differs from any *Hamlet* we know. The explanation appears to be that in the 1710 version we are dealing with the descendant of two lost plays: first, the English "Ur-Hamlet," and second, the earliest German adaptation of the

---

[1]In Thomas Lodge's *Wits miserie, and the Worlds madnesse, discovering the Devils incarnat of this Age* (1596), one of the devils is *Hate-Virtue or Sorrow for another mans good Success* whom Dr. Lodge describes as *"a foule lubber, and looks as pale as the visard of ye ghost, which cried so miserally [sic] at ye theator, like an oisterwife, Hamlet revenge."* Quoted with other contemporary references to the phrase "Hamlet, revenge!" in *A New Variorum Edition of Shakespeare,* ed. H. H. Furness, vol. 2 of *Hamlet,* pp. 9-11.
  The following is quoted from an epistle prefixed by Thomas Nash to Robert Greene's *Menaphon,* printed in 1589: "...yet English Seneca read by candle-light yeeldes manie good sentences...and if you intreate him faire in a frostie morning, he will affoord you whole *Hamlets,* I should say Handfulls of tragical speaches." *A New Variorum Edition of Shakespeare,* ed. H. H. Furness, vol. 2 of *Hamlet,* p. 5.

"Ur-Hamlet."[1] A scenario of *Der Bestrafte Brudermord* is included in Chapter One.

Chapter Two is a scene-by-scene discussion of the First Quarto. Foster considered it an early version written before the script was enlarged to "almost as much againe," as stated on the title page of Quarto Two. In Q1 events follow the sequence of the sources more closely than they do in Q2, and the character of the hero is more directly in line with that of his predecessors. Hamlet is doomed to the same mission as was Amleth, and although he has been transformed from the legendary Danish superman into a human, thoughtful Elizabethan, he pursues the mission in much the same spirit. He assumes his mask, parries the probes of his adversaries, and then moves toward his revenge as best he can. The shorter script of Q1 makes his delay seem less protracted; and the steadily unfolding action toward the play-within-a-play, and then toward an understanding with his mother, show him as a more resolute character than he seems in Q2. This Q1 Hamlet sometimes acts on impulse, but he is not insane; he is not held back by overmuch thinking; he cannot be viewed as the victim of complexes. He is a victim, however, a victim of Fate. And when, in an impulsive moment, he stabs the Counsellor, his doom is sealed. He becomes murderer as well as avenger and must suffer the consequences. But before he succumbs, he out-duels a treacherous opponent and then kills the King with the King's own weapons. He is borne as a soldier to his grave and the Danes (as well as the audience) share in the tribute accorded by his successor: "For he was likely, had he lived, / To a prov'd most royall."

It is a good thing to become acquainted with this heroic Hamlet, because once he is made clear he will be seen to persist in Q2. There he accomplishes the same feats and is accorded the same tribute. In fact, there is new imagery which enhances his royal

---

[1]For details cited to support the theory that the original German manuscript was dated about 1589 and that in it the "Ur-Hamlet" was preserved wholly or in part, see *A New Variorum Edition of Shakespeare,* ed. H. H. Furness, vol. 2 of *Hamlet,* pp. 117-120.

attributes.[1] But among the lines added in Q2 are some in which his melancholy and self-reproach are so forcefully expressed that these become the memorable traits, and we are prone to see Hamlet as he depicts himself, not as he is described by others in the play. Thus by his own eloquence, ambiguities are created. The revisions introduced into his role, as well as those added throughout the text of Q2, have turned a terse but ingenious play into an enigmatic masterpiece that has been variously interpreted for nearly four centuries. Undoubtedly the leading actor, Richard Burbage, and the rest of Shakespeare's troop played the new lines to the hilt. But it may also be true that Q1 was the play they had started with, and Q1 was still the play they were building upon. If so, we are following in their footsteps when we search Quarto One for help with the obscurities of Quarto Two.

This estimate of the First Quarto as an important link in the evolution of *Hamlet* runs counter to the opinions held by many Shakespearean scholars. Therefore when, as long-time collaborator and literary executor, I was preparing this manuscript for the press, I added a selection from the notes Foster had made over the years, showing his reasons for believing that the text of Q1 is partly — probably mostly — the work of Shakespeare, and that consequently Q2 is a revision, magnificent as literature, but as drama posing problems that it does not solve. These notes constitute Chapter Three.

A word about the supplementary material: Appendix A is a short essay by Max Foster giving his solution to four of the textual puzzles that appear in the canon *Hamlet*. He has interpreted them by studying the idioms and word usage in three texts, Quarto One, Quarto Two, and the Folio. Appendix B outlines the major differences in the scenario of Q1 as compared to the scenario of Q2. This outline is followed by the Huntington Library facsimile of the First Quarto, reproduced in full since most editions are now out of print. Finally, a chronology of the action in Q1 has been added after the index as a convenient reference to the sequence of events.

[1]See Chapter Three, p. 107.

I have had the help of a second literary executor, Foster's son Vincent, both in editing the original manuscript and in the choice of additional work. He and I must assume responsibility for the book as it now stands.

We would like to acknowledge the assistance that was crucial to the typing, further editing, and printing of the manuscript given by Deborah Lapp, John Spanos, and James J. Sommer.

ANNE SHIRAS, 1991

A NOTE TO THE READER

When quoted passages include words or lines in bold print, the bold printing is ours, used for emphasis. Brackets are used whenever we have interpolated explanatory material into quoted passages.

Readers who may wish to refer to the texts quoted or discussed in this book will find the following information helpful.

The Texts Used for the Sources of Shakespeare's "Hamlet"

The page numbers cited for passages quoted from Saxo Grammaticus and Belleforest are from *The Sources of "Hamlet": With Essay on the Legend by Sir Israel Gollancz* (London: Oxford University Press, 1926).

The citations (acts and pages) for *Der Bestrafte Brudermord oder Prinz Hamlet aus Dänemarck* refer to *Shakespeare in Germany, 1590-1700, With Translations of Five Early Plays,* edited and translated by Ernest Brennecke (University of Chicago Press, 1964).

The Shakespearean Texts

The early texts of Shakespeare's *Hamlet* (the 1603 printing of Quarto One and the 1604 printing of Quarto Two) were not divided into acts and scenes. The 1623 Folio made a brave beginning, but gave up act and scene divisions after scene ii of the second act. In order to place the passages quoted in this book we have divided each of the three texts[1] into the five acts used in modern editions. And since Quarto Two and the structurally identical Folio are the basic texts on which the canon *Hamlet* is based, our division of these texts into scenes also corresponds to the scene divisions in modern usage. Quarto One is not structurally identical; it has fewer scenes and at one point a different scene altogether. We have numbered its scenes consecutively as they appear in each act.

[1]For publication data related to the three texts (The First Quarto, 1603; The Second Quarto, 1604; and the First Folio, 1623) see Acknowledgments, p. 113.

Neither Quarto One nor Quarto Two has numbered pages. We have numbered the pages consecutively throughout each Quarto, starting with the pages on which act I, scene i begins. As to the Folio collection of plays its editors (or its printer) did in fact assign page numbers, but there seems to have been some confusion in the mind of the compositor.[1] In our citations from the Folio we follow its pagination, erratic though that is.

As noted in the Introduction, further help in locating passages cited from Quarto One will be found in the supplementary material at the end of this book.

[1]*Hamlet* begins on page 152 of the Folio and continues consecutively through page 156, when the pagination suddenly goes from 257 to 278; then to a second page 259, followed immediately by pages 280, 281 and the final page, which is a second 280.

EVOLUTION OF CHARACTERS

Evolution of Characters in Five Texts: The Saxo Grammaticus *Hamlet;*
The Belleforest *Hamlet; Der Bestrafte Brudermord (Der BB);*
Quarto One (Q1); and Quarto Two (Q2)

THE ROLES	SAXO	BELLEFOREST
The murdered King	Horwendil	Horvendile
The widowed Queen	Gerutha	Geruth
Their son	Amleth	Hamblet/Hamlet
The usurping King	Feng	Fengon
The Counselor (Lord Chamberlain)	No name	No name
His son		
The woman-decoy	Amleth's foster-sister	The soeur-de-lait
Friend of Hamlet	Amleth's foster-brother	The frere-de-lait
Companions for the English trip	Fen's courtiers	Fengon's courtiers
Leader of the Players		
Play-Ruler		
Play-Lady		
Play-Villain		
Officer of the Watch		
Duke of Norway		
Captain		
Clown(s)		
Soldiers		
Ambassadors		
Courtier		
Peasant		
Servant to Lord Chamberlain		
Churchman		

There are slight variations in the names of most of the characters, but the
only change likely to confuse the reader is that of the Lord Chamberlain.
His is Corambis in Q1 but becomes Polonius in Q2. Among the minor
characters there are some definite changes, such as Montano as the Lord
Chamberlain's servant in Q1, changed to Reynaldo in Q2. Otherwise the

Throughout his book we give each character the name appropriate to the text we are dealing with. If the discussion involves both versions of the old prose stories, we use the *Saxo* names, as being the originals. If both Shakespearean versions (Q1 and Q2) are under discussion, we use the Q2 versions, as being more familiar to the reader.

DER BB	Q1	Q2
Ghost	Ghost (Hamlet I)	Ghost (Hamlet I)
The Queen/Sigrie	The Queen/Gertred	The Queen/Gertrard
Hamlet	Hamlet (II)	Hamlet (II)
Erico	The King	The King/Claudius
Corambus	Corambis	Polonius
Leonhardus	Leartes	Laertes
Ophelia	Ofelia	Ophelia
Horatio	Horatio	Horatio
Bandits	Rossencraft & Gilderstone	Rosencraus & Guyldensterne
Carl	Player	Player
King	Duke	King
Queen	Dutchesse	Queene
King's brother	Lucianus	Lucianus
Francisco	Marcellus	Marcellus
Fortempras	Fortenbrasse	Fortinbrasse/Fortenbrasse
	Captain	Captain
Phantasmo	Gravediggers	Gravediggers
2 Sentries	Bernardo & Centinel	Barnardo & Francisco
	Voltemar & Cornelia	Votlimand & Cornelius
	Braggart Gentleman	Courtier/Ostrick(e)
Jens		
	Montano	Reynaldo
	Priest	Priest/Doctor

changes are mostly variations in spelling. The Folio follows Q2 in general but spells the Queen *Gertrude* and the two schoolfellows *Rosincrance* and *Guildensterne*. Modern versions use the Folio spelling with the exception of the two schoolfellows who have become Rosencrantz and Guildenstern.

CHAPTER ONE

THE SOURCES

The sources of *Hamlet* are multilingual. They consist of (1) some episodes in the Latin *Historia Danica* by the 13th-century Danish author Saxo Grammaticus; (2) a 16th-century French "novel" based on the Danish history, but altered and much embellished, in the *Histoires Tragiques* of F. De Belleforest; and (3) clues suggested by the German manuscript of a play, *Der Bestrafte Brudermord, oder Prinz Hamlet aus Dänemarck,* which is dated much later (1710) but which apparently derives from a 16th-century English play about Hamlet earlier than any Shakespearean version, the so-called "Ur-Hamlet," no longer extant.

The Latin history and the French novel tell the story of Amleth, whose father, a ruler, is murdered openly by his brother (Amleth's uncle) abetted by a gang, now his courtiers. The uncle takes over the rule and marries his brother's widow, Amleth's mother. In Saxo the mother is true to her first husband during his lifetime. In Belleforest she is seduced by the murderer before the murder.

In both, Amleth pretends to be mad,[1] as a protection against being murdered by his usurping uncle, now his stepfather. The early part of the story has to do with the probes the uncle and his courtiers make to determine whether Amleth is really mad or only pretending to be mad, and with Amleth's foiling of those probes. When Amleth is asked a question, he always in answering tells the truth, but in such a way that the probers think he is mad and the answer meaningless. One test—based on the theory that if he is

---

[1]Saxo's *Hamlet* is Northern in origin but it also contains incidents apparently borrowed from legendary Roman history. Thus Amleth's madness resembles the madness feigned by Lucius Junius Brutus in order to escape death at the hands of Tarquin. For this and other parallels with the Roman saga see *The Sources of "Hamlet": With Essay on the Legend by Sir Israel Gollancz,* pp. 27-28.

really mad, he will be without sexual desire—consists of arranging for Amleth to find a pretty girl in a secluded woodland, ostensibly alone, but with hidden courtiers watching. Amleth is warned of this plot by one of the courtiers, his foster-brother, so Amleth makes no attempt to have intercourse with her there. Later, however—according to Saxo, but not Belleforest—he has intercourse with her in an impenetrable fen far from prying eyes. She turns out to be his foster-sister and on their return, when asked, she replies, as she promised Amleth she would, that they did not have intercourse (a lie, but believed), while he says that they did (the truth, but not believed).

In both texts, this probe is followed by another. There is a courtier who, as Saxo puts it, was "gifted more with assurance than judgment" (p. 111). This courtier suggests that the uncle go on a trip so that Amleth alone with his mother will disclose his state of mind. Meanwhile, unbeknownst to either Amleth or his mother, the courtier will hide in Amleth's mother's chamber to overhear their conversation. This he does under a mattress. Amleth discovers him, kills him, cuts his body up, boils it, and puts it down the privy, where the hogs eat the flesh and scatter the bones in the filth.

In Saxo, after killing the courtier and disposing of his body, Amleth returns to his mother's chamber and reproaches her for marrying her first husband's murderer. He then discloses the fact that the eavesdropper had craved to hear: his, Amleth's, madness is assumed. He wears, he says, the appearance of a fool while waiting the occasion and the opportunity to avenge his father's death. He tells her she should "weep for the blemish in thine own mind, not for that in another's. On the rest see thou keep silence."[1] The scene between the Queen and Amleth ends: "With such reproaches he rent the heart of his mother and redeemed her to walk in the ways of virtue; teaching her to set the fires of the past

---

[1]One wonders whether, when Shakespeare came to writing Hamlet's last speech as it appears in the canon *Hamlet,* those perfect final words, "The rest is silence," sprang from some echo of this scene in Saxo.

above the seductions of the present" (pp. 115, 117).

In Belleforest, while Hamblet is cutting up and boiling the eavesdropper's body, the Queen

> in the meane time wepte and tormented her selfe to see all her hopes frustrate, for that what fault soever she had committed, yet was shee sore grieved to see her onely child made a meere mockery, every man reproaching her with his folly, one point whereof she had as then seene before her eyes, which was no small pricke to her conscience, esteeming that the gods sent her that punishment for joyning incestuously in marriage with the tyrannnous murtherer of her husband.
>
> pp. 207, 209

Hamblet returns to his mother's chamber and castigates her for marrying her first husband's murdcrcr, cven expressing the suspicion that she consented to the death of her husband. He reveals that his ill fortune and her "over great lightnesse" have constrained him to play the madman to save his life, adding that if he does not die shortly he hopes to "take such and so great vcngcancc, that these countryes shall for ever speake thereof" (p. 217), and warning her not to let the King or any other know of his intent. She defends herself on the grounds that King Fengon had compelled her to marry him through fcar of thc conscqucnccs to her and to Hamblet if she refused. (In this interview neither she nor Hamblet refer to her adultery with Fengon before the murder, although she stands accused of it earlier in the Belleforest text.) Nevertheless, "the wise admonitions" given her by Hamblet

> quenched the flames of unbridled desire that before had moved her to affect K. Fengon, to ingraff in her heart the vertuous actions of her lawfull spouse, whom inwardly she much lamented, when she beheld the lively image and portraiture of his vertue and great wisedome in her childe, representing his fathers haughtie and valiant heart.
>
> p. 219

Hamblet now tells her he will put his trust in her, and as he leaves, adds that he has so great confidence in his fortune that he believes he will "not dye without revenging my selfe upon mine enemie, and that himselfe shall be the instrument of his owne decay, and to execute that which of my selfe I durst not have enterprised" (pp. 227, 229).

In both texts, the uncle, on returning, seeks out the spying courtier and cannot find him. He asks Amleth[1] *inter alios* where the courtier is. Amleth answers truthfully but is not believed when he says the courtier has fallen through the privy and been eaten by the pigs. Although Amleth has foiled this probe, King Feng decides to treat him as guilty and to send him to England accompanied by two courtiers who will carry a mandate to the King of England to kill Amleth forthwith. Before leaving for England, Amleth tells his mother that he will be back in a year, and that she is to hang tapestries in the banqueting hall.

During the voyage he finds the mandate, and changes its terms to make the two courtiers instead of himself the victims. In England he wins the King's admiration by showing a perspicacity that amounts to second sight. His divinations reveal hidden truths about the English Court, including the fact that both the King and Queen have lowborn antecedents.

In a year Amleth returns to Denmark. In both stories the courtiers are celebrating his funeral in the great banqueting hall. They are drinking, drunk. Amleth, resuming his role of madman, induces them to nail his sword in its scabbard. Then he pulls the tapestries down on them and sets fire to the building. Meanwhile his uncle has gone to bed. Amleth goes to his bedroom and changes his (Amleth's) sword, nailed in its scabbard, for his uncle's sword, hanging at the end of the bed. He wakes his uncle and taunts him. His uncle seizes Amleth's sword and tries to draw it. While he is doing this, Amleth, with his uncle's sword, kills him.

In an oration to the Danes, Amleth explains his actions: how he assumed madness to rid the country of a tyrant and to quench

---

[1]A return to the Saxo nomenclature, since we are now discussing that text as well as Belleforest's. Refer to Evolution of Characters, p. xxviii.

the infamy of his mother. He succeeds in moving the hearts of his hearers and is appointed King by general acclaim. After his coronation he goes on to other achievements until he dies in battle, betrayed by a disloyal wife.

So much for the pertinent episodes in Saxo and Belleforest. Now to the prose play, *Der Bestrafte Brudermord, oder Prinz Hamlet aus Dänemarck.*

The story line that *Der Bestrafte Brudermord (Der BB)* has in common with Belleforest and Saxo concerns the murder of a ruler by his brother, who then takes over the rule and marries his murdered brother's wife. But the murder in *Der BB* is not open as in Belleforest and Saxo; it is perpetrated in secret and revealed by the Ghost of the victim. The son of the late King, fearing to be, like his father, murdered by his uncle, feigns madness as a shield against that threat. (If he is really mad, he will be considered harmless.) The King, who shows no enmity toward Hamlet at first, probes variously to discover the cause of the madness, not, as in Belleforest and Saxo, to discover whether the madness is real or feigned. The probers in *Der BB* are not hostile to Hamlet. In Saxo and Belleforest the only probers not hostile to Amleth are the foster-brother and the foster-sister.

In *Der BB* the counterpart of the courtier who suggests the eavesdrop on Amleth and his mother, and whom Amleth kills, is old Corambus, the Chamberlain. This Corambus, furthermore, in *Der BB,* has two children, a son, Leonhardus, about Hamlet's age, and a daughter, Ophelia. Ophelia derives from the foster-sister in the old stories, while the foster-brother in the old stories becomes Horatio, Hamlet's trusted friend. It is probable that the relationships in the cast of *Der BB* originated in the "Ur-Hamlet," the lost English play. They hold true for all the extant stage versions of the Hamlet story.

The dramatic devices in *Der BB* which do not stem from the old stories have to do with the Ghost, his story and his honesty; Ophelia's madness; and the King's plot to have Leonhardus kill Hamlet. Persons in *Der BB* with no counterpart in Belleforest or

Saxo are the Ghost of the murdered ruler; a jester, Phantasmo; and a peasant, Jens, a very minor character, present only with Phantasmo.

Der Bestrafte Brudermord begins with passages in no way derived from Saxo or Belleforest. First there is an invocation by Night, bidding three of her Furies to spread discord and kindle the fire of revenge in a kingdom where an incestuous marriage is about to be consummated between a fratricide and the murdered brother's wife. This prologue is a mixture of free verse, rhymed couplets and prose, but such as it is, it constitutes the only flight of poetic imagery in the play. When act I opens with two soldiers on the battlements of the Danish castle, the writing settles into prose. Night and her attendants are never mentioned again. The Ghost—a second departure from the prose stories—enters and in the space of a few moments appears first to a sentinel; then to Francisco (officer of the watch) and Horatio; then to Francisco, Horatio, and Hamlet; and finally, having beckoned Hamlet away from the others, to Hamlet alone. The Ghost then relates how his brother murdered him by pouring poison in his ears when he was asleep in the afternoon in his orchard. (It was thus a perfect crime, in that no one knew of it, except the murderer—and perhaps the widow, if she was an accessory before, during, or after the crime.) It was given out and believed that the victim died of apoplexy. Replying to the Ghost, Hamlet says:

Act I,[1]
pp. 256-264

> Just heavens! If this be true, I swear you my revenge.
> *Ghost* I shall not rest until my unnatural death is avenged.
> *Exit.*
> *Hamlet* I swear never to rest until I have taken vengeance upon this fratricide.

Hamlet swears Francisco and Horatio to secrecy and asks their aid in a matter he does not disclose, except to say it demands revenge. Each time they say, "We swear," the Ghost repeats "We

---

[1]Scenes are omitted from *Der BB* citations because its script follows the classical convention of introducing a new scene whenever a character comes on stage, in this case producing forty scenes in thirty-six pages of text.

swear," till finally, after the fourth time the Ghost repeats "We swear," Hamlet says:

> Oh, now I understand. It seems that the ghost of my father does not wish me to reveal this matter. Gentlemen, I pray you leave me. Tomorrow I shall tell you all.

Francisco leaves, but as Horatio is leaving, Hamlet calls him back and (although the audience has already heard it) tells him what the Ghost has said. Hamlet concludes:

> But from this hour on I shall pretend to be mad, and in this pretense I shall play my role artfully, until I find an opportunity to avenge my father's death.

Following this scene on the battlements, there is a court scene, in which the King says that it is time to end the mourning for the late King and change from black clothes to crimson, purple, and scarlet; and, the late King's widow having become the present King's spouse, that he is going to hold a carousal to put an end to the Queen's grief. He points out that the Queen is sad and disturbed over her son's melancholy and he beseeches Hamlet to stay at court and not to resume his studies in Wittenberg. The Queen joins in this entreaty, and to her Hamlet says: "I shall obey your command with all my heart. And so for the present I shall remain here and not go away."

The King inquires of Corambus if his son Leonhardus, not mentioned up to this point, has gone to France, and Corambus says he has. This scene ends the act as dawn breaks and the King and Queen retire to their bedchamber.

Act II, pp. 264-272   Act II begins with the King and Queen alone together. The King asks the Queen why she is so sad. She says she is greatly troubled at Hamlet's melancholy. The King (surprisingly) asks, "What, is he melancholy?" and says he will gather all the doctors in the kingdom to give him aid.

Corambus enters to say Hamlet is mad. Ophelia enters to say Hamlet has been pestering her. Corambus immediately concludes Hamlet is mad for love of Ophelia. The King says:

But may we not ourself observe his frenzy and his madness?

Corambus Indeed, your Majesty. Therefore let us stand somewhat aside, while my daughter shows him the trinket he presented her; your Majesty may then observe his madness.

King Dearest consort, may it please you to retire to your chamber? We shall in the meantime take note of his madness.

Conceal themselves.

The ensuing Hamlet-Ophelia scene is, of course, the counterpart of the scene in Belleforest and Saxo where the foster-sister is put in a secluded spot in the woods for Amleth to come upon, to see if he will make love to her (if so, he is sane) or not (if not, he is insane). In those tales he receives a warning from his foster-brother that the meeting is a trap, and he maintains his mask of insanity. The Hamlet of *Der BB* dissembles in the same way, though in this case we are not told how he becomes aware of eavesdroppers.

Ophelia May I return to your Highness the trinket which you gave me?

Hamlet What, girl! Are you eager for a husband? Go away from me! But stay. Listen, girl, you virgins do nothing but deceive young men; you buy your beauty from chemists and shopkeepers.

Then he tells the story of the cavalier of Anion, who, when his bride had removed all the artifices of her makeup, took her for a spectre. He concludes:

Thus do you deceive young men, and therefore listen to me! Pause, girl. Get you off to a nunnery, but not to a nunnery in which two pairs of slippers stand beside each bed.

Exit.

It is not clear what happens to Ophelia, but evidently she exits, and Corambus and the King come out of hiding:

Corambus Is he not perfectly and veritably mad, gracious lord and King?

> *King* Corambus, leave us. If we need you, we shall summon
> you. (Corambus *exit*.) We have observed the Prince's madness
> and raving with much wonderment. We suspect, however, that
> this is no true madness, but more likely a pretended madness.
> We must take steps to see that he is put out of the way, or even
> out of his life; otherwise great misfortune may come out of this.

We come now to the passages which pertain to the arrival of the
Players and the consequent testing of the Ghost's honesty. These plot
developments probably originated in the "Ur-Hamlet." In Saxo and
Belleforest there is, of course, no need for a Ghost nor a play since
the murder is open and notorious, and the murderer is known to all.
We do not know how the "Ur-Hamlet" handled the question of the
Ghost's honesty and the preparation for the play-within-a-play, but it
may be that *Der BB* follows that early English play quite faithfully.[1]

In *Der BB* the exposition is brief and to the point. Horatio and
Hamlet are alone together. Hamlet says that he is going to try to kill
the King and as the King always has guards around him, he (Hamlet)
may himself be killed and he asks Horatio, if that happens, to bury
him honorably.

> *Horatio* Your Highness, I beg you to do no such thing.
> Perhaps the ghost has deceived you.
> *Hamlet* Oh no! Its words were spoken all too clearly, and I
> may put my trust in it. But what news is the old fool bringing us?
> *Enter* Corambus.
> *Corambus* News, gracious Sir! The players have arrived.

After he has sent Corambus out to bring the leader of the Players
in, Hamlet says to Horatio:

> These players come at the right moment, for through them I
> shall discover whether the ghost has given me the truth or
> not. I once saw a tragedy in which one brother murders another
> in a garden. This story they shall enact. If the King grows pale,
> then he did the deed of which the ghost told me.

[1]For a discussion of Shakespeare's quite different preparation for the play-within-
a-play, see Chapter Two, pp. 36-38.

The Players enter. Hamlet and Carl, the leading Player, discuss acting. Hamlet offers some advice on the matter, recommending natural ease and elegance. He then draws out of Carl the fact that there is a play where "King Pir—Pir—Pir-something" (Carl supplies "Pyrro") is murdered in his garden by his brother. They agree that this shall be the play performed that night.

The Players go to get ready for the performance. Hamlet tells Horatio to watch the King carefully, for if he "changes color or is agitated, then he has certainly done the deed." He tells Horatio the story of the woman in Strasbourg whose conscience was so much stirred by witnessing a tragedy wherein a woman murdered her husband that she tore her hair, rushed out of the theatre and confessed she had committed the same crime. Then Hamlet says since he must dissemble, Horatio is to "observe all things closely"; and Horatio promises to "keep a sharp eye on all that may happen."

The Court now convenes for the play. The King questions Hamlet about the plot, asking if it contains anything offensive or in bad taste. Hamlet says it is a good plot: "It does not concern us, who have good consciences."

The play is only a dumb show. Hamlet acts as Chorus, interpreting the action.

> *Now the play begins: the* King *with his consort. He wishes to lie down to sleep. The* Queen *begs him not to do so; nevertheless he lies down. The* Queen *takes her leave with a kiss, and exit. The* King's *brother enters with a flask, pours something into his ear, and exit.*
>
> *Hamlet* That is King Pyrrus. He goes into the garden to sleep. The Queen begs him not to do so; he lies down nevertheless. The poor lady departs; and see, the King's brother comes with henbane poison and pours it into his ear—poison which, once introduced into the body's bloodstream, kills that body.
>
> *King* Torches, candles! The play does not please us!

Hamlet and Horatio agree that the King blenched. It is an honest Ghost.

A brief scene follows where Hamlet bids Corambus see the actors well bestowed, for their work is worth it: they punish vices and exalt virtues.

Act III, pp. 272-279 The next scene shows the King at an altar, kneeling. Hamlet enters with a drawn sword, but reasons himself out of using it lest he take the King's sins upon himself.

Now comes a scene comparable to an episode in Belleforest and Saxo: the eavesdropping courtier killed, and the ensuing private interview between Hamlet and the Queen. It is, however, by no means identical, and the differences may be a legacy from the author of the "Ur-Hamlet." In the old stories the Queen does not know of the eavesdropping any more than Hamlet does; the scheming courtier maneuvers the interview and stealthily secrets himself in the Queen's bedchamber. But in *Der BB* it is Hamlet himself who requests an audience; and while his mother awaits him, she orders Corambus, who happens to be present, to conceal himself until she summons him. He hides, not under a mattress as in Belleforest and Saxo, but in a more stage-worthy retreat behind the tapestry.

Hamlet Lady Mother, did you really know your first husband?

Queen Oh, remind me no more of my recent grief. I cannot restrain my tears when I think of him.

Hamlet You weep? Oh, let be! These are but crocodile tears. But see, there in that gallery hangs the portrait of your first husband, and here hangs the portrait of your present one. How does it seem to you, which one of them is the handsomer? Is not the first a majestic figure?

Queen Yes, indeed, that is true.

Hamlet How could you have forgotten him so soon? Fie! Shame! Almost on the same day you celebrated the funeral and the nuptial rites. But hold! Are all the doors securely locked?

Queen Why do you ask that?

Corambus *coughs behind the tapestry.*

Hamlet Who is spying upon us?

> *Stabs him.*

Corambus Alas, Prince, what are you doing? I die.

Queen Oh heavens, my son, what are you doing? It is Corambus, the court chamberlain.

> Ghost *crosses the stage.*
> *Lightning.*

Hamlet Oh revered shade of my father, stay! Oh, oh, what do you desire? Do you demand revenge? I shall exact it at the proper time.

Queen What are you doing, and with whom are you speaking?

Hamlet Do you not see the ghost of your departed husband? See, it gestures as though it would speak with you.

Queen What! I see nothing.

Hamlet I indeed believe that you see nothing, for you are no longer worthy to behold its form. Fie! Shame upon you. I wish no further word with you.

> *Exit.*

After Hamlet exits, the Queen has a soliloquy:

> *Queen (alone)* Oh heavens, to what excess of frenzy has this Prince's melancholy driven him! Ah, my only Prince has entirely lost his wits. If I had not taken in marriage my brother-in-law, my former husband's brother, I would not have maneuvered the crown of Denmark out of my son's grasp. But what can one do about things already done? Nothing. Things must remain as they are. If the Pope had forbidden me such a marriage, this would never have happened. I shall go and take most careful thought, how I may help my son to regain his former sanity and health.

Plainly she has no idea of the murder. It is only the results of her second marriage that she regrets: she has maneuvered the crown of Denmark out of her son's grasp. Indeed, this had been Hamlet's complaint in the first act before the Ghost appeared to him. At that time he had said:

> Oh Horatio, I do not know why my heart has felt such distress over my father's death, since my royal mother has

so soon forgotten him, and our present King even sooner. For while I was in Germany he swiftly had himself crowned as King of Denmark. But he granted me, as a semblance of justice, the crown of Norway, to be confirmed by a state election.

Act I, p. 259

After the Queen's soliloquy there is evidently a lapse of time, for by the time the action resumes, Ophelia has gone mad. No reason is given for her madness. Since she makes no mention of her murdered father, we are apparently meant to assume that she is grieving for the lover who rejected her, though the audience has seen no previous evidence of either love or grief. Phantasmo, the Court Jester, first informs us of her condition:

Strange things are going on at court nowadays. Prince Hamlet is mad. Ophelia is likewise mad. To sum it up, things go most strangely there...

. . . .

Enter Ophelia, *mad.*

Ophelia   I hasten, I run, and yet I cannot find my sweetheart. He has sent me messages; I am to come to him; we are to be wed; I have arrayed myself. But there is my lover! Look, are you there, my little lamb? I have searched for you, yes, for you I have searched. Only think! The tailor has completely ruined my calico dress. Here, take this pretty flower, my heart!

Phantasmo   Oh, the devil! If only I could get away from her! She thinks I'm her lover.

Ophelia   What say you, my love? Let us to bed together; I shall wash you quite clean.

Phantasmo   Yes indeed. And I shall soap you well and rinse you.

Ophelia   Hear me, my love. Have you put on your new garment? Ah, it is well made, exactly after the new fashion.

Phantasmo   I know that well, without...

Ophelia   Oh heavens, I had almost forgotten! The King has invited me as his guest, I must run! See there! My little coach, my little coach!

Exit.

Phantasmo Oh Hecate, Queen of witches, I'm so glad that this mad thing has gone. If she'd stayed any longer, I'd have gone mad myself. I'd better go now, before the crazy thing comes back.

In *Der BB,* as in Belleforest and Saxo, after Hamlet kills the eavesdropper, he is sent by his uncle to England to be killed. But in *Der BB* the King of England is not involved. The uncle sends two ruffians with Hamlet, who themselves are to do the killing. (If they are unable to kill Hamlet themselves, there is a backup letter addressed to an expert assassin in England, bidding him to do away with Hamlet.)

No sooner have the travellers departed than Ophelia enters for a second mad scene with Phantasmo. Phantasmo in a soliloquy is complaining that Ophelia thinks him her lover (which he isn't) and runs at him from every corner. Ophelia enters, corners him and begins planning the wedding. The tone is like that of their first scene. It is leer-humor: Phantasmo seems willing to comply with her proposals, short of marriage. But suddenly she turns against him and runs off to another lover she thinks she sees beckoning her.

Act IV, pp. 279-284   Following this scene, we have Hamlet and the two ruffians on an island en route to England, where Hamlet cleverly arranges matters so that they, in attempting to kill him, kill each other. This he does by obtaining time to pray, and at the end of his prayer, calling "Shoot!" and falling flat, whereupon each ruffian shoots the other through the space occupied by Hamlet before his fall. This rather absurd episode continues with Hamlet thanking Heaven for the guardian angel who has saved his life. Thus, the second sight (divination) of Amleth in the stories has in this play become angelic inspiration.

After the scene on the island the action moves back to Denmark. Phantasmo brings the news that Leonhardus has returned, and the King orders that he be admitted. Leonhardus demands his father of the King, who replies that he is innocent of Corambus's death: "Prince

Hamlet stabbed him accidentally behind the tapestry, but we are resolved that he shall be punished for it." Phantasmo announces that Hamlet is back. The King forthwith proposes to Leonhardus a plot by which he, Leonhardus, will have revenge on Hamlet: the King will arrange a fencing match between them for a wager; he who makes the first three hits shall win a white Neapolitan horse.

King ...in the midst of this bout you must drop your foil, and in its place you must have ready to hand a sharply pointed rapier, made to resemble the foil closely — but you must anoint its point with deadly poison. The moment you wound his body with this, he will instantly die. Thus you will win both the prize and the King's favor.

Leonhardus Forgive me, your Majesty, but I may not undertake this thing. The Prince is an accomplished swordsman, and he might easily do the same to me.

King Leonhardus, do not refuse this, but do it as a favor to your King. In order to avenge your father's death you must indeed do this. You know that the Prince, as your father's assassin, has deserved such a death. We may not, to be sure, bring him to justice, since he has the support of his mother and is well beloved by our subjects. Therefore, if we openly took vengeance upon him, an insurrection might easily occur. The fact that we disown him as our stepson and nephew is only for the sake of divine justice, for he is murderous and insane, and we ourselves must remain in perpetual fear of such an evil person. Therefore do what we require of you; thus you will relieve the King of his fear and at the same time take secret revenge on your father's murderer.

Leonhardus This is a difficult matter, and I can hardly undertake it. For if this should be discovered, it would surely cost me my life.

King Have no doubts. Should it miscarry, we have already thought of another device. We shall have a small oriental diamond crushed into bits, and when he is over-heated we shall bring it to him in a goblet, mixed with wine and sugar; thus to our health, he shall drink his own death.

Leonhardus Very well, your Majesty. Under such protection I shall undertake it.

Here enters the Queen with news that Ophelia is mad. Then,

> *Enter* Ophelia, *with flowers.*
> *Ophelia*   See, here is a blossom for you—and you, and
> you.
>
> *Gives each one a flower.*
> But heavens! I had almost forgotten! I must run quickly; I
> have forgotten my jewelry. Ah, my forehead! I must go
> quickly to the court jeweler and ask what new styles he
> has received. There, there, set the table quickly; I shall
> soon return.
>
> *Runs off.*

The others exit, with Leonhardus bewailing his father's death
and his sister's madness, and the King promising Leonhardus his
royal favor.

Act V, pp. 285-290   At the beginning of the next and final act, Hamlet, returning to Denmark, swears he will wreak vengeance on the
King that very day. Horatio joins him and, although the
audience has seen it occur, Hamlet recounts the island episode to
Horatio, attributing his safe return to divine Omnipotence. At the
conclusion of Hamlet's report Horatio exclaims: "Oh, unheard-of
treachery!" Phantasmo now enters. As usual he is bringing news:

> *Phantasmo*   Welcome home, Prince Hamlet! Do you know
> the latest? The King has placed a wager on you and young
> Leonhardus. You are to fence together with rapiers, and
> whichever of you makes the first two [*sic*] hits shall win a
> white Neapolitan horse.
> *Hamlet*   Is this true, what you say?
> *Phantasmo*   Yes, it is nothing else.
> *Hamlet*   Horatio, what may this mean? Leonhardus and I
> are to fence together. I believe they have gulled this fool, so
> that one may make him imagine whatever one will. Look
> here, Signora Phantasmo, it is horribly cold.
> *Phantasmo*   Yes, yes; it is horribly cold.
>
> *His teeth chatter.*

Hamlet But now it's no longer so cold.

Phantasmo Yes, yes; it's now just moderate.

Hamlet But now it is very hot.

> *Wipes his face.*

Phantasmo Oh, what a horrible heat!

> *Wipes the sweat from his face.*

Hamlet Now it is not very cold, nor yet very warm.

Phantasmo Yes, it now seems quite temperate.

Hamlet You see, Horatio, that one may make him imagine what one will. Phantasmo, return to the King, and tell him that I shall soon wait upon him.

After Phantasmo leaves, Hamlet and Horatio are alone together.

Hamlet Now come, Horatio. No matter what, I shall go and present myself to the King. But oh! What does this mean? Drops of blood fall from my nose; my whole body is trembling! Alas, what is happening to me?

> *Faints.*

Horatio Noble Prince! Oh heavens, what does this mean? May your Highness come to yourself again! Noble Prince, what is it? What is happening to you?

Hamlet I do not know, Horatio. While I was thinking of going to the court a sudden faintness came over me. What this means only the gods can tell.

Horatio Ah, may heaven grant that this omen betokens no evil.

Hamlet Be it as it may, I shall proceed to the court, even if it costs me my life.

> *Exeunt.*

Here the action shifts to the court, where the final scenes take place. The King, Leonhardus, and Phantasmo enter.

King Leonhardus, make ready, for Prince Hamlet will soon be here.

Leonhardus Your Majesty, I am ready, and I shall do my best.

King See to it. Here comes the Prince.

> *Enter* Hamlet *and* Horatio.

Hamlet May all good fortune wait upon your Majesty!

King We thank you, Prince. We are most happy that your melancholy has somewhat abated. Therefore we have today arranged a festive match between you and young Leonhardus. You shall fence with him with rapiers, and whichever of you two makes the first three hits shall win a white Neapolitan horse, with saddle and all trappings.

Hamlet Your Majesty will forgive me; I am not in good practice with the rapiers. But Leonhardus has just returned from France; there he without doubt had good practice. So I beg you to excuse me.

King Prince Hamlet, do this as a favor to us, for we are eager to learn what feints are practiced by Germans and Frenchmen.

Enter Queen.

Queen Gracious Lord and King, I must inform you of a great calamity.

King Heaven preserve us! What is it?

Queen Ophelia has climbed a high hill, and has thrown herself down and killed herself.

Leonhardus Oh, unhappy Leonhardus! In this brief time you have lost a father and a sister! Where will your misfortune still lead you? I wish I myself were dead in this misery.

King Be comforted, Leonhardus. You have our good will— so begin the match. Phantasmo, bring the rapiers. You, Horatio, shall be the referee.

. . . .

Hamlet Very well, then, Leonhardus, come on! We shall see which one of us will make a fool of the other. But if I should break any of the rules, pray excuse me, for I have not fenced for a long time.

Leonhardus I am your Highness' servant; you only jest. *In the first bout they fight clean.* Leonhardus *receives a hit.*

Hamlet That was one, Leonhardus!

Leonhardus True, your Highness. And so—revenge! *He drops his foil, seizes the poisoned rapier which lies at hand, and gives the* Prince *a thrust* en carte, *in the arm.* Hamlet *parries* Leonhardus, *so that they both drop their weapons. They both reach for a foil.* Hamlet *picks up the poisoned rapier, and mortally wounds* Leonhardus.

Leonhardus Alas, I have a mortal hit! I receive the payment which I thought to pay to another. May heaven help me!

Hamlet What the devil is this! Leonhardus, have I wounded you with the foil? What is going on here?

King Go quickly, bring forth my goblet with wine, so that the contestants may refresh themselves. Go, Phantasmo, fetch it. *(Steps down from the throne. Aside.)* I hope that when they have both drunk of the wine they will die at once, and this trick remain undiscovered.

Hamlet Tell me, Leonhardus, how did this happen?

Leonhardus Ah, Prince, I was seduced into this mischief by the King. See what you hold in your hand. It is a poisoned sword.

Hamlet Oh heaven, what is this! Protect me from it!

Leonhardus I was to wound you with it, for it is so powerfully poisoned that he who receives the slightest wound from it must instantly die.

King Ho, my lords, refresh yourselves a little, and drink. *(While the* King *rises from his seat and speaks these words, the* Queen *takes the goblet from* Phantasmo's *hand and drinks. The* King *cries out:)* Ho! Where is the goblet? Oh dearest wife, what are you doing? What has been poured into this has been mixed with most powerful poison! Alas, what have you done!

Queen Alas, I die!

The King *stands
before the* Queen.

Hamlet And you, tyrant, shall be her companion in death!

Hamlet *stabs him
from behind.*

King Alas, I am rewarded for my wickedness.

Leonhardus Farewell, Prince Hamlet. Oh world, farewell. I also die. Oh, forgive me, Prince!

Hamlet May heaven guide your soul, for you are innocent. As for this tyrant, I hope that his black sins will be washed away in hell! Ah, Horatio, my soul is now at rest, since I have wreaked revenge upon my foes. Indeed I have a wound in my arm, but I hope it means nothing. I am sorry to have stabbed Leonhardus to death, but I do not know how the fatal blade found its way to my hand. But as the deed is, so is its reward, and he has received his payment. Nothing grieves me further except my mother. Yet because of her sins she has merited her death. But tell me, who gave her the goblet that poisoned her?

Phantasmo I, my lord Prince. I also brought the poisoned sword. But the poisoned wine was intended only for you to drink.

Hamlet Were you also a party to this crime? Well, you also have your reward!

Stabs him to death.

Phantasmo Stab away until the blade is broken!

Hamlet Ah, Horatio, I fear that my fulfilled revenge will cost me my life, for I am badly wounded in the arm. I feel quite faint, my limbs grow weak, and my legs support me no more. My speech fails me; I feel the poison working in all my limbs. Yet I beg you, dear Horatio, convey the crown to Norway, to my cousin the Duke Fortempras,[1] so that the kingdom may not fall into other hands. Ah, alas, I die!

Horatio Ah, noble Prince, wait for help! Oh heavens, he sinks into my hands. Ah, what dreadful wars has this kingdom waged in recent times. No sooner has it peace than it is filled with internal unrest, contention for the crown, and murderous ambition. So sad a misfortune as we have suffered at this court may well have never happened in any age of the world's history. With the help of trusted counsellors I shall make all provision for the burial of these noble personages, according to their rank. Then I shall proceed quickly to Norway with the crown and deliver it according to the orders of this unhappy Prince.

VERSE

Thus, when a potentate with stealth grasps for the throne,
And with the vilest treachery attains it for his own,
He finds himself with scorn and mockery abhorred,
For as the deed has been, so follows the reward.

END

[1]There has been no previous mention of Fortempras in the play.

There is no temptation to linger over this meager script. The action moves along fast, propelled mainly by the needs of the plot. Characterization is incidental. For instance, Ophelia goes mad, but her madness motivates nothing as Leonhardus has already acceded to the King's scheme against Hamlet before her madness becomes known. Similarly, the news of her death comes late, just as the fatal duel is about to begin; she has been an absentee heroine with no thought given to her since her flower scene. Hamlet's interview with his mother is not a probe planned by others; he requests the interview himself for no reason, apparently, but to scold her for remarrying so soon. Nothing is accomplished except the killing of Corambus. Hamlet does not disclose the important fact that his madness is assumed; the Queen is still mourning the loss of his wits when he leaves her. In the final scene there is no motivation for the Queen's drinking from the poisoned cup. No healths have been proposed for her to wish to join in. She takes the cup, apparently on an impulse, drinks and dies almost immediately.

Yet because this play, although dated later than the Shakespearean Quartos, seems to derive in part from the early lost English *Hamlet,* it gives some idea of how the rambling prose tales may first have been compressed into a revenge drama.[1] It is doubtful that Shakespeare had a hand in plotting or writing this early *Hamlet;* contemporary allusions to the play make no mention of him. But certainly he was familiar with it, as was some of the theatre-going public. Thus the tale was not new when it appeared in the first printed version bearing Shakespeare's name: the First Quarto of 1603. In that version, however, we are in a different world. Though the plot is fast-moving, it is no longer the mainspring of the action. The characters have taken over.

[1]See note, p. xxi(n).

CHAPTER TWO

THE FIRST QUARTO

A vengeance play is made up of great wrongs accumulated on the hero at the instigation of the villain, interspersed with opportunities for revenge that are thwarted by external circumstances or mental barriers, until at the end the avenging hero seizes a last opportunity in a fit of vindictive rage. The Hamlet of the old stories and even of *Der Bestrafte Brudermord* is, beneath his mask of madness, brave and self-sufficient. He will act: only outward circumstances prolong the villain's days. But now, in the Shakespearean Quartos, the hero's inner thoughts have a share in determining the course of events. In contemplative speeches and soliloquies, Hamlet considers his world and the fate that has been thrust upon him. Death becomes a theme, death not only as punishment but as the universal end which time brings to pass.

And, under its guise as a vengeance play, Shakespeare's *Hamlet* is also a play about women. The perfidy of women, taken from the old stories as a theme to be dramatized and turned into poetry ("Frailty, thy name is woman"), is *en ieu* throughout. Mistakenly attributed to Ophelia, it results in the cruel rejection which contributes to her madness, her death, and the vengeful rage of her brother. Rightly attributed to the Queen, it adds to the infamy of a Court so corrupt that only "some strange eruption to the state" can cleanse it. The Queen is pivotal to the way the play's antagonists act toward one another. The King, because of his love for her and her love for her son, cannot overtly accomplish the thing he most desires: to rid himself of Hamlet. Hamlet, on the other hand, cannot avenge his father unless the Queen sides with him. For it is clearly a fact (though never explicitly stated) that if she is against him, he will be dealt with as a madman or a regicide, and the State will not be cleansed.

Quarto One, being as I believe one step nearer its sources, develops these themes more clearly than does the much-altered Quarto Two. One important difference is structural; it concerns the placement of the passage which shows Hamlet assuming the antic disposition. In Q1 the audience first sees Hamlet "mad" when, after entering with "To be, or not to be," he has the seemingly chance encounter with Ofelia, overheard by the King and his Chamberlain. There are textual indications that the action was intended to follow the same pattern in Q2 and subsequent versions, but a change has taken place. Hamlet enters in act II, scene ii, but now his first encounter is with the Chamberlain ("You are a Fishmonger.") The "To be, or not to be" soliloquy and ensuing passage with Ophelia have been postponed to act III, scene i, where they no longer serve as an introduction to the antic disposition, but as a sort of counterpoint to and (in my view) an interruption of the action having to do with the play-within-a-play.

The scene between Hamlet and his mother after the play is more eloquent in Q2, but the all-important question as to whether she was an accessory to her husband's murder is lost along the way. Similarly, Hamlet's redemption of his mother from infamy, stressed in the stories and still viable in Q1, is questionable in Q2. Indeed, Hamlet's own character becomes clouded in the alterations. His calling himself a coward, which has caused many years of controversy, comes in Q2 as a result of Shakespeare's more expansive use of soliloquies. In Q1 Hamlet charges himself with cowardice only once. He has just heard the Player's passionate speech and it has touched his conscience. He compares his own inaction with the Player's powerful eloquence. The passage furnishes the exposition which prepares for the play-within-a-play. I do not think his self-castigation is intended to throw any doubt on his ultimate will to act. Because his conscience has been roused by the Player, he conceives the idea of using the Players to catch the conscience of the King. However, in Q2 the question of cowardice is reopened and thus gains added weight in a new soliloquy "How all occasions doe informe against me" (IV. iv, pp. 69-70) introduced as Hamlet is departing for England.

These and other differences between the Quartos will be considered in Chapter Three and in the Appendices. The discussion that follows here is concerned with Quarto One as drama. This play is, I believe, an enlightening precursor to the texts printed later. It is sparse, but though it moves fast, it is a well-structured play and its dramatic course is true.

ACT I

I.i, pp. 1-5   It is the middle of the night, dark, cold. (It does not matter that it may be a hot sunny afternoon. The Elizabethan, the Jacobean audience will not laugh. Most likely they will shiver.) There are sentinels changing the watch. An officer of the watch who joins them has brought along a skeptical scholar, Horatio, to speak to the apparition they have seen the two past nights. Horatio thinks it is their fantasy, a trick of their mind's eye.

To that audience there were at least three sorts of ghosts: the illusion of the mind's eye; the ghost from hell, putting on someone else's likeness to damn the one he appears to; and an honest ghost, but still unhallowed: he cannot go about in hallowed season, such as Christmas.

The Ghost appears. It is not fantasy; Horatio is disabused. He recognizes it as a ghost, in looks and armor like the late King of Denmark. He speaks to it, but it makes no answer and fades away with the crowing of the cock.

Actually, the Ghost appears and leaves twice during this first scene. In between its two appearances Horatio explains to the sentry and to the officer, Marcellus, why this strict watch is being kept and why the country is so busily carrying on warlike preparations: it is because the late King (Hamlet I), in a lawful single combat for a gage, killed Fortenbrasse I of Norway. The gage was all the lands that Fortenbrasse ruled. Young Fortenbrasse (Fortenbrasse II), the son, has gathered an army to regain these lands by fighting Denmark. At Horatio's suggestion, the watch breaks up with the expressed intent of reporting the appearances of the Ghost to young Hamlet: "This Spirite dumbe to us will speake to him."

I.ii, pp. 5-10   The first court scene follows, in which the King sends the ambassadors, Cornelia and Voltemar, to negotiate with Old Norway to restrain young Fortenbrasse, his nephew, from warring against Denmark; gives permission to the Chamberlain's son, Leartes, to return to France; entreats Hamlet to stay in Denmark; and rebukes him for continuing to mourn for his father. When the Queen intervenes to beg Hamlet not to go back to Wittenberg, he says, "I shall in all my best obay you madam." Then follows Hamlet's first soliloquy, when, left alone onstage, he rails against his mother for marrying the King so soon after the death of her first husband, the King's brother. We are already in the midst of things, even before we know there has been a murder. For Hamlet, the marriage itself pollutes the realm. He wishes his "too much griev'd and sallied flesh / Would melt to nothing, or that the universall / Globe of heaven would turne al to a Chaos!" His foreboding increases when Horatio and Marcellus report on their watch of the night before. He agrees to join them that night.

I.iii, pp. 10-12   Meanwhile, the Chamberlain's son and daughter, Leartes and Ofelia, have a scene in which Leartes warns Ofelia against Hamlet's suit. The Chamberlain, Corambis, joins them and gives precepts to Leartes on friends and foes, apparel (the outward semblance) and the inward spirit. After Leartes's departure, he too warns Ofelia against Hamlet's suit and finally bids her deny him access, refuse his gifts, reject his letters. The reason for these warnings is that the only honorable conclusion of this suit is marriage, and because of the difference of their stations such a marriage is out of the question. Even in this brief scene, Ofelia flowers. She speaks only sixteen lines; she is the obedient girl. Yet doubly warned against Hamlet's suit, she makes it doubly clear that she is in love with Hamlet and he with her.

I.iv, v, pp. 12-19   Now, in the second and third platform scenes, Hamlet and the Ghost of Hamlet's father, the late King, have a talk apart from the others. The Ghost tells Hamlet that the story of his being stung to death by a serpent, which all Denmark believes, is a lie. He tells Hamlet he was killed by his brother, the present King, who had seduced his wife, Hamlet's mother, whom this murderer has now married. His description shows it to have been a perfect crime, committed in the royal garden in the afternoon, where the late King, as was his custom, was asleep. No one else was there. His brother killed him by pouring juice of hebona in his ear.

> *Ghost* If thou hast nature in thee, beare it not,
> But howsoever, let not thy heart
> Conspire against thy mother aught,
> Leave her to heaven,
> And to the burthen that her conscience beares.

The Ghost exits. In the soliloquy "O all you hoste of heaven! O earth, what else?" Hamlet swears to put out of his mind everything other than memory of the Ghost, who has bidden Hamlet revenge his murder. Marcellus and Horatio, his fellows on the watch, rejoin Hamlet. Hamlet does not tell them what the Ghost has said, but swears them to secrecy as to that night's events, and also as to his behavior if he decides to put on an antic disposition. As they go off together, Hamlet, in a very different mood from the one which prompted his ardent response to the Ghost regarding the murder (viz., "Haste me to knowe it, that (I)[1] with wings as swift as meditation, or the thought of it, may sweepe to my revenge"), now says (perhaps as an aside), "The time is out of joynt, O cursed spite, / That ever I was borne to set it right."

This is the first example of a characteristic of the hero. He meets an event or an idea first with a swift impulsive response, which reason then qualifies or rejects.

---

[1] "I" evidently omitted by printer's error from Q1, inserted by Q2 (I.v, p. 20).

ACT II

II.i,
pp. 19-
21   Time elapses. Corambis is sending his man Montano to Paris with letters and money for Leartes. Montano leaves.

Ofelia enters to tell Corambis how she met Hamlet in the gallery, and how he was dressed and acting like a madman. Corambis immediately jumps to the conclusion that Hamlet's madness is due to Ofelia's rejection of his suit. Corambis also sees the advantage to Ofelia of this condition. For—though in ordinary circumstances their differences in station would preclude marriage—as a cure of the young Prince's madness, such a marriage would be welcomed. "Lets to the King," Corambis says, "this madnesse may proove,/ Though wilde a while, yet more true to thy love." *Exeunt.*

Though no more is staged, it is reasonable to infer that, before they left Corambis's house, Corambis and Ofelia picked up some gift or gifts Hamlet had given to Ofelia and that Corambis coached Ofelia on how to behave if she were to meet Hamlet (with Corambis and the King eavesdropping).

II.ii,
pp. 21-
33   They arrive in the middle of the second court scene. The King and Queen have just welcomed Hamlet's school-fellows, Rossencraft and Gilderstone, who have come from Wittenberg in answer to a royal summons. The King asks them to see if they cannot find out from Hamlet the cause of his madness. As they exit, Corambis and Ofelia enter. The ambassadors, Cornelia and Voltemar, return from Norway and make their report of complete success: Old Norway has rebuked young Fortenbrasse, who, seeing reason, has sworn never to attack Denmark. He has agreed to use his army against the Pollacks instead, and has asked for passage across Denmark for that purpose. Cornelia and Voltemar are dismissed. Now Corambis, who on his first entrance said he believed he had found "The very depth of Hamlets lunacie," expounds his theory. At the conclusion of Corambis's exposition:

> *King* How should wee trie this same?
> *Cor.* Mary my good lord thus,
> The Princes walke is here in the galery,

There let *Ofelia* walke untill hee comes:
Your selfe and I will stand close in the study,
There shall you heare the effect of all his hart,
And if it prove any otherwise then love,
Then let my censure faile another time.
    King See where hee comes poring uppon a booke.
(Q2)[1]   *Enter Hamlet.*
    Cor. Madame, will it please your grace
To leave us here?
    Que. With all my hart.
                        Exit.
    Cor. And here *Ofelia,* reade you on this booke,
And walke aloofe, the King shal be unseene.

If Ofelia's previous conduct has made Hamlet mad, the return of his gifts will exacerbate his madness, and his consequent behavior will make that clear to the King.

All this depends on Hamlet's thinking he is alone. But he doesn't. With Corambis's "The King shal be unseene" Hamlet has seen the King and Corambis bustling into the study, and the audience is aware that he saw them. An understanding of the soliloquy, and the scene following it, as they appear in Q1, depends on having the audience know that Hamlet knows he and Ofelia are being overheard.

The protagonists are here with one exception. She has just left: the Queen. Hidden in the study are power (satanic), and wile (here beneficent). In the gallery is young love set all awry by wile and by death. Hamlet, who loves Ofelia, has been jilted (at the command of wile) by Ofelia, who loves Hamlet. Death has reached out and charged Hamlet with the duty to kill, and he has sworn to forgo all else (obviously including love) until that bestial duty is performed.

Hamlet will be talking to Ofelia but his thoughts are also on the nearby King, and because in Hamlet's mind the existence of the Queen makes itself felt wherever the King is, he is also thinking of his mother. The Queen is beautiful—to Hamlet, to the King, and to

---

[1]Q2 postpones this *Enter Hamlet* and the passage following it—the "To be, or not to be" soliloquy and the "Get thee to a nunnery" scene with Ophelia—to III.i. See Appendix B for differences between the scenarios of Q1 and Q2.

the Ghost. That is her outward semblance. They all recognize it. As of now the King possesses it. It had once been the Ghost's:

> *Ham.* Why she would hang on him, as if increase
> Of appetite had growne by what it looked on.
>   I.ii, p. 7

But no longer: that "half-heart" of the Queen—her body, her flesh in its beauty, in its lust—belongs to the King. The other half—her inward spirit, her moral instinct, her soul—belongs to Hamlet.

Ultimately the issue will be whether her flesh will overcome her spirit and her body damn her soul, or whether her soul will prevail and win her to salvation. The King is the force moving her toward damnation: Hamlet's aim throughout the play is to turn her toward salvation. In this Quarto Hamlet succeeds. At the end she wholly forsakes the King. The Christian souls are all redeemed— Hamlet's, the Queen's and Leartes's, though the King's satanic powers have delivered their bodies to death. Only the heroic friend and great pagan spirit of the play survives. Horatio will remain alive to tell the story of their deaths.

Now, however, in this second-act scene, with Ofelia waiting, the philosophic issue of salvation versus damnation is raised by Hamlet in the soliloquy with which he enters: "To be, or not to be..."[1] This soliloquy is multipurposed. It is, to the ears of the King and Corambis, supportive of Hamlet's mask—that is, of his insanity. Thoughts of death are expected in a young man mad from melancholy. The picture of the Last Judgment is an image in taunt of the King, who—satanic as he is—cannot (as we shall see later) repent, cannot with any hope ask Grace to save him from despair. But the main issue raised by the soliloquy is that of suicide, the bravest and most honorable of deaths in the pagan world. However, the Christian concept of doomsday changes that, and to the heathen perception of suicide as a noble end, a twist is given by the hope of eternal bliss that would be forfeited by self-slaughter. The dread of that

---

[1] The text of this soliloquy is quoted and discussed further in Chapter Three, pp. 95-99.

forfeiture makes all Christians cowards in this regard, fearful of self-slaughter. In other words, since by salvation lost, damnation is certain, the Christian cowardice toward self-slaughter can be characterized as fear of damnation. All this the soliloquy in Q1 describes, suggesting also the opposite possibility: that suicide is a rational and noble act in the hostile circumstances predicated, if death is a sleep—no more.

The "cowardice" of the Christian here announced provides a philosophic contrast to the pagan courage of Horatio at the end. As such, it is obviously a prelude to that.

The soliloquy ends as the lovers encounter one another. The scene breaks into dialogue. Ofelia says she has sought the opportunity which now she has (a patent lie committed to memory) to "redeliver to your worthy handes, a small remembrance, such tokens which I have received of you."

Hamlet's response is revealing. He knows not only that the King and Corambis are in the study—watching, listening—but also that Ofelia is doing something she has been put up to and saying words she has been taught:

> *Ham.* Are you faire? [outward semblance, beauty]
> *Ofel.* My Lord.
> *Ham.* Are you honest? [inward spirit, virtue]
> *Ofel.* What meanes my Lord?
> *Ham* That if you be faire and honest,
> Your beauty should admit no discourse to your honesty.
> *Ofel.* My Lord, can beauty have better priviledge than
> with honesty?

Hamlet answers, yes, since beauty can transform virtue into a bawd sooner than honesty can transform beauty. And when he says, "This was sometimes a Paradox, / But now the time gives it scope," we are reminded of how the beauteous Queen was won—the Ghost has said—by the King to his adulterous sheets by gifts. *By gifts.*

> *Ham.* I never gave you nothing.
> *Ofel.* My Lord, you know right well you did,
> And with them such earnest vowes of love,
> As would have moov'd the stoniest breast alive.

And *vows*. Does the word move Hamlet to imagine the King's vows when he seduced the Queen? And will such earnest vows of love re-echo in Ofelia's mind when, later, she sings the valentine song (IV.iii, p. 51) about the false steward who does what her father has warned her young men do, unlocking "Chastitie unto Desire"? (I.iii, p. 12).

Hamlet knows by the reaction of Ofelia (who had no stony heart) that she has loved him, perhaps still loves him of her own will. Now, however, her will appears not to be her own, but her father's. Hamlet cannot trust her under these circumstances.

> *Ham.* I never loved you.
> *Ofel.* You made me beleeve you did.
> *Ham.* O thou shouldst not a beleeved me!

Hamlet now shifts his denunciations from women to men, offering his own character as proof of their knavery. But there are adjectives in his self-denigration which are carefully chosen as threats for the ears of the eavesdropping King.

> Go to a Nunnery goe, why shouldst thou
> Be a breeder of sinners? I am myselfe indifferent honest,
> But I could accuse myselfe of such crimes
> It had beene better my mother had ne're borne me,
> O I am very prowde, ambitious, disdainefull,[1]
> With more sinnes at my backe, then I have thoughts
> To put them in, what should such fellowes as I
> Do, crawling between heaven and earth?
> To a Nunnery goe, we are arrant knaves all,
> Beleeve none of us, to a Nunnery goe.
>   *Ofel.* O heavens secure him!

She has no answers now. She has not been coached on how to counter such an onslaught, and certainly she is not prepared for the question Hamlet suddenly propounds:

---

[1]"Disdainefull" should be "revengefull" as it appears in Q2 (III.i, p. 45). But there it is misplaced as the middle word: "I am very proude, revengefull, ambitious." Surely "revengefull" should be the third word, to emphasize the taunt to the King.

Wher's thy father?
Ofel. At home my lord.

Her reply gives Hamlet an opportunity to insult Corambis—as from
now on he always will. Just as he sees the King as the satanic
influence on the Queen, so he sees Corambis as the perverting
influence on Ofelia, and as such he will take every opportunity to
mock him.

> *Ham.* For Gods sake let the doores be shut on him,
> He may play the foole no where but in his
> Owne house: to a Nunnery goe.

The taunts to the King involve the transformation of beauty
into a bawd (his seduction of the Queen) and wise men made into
monsters (cuckolds; imaging the King and Queen cuckolding Hamlet's
father during his lifetime). When after his self-denigration he returns
to the subject of women he will climax his accusations with an
outburst against marriage which will contain a threat against the
King's very life. But first:

> *Ham.* If thou dost marry, Ile give thee
> This plague to thy dowry:
> Be thou as chaste as yce, as pure as snowe,
> 'Thou shalt not scape calumny....

Ofelia can only respond with prayerful interjections—"Help him
good God," "Alas, what change is this?" "Pray God restore him"—as
Hamlet presses his charges against her sex (and his mother's). He
condemns women for their mannerisms and their seductive wiles
whereby they make themselves seem lovelier than they are. Then
he bursts out:

> A pox, t'is scurvy, Ile no more of it,
> It hath made me madde: Ile no more marriages,
> All that are married but one, shall live,
> The rest shall keepe as they are, to a Nunnery goe,

a sweeping indictment that not only threatens the King but pre-
cludes any marriage between these lovers, Hamlet and Ofelia. We
shall see how this conclusion contrasts with (and by contrast
explains) the conclusion of the only other conversation between
Hamlet and Ofelia, at the *Murder of Gonzago* (III.ii, p. 39).

With a final "To a Nunnery goe," Hamlet departs. So, in a
moment, does the heartbroken Ofelia. The King and Corambis
enter. The King expresses doubt that love is deranging Hamlet,
adding "Some deeper thing it is." Corambis is not content to let
matters rest. He persuades the King to leave him alone to probe
Hamlet, who is conveniently re-entering.

> *Cor.* Now my good Lord, do you know me?
> *Ham.* Yea very well, y'are a fishmonger.

("Fishmonger" meaning a pander, for having loosed his daughter to
Hamlet for the benefit of the King.) Hamlet proceeds to make a fool
of Corambis, who ends his questioning with: "Will you walke out of
the aire my Lord?" only to be confounded by Hamlet's answering:
"Into my grave."

Exit Corambis as the next probe begins. Rossencraft and
Gilderstone come in. Hamlet, who has been rendered suspicious
by the fact that he now knows the King and Corambis are testing
him, questions them. They admit that they have been sent for by
the King and Queen to find the cause of his discontent. Hamlet
says he wants preferment and then plays upon the word discontent,
saying neither the world, nor the heavens, nor the sea, nor Man,
contents him; no, nor woman too. Rossencraft and Gilderstone
then announce the approach of the Players. The action will now
change tracks, switching from the testing of Hamlet to preparations
for Hamlet's own test, the play-within-a-play. Corambis returns to
report that the Players have arrived.

Hamlet talks with the Players and requests a "passionate
speech." They ask what speech. He starts off, after praising the

play from which it (allegedly) comes,[1]

> The rugged *Pyrrus,* like th'arganian beast:
> No t'is not so, it begins with *Pirrus:*
> O I have it.
> The rugged *Pirrus,* he whose sable armes…[2]

and continues with a description of Pyrrhus, as he searches out his Trojan foes:

> …horridely tricked
> With blood of fathers, mothers, daughters, sonnes,
> Back't and imparched in calagulate gore,
> Rifted in earth and fire, olde grandsire *Pryam* seekes:
> So goe on.

The Player takes up.

> Anone he finds him striking too short at Greeks,
> His antike sword rebellious to his Arme,
> Lies where it falles, unable to resist.
> *Pyrrus* at *Pryam* drives, but all in rage,
> Strikes wide, but with the whiffe and winde
> Of his fell sword, th'unnerved father falles.

Here Corambis, as old and feeble as Priam (as Hamlet has made clear in his treatment of Corambis), cannot stand to see his image,

---

[1]The praise may have been a tribute to Marlowe, whose *Dido, Queen of Carthage,* unfinished at the time of his death in 1593, was completed by Nash and published in 1594. The "passionate speech," however, was not quoted from that play. It is all Shakespeare's.

[2]In *Der Bestrafte Brudermord* (and perhaps in the lost "Ur-Hamlet") Pirrus is the name of the King in the play Hamlet wants the Players to enact. It is Pirrus who lies down to sleep in his garden and is murdered by his brother. Hamlet is perhaps trying to make his choice of that play seem casual when he appears to search his memory for the King's name: "King Pir—Pir—Pir-something" (*Der BB,* act II, p. 268).

In Shakespeare's versions Hamlet appears to search his memory for the lines he will quote about Pyrrhus ("Pyrrus" or "Pirrus"), but here, Pyrrhus is the son of Achilles whom Aeneas described to Dido, and is in no way connected with the play Hamlet will request from the Players. The halting recollection seems to be a bit of stage-business that persisted, though there is no apparent motive in Hamlet's groping for the lines about the Grecian Pyrrhus. The compositors of Q1 apparently made no distinction between the spellings *Pyrrus* and *Pirrus* and used them interchangeably in referring to Achilles's son, *Pyrrhus.*

unable to resist, falling under the wind of Pyrrhus's sword, and he cries out, "Enough my friend, t'is too long." But Hamlet brushes Corambis aside saying,

> ...come on to *Hecuba,* come.
> *Play.* But who, O who had seene the mobled Queene?
> *Cor.* Mobled Queen is good, faith very good.
> *Play.* All in the alarum and feare of death rose up,
> And 'o're her weake and all ore-teeming loynes, a blancket
> And a kercher on that head, where late the diademe stoode,
> Who this had seene with tongue in venom steept,[1]
> (Gainst fortunes state)[2] would treason have pronounced,
> For if the gods themselves had seene her then,
> When she saw *Pirrus* with malitious strokes,
> Mincing her husbandes limbs,
> It would have made milch the burning eyes of heaven,
> And passion in the gods.
> *Cor.* Looke my lord if he hath not changde his colour,
> And hath teares in his eyes: no more good heart, no more.
> *Ham.* T'is well, t'is very well....

He praises the Players as being Chronicles and "briefe abstracts" of the time, and asks Corambis to see them well bestowed. *Exit Corambis.* Rossencraft and Gilderstone are still onstage, but clearly out of hearing.

> *Ham.* Come hither maisters, can you not play the murder of
> *Gonzago?*
> *Players* Yes my Lord.
> *Ham.* And could'st not thou for a neede study me
> Some dozen or sixteene lines,
> Which I would set downe and insert?
> *Players* Yes very easily my good Lord.
> *Ham.* T'is well, I thanke you: follow that lord.

The Players go off, following Corambis. And so Hamlet has conceived the plan of having the *Murder of Gonzago* enacted, with

---

[1]Q1's misprint of "with tongue invenom'd speech" is revised by Q2 (II.ii, p. 39) to "with tongue in venom steept."

[2]Q1's omission of "Gainst fortunes state" is corrected by its inclusion in Q2 (ibid.).

some twelve or sixteen lines inserted, and the Players have agreed to carry it out—all prior to the soliloquy in which the idea seems to occur to him. A soliloquy is the medium by which inmost thoughts can be conveyed to an audience. The "passionate speech" has stirred Hamlet's emotions. It has also given him an idea. He cannot express it at once, for the stage is thronged with people: the Players, Corambis, Rossencraft and Gilderstone. Not until they are gone can Hamlet share his thoughts with the audience. Yet these several characters cannot exit immediately; there is exposition to attend to. Plans must be laid for the production to be given the following night. The plot to catch the conscience of the King must be prepared by having the Players ready to re-enact (unconsciously) a murder carried out precisely as the Ghost has described the crime committed by the King. Hamlet makes suggestions; the Players readily agree. They are dismissed; Rossencraft and Gilderstone are dismissed. Then—only then—is Hamlet free to think the thoughts that lie behind the actions already taken.

> *Ham.* Why what a dunghill idiote slave am I?
> Why these Players here draw water from eyes:
> For Hecuba, why what is Hecuba to him, or he to Hecuba?
> What would he do and if he had my losse?
> His father murdred, and a Crowne bereft him,
> He would turne all his teares to droppes of blood,
> Amaze the standers by with his laments,
> Strike more then wonder in the judiciall eares,
> Confound the ignorant, and make mute the wise,
> Indeede his passion would be generall.
> Yet I like to an asse and John a Dreames,
> Having my father murdred by a villaine,
> Stand still, and let it passe, why sure I am a coward:
> Who pluckes me by the beard, or twites my nose,
> Give's me the lie i'th throate downe to the lungs,
> Sure I should take it, or else I have no gall,
> Or by this I should a fatted all the region kites
> With this slaves offell, this damned villaine,
> Treacherous, bawdy, murderous villaine:
> Why this is brave, that I the sonne of my deare father,

Should like a scalion, like a very drabbe
Thus raile in wordes. About my braine,
I have heard that guilty creatures sitting at a play,
Hath, by the very cunning of the scene, confest a murder
Committed long before.
This spirit that I have seene may be the Divell,
And out of my weakenesse and my melancholy,
As he is very potent with such men,
Doth seeke to damne me, I will have sounder proofes,
The play's the thing,
Wherein I'le catch the conscience of the King.

Exit.

The passionate speech, as we have said, must arouse Hamlet's conscience in order to explain his use of the Players to catch the conscience of the King. Plainly, Hamlet's conscience, aroused, reproaches him for his delay in revenging his father's murder. He reflects that the Player can stir himself and his listeners to tears with the sufferings of a fictitious character. A wronged person whose sorrows are real should go far beyond; should turn his tears to drops of blood, should, in fact, out-Pyrrhus Pyrrhus. Hamlet condemns himself as a coward because, in contrast to that raging avenger, he rails in words. And then...and then comes "About my braine." Reason has taken over, pointing out that he doesn't even know for sure that the King has killed his father. Reason insists that the murder be established beyond a reasonable doubt and shows a way to use the Players as a test.[1] The Elizabethans, who believed

---

[1]The reasoning and planning which lead to the play-within-a-play must be appended to this soliloquy because of the fact that Rossencraft and Gilderstone have displaced Horatio in this scene. In *Der BB,* and probably in the lost *Hamlet,* Horatio is Hamlet's only friend and confidant. Early in *Der BB* (act II, pp. 266-267) Hamlet discusses the Ghost's revelation with Horatio, who warns him that the Ghost may be deceiving him. It is just after this warning that the Players arrive "at the right moment" for Hamlet to test the Ghost's honesty. He tells Horatio of his plan for the play-within-a-play, and the preparations to put that plan into effect then follow. When, later, Hamlet is sent away, the two who accompany him are enlisted as "bandits" and have no connection with any earlier part of the play. As revised by Shakespeare, Rossencraft and Gilderstone will accompany Hamlet. By making them schoolfellows, and introducing them early, he has enriched his play, but the revision causes complications of its own. Horatio is shunted to one side, and there is no opportunity for Hamlet to discuss the motivation and the planning of the play-within-a-play. What cannot be put into dialogue must be thus communicated by Hamlet solus.

in ghosts honest and dishonest, would have found the logic more compelling than we do today.

I believe that Hamlet has more than the testing of the King in mind when he talks to the Players about inserting the twelve to sixteen lines. Is he not also thinking of the lines he will write into the upcoming play to test his mother? From the moment the Ghost told him of the murder and bade him contrive nothing against his mother, rather to leave her to her conscience and to Heaven, Hamlet must have had in his mind the question of her complicity in the murder. This question he can mention to no one. It has to remain his secret quest. Believing, as he does, that his mother's tears at his father's burial were hypocritical, that, while following his corpse in her new shoes, she was thinking of running in them to the new King's incestuous sheets—with these beliefs, it is reasonable for Hamlet to think the Queen might well have been an accessory to the murder. While he tests the King's guilt by the Players, I believe he has decided to test hers, too. The ten lines for the Play-Duchess to speak will try the Queen: was she an accessory?

If she was an accessory, she is as guilty as the King. Perhaps more so. But if she is innocent, if she knows nothing of the murder, and if Hamlet can persuade her to aid him in his revenge, she can thereby redeem herself. He will have won her back to salvation. Thus, throughout Quarto One, in addition to Hamlot's wreaking of vengeance on the King (bestial), is Hamlet's quest to save his mother's soul (heavenly).

ACT III

III.i, In the court scene that follows, Rossencraft and Gilder-
pp. 33-34 stone announce the play, and the King and Queen agree
(Q2)[1] to attend. After Rossencraft and Gilderstone leave,
Corambis suggests a second eavesdrop scene as a way to discover the cause of Hamlet's madness: after the play the Queen will send

---

[1]In Q2 and all subsequent versions, the overheard passages ("To be, or not to be" and "Get thee to a nunnery") are inserted into this scene after the departure of Rosencraus and Guyldensterne.

for Hamlet, and (with Corambis hiding behind the arras) she and
nature will induce him to tell all. Both King and Queen agree
enthusiastically to the plan.

> *King* It likes us well, Gerterd, what say you?
> *Queene* With all my heart, soone will I send for him.
> *Cor.* My selfe will be that happy messenger,
> Who hopes his griefe will be reveal'd to her.
>
> > *Exeunt omnes.*

The irony is poignant. The old man will be a stand-in for the King,
behind the arras. As a happy messenger, he will summon the
young Prince to the meeting where the young Prince will kill him,
taking him for the King.

III.ii,   *Enter Hamlet and the Players.*
pp. 35-42   *Ham.* Pronounce me this speech trippingly a the tongue as I
       taught thee.

If he mouths it, Hamlet would rather hear a "towne bull bellow."
He offers the Player his views on moderation rather than exag-
geration in acting, and then proceeds to castigate clowns whose
pantomime interrupts the action of a play. On the subject of clowns,
he takes a swipe at Ben Jonson, alluding to a line in *Every Man Out
of His Humour* about coats that needed a cullison (a "cullison" was a
badge worn by a servant). "My coate wants a cullison," Hamlet
says, as an example of the stale jests in a clown's "sute of jeasts."
The line was evidently well known and good for a laugh.[1]

    Hamlet sends the Players in to get ready. He calls Horatio to him
and tells him about his plot to catch the King. This is their first
scene alone. Horatio has not been on since the "swear scene" on the
battlements. But we infer from their talk now that he has been told,

---

[1]The first recorded use of this form appears in the Jonson play which Shakespeare's company acted in 1599. The line reads: "I'll keepe men....and I'll give
coats...but I lacke a cullisen." *The Complete Plays of Ben Jonson,* ed. E. Rhys,
vol. 1, p. 70. The reference does not appear in later *Hamlet* texts, perhaps
because it was no longer topical.

offstage, about the Ghost's story of the murder. Hamlet now asks
Horatio to watch the King closely when the murder scene comes on:

> Marke thou the King, doe but observe his lookes,
> For I mine eies will rivet to his face:
> And if he doe not bleach, and change at that,
> It is a damned ghost that we have seene.

The murder scene will show the poisoning of the Play-Duke,
while Lucianus, the Play-Murderer, speaks the six lines Hamlet has
written for him. Those six plus the ten written for the Play-Duchess
comprise the designated sixteen inserted lines.

And now the Court arrives for the *Murder of Gonzago.*

Horatio takes his place to one side, aware of one aim only: to
watch the King. Hamlet's motives are more complex. He will watch
the Queen as well as the King. And he must maintain his mask.

The Queen's second marriage was suspiciously close to her
husband's death. The Ghost has said that before his brother
murdered him, his brother had seduced his wife, the Queen. This
seduction is not mentioned in Saxo but is true of Queen Geruth in
Belleforest. There were people—so Belleforest says—who suspected
that Geruth knew of the planned murder and abetted it. On this
point the Ghost has been silent. Does Gertred know?

Hamlet has written "some dozen or sixteene lines" to be inserted
in the script. "Twelve to sixteen" might be a way of saying "several"
but does seem to indicate more lines than the six we believe he
contrived for the murderer, Lucianus. In Q1, the Play-Duchess has
two speeches only, and, as we have said, they add up to ten lines.
Clearly, I think, Hamlet inserted those lines and for a purpose.

We do not know how the Players speak Hamlet's lines. Lucianus,
evidently no subtle actor ("leave thy damnable faces," Hamlet cries),
may "mouth" his lines. Does the "Lady" who plays the Duchess
observe Hamlet's directive and speak "trippingly a the tongue"? If
so, her quick, light delivery plus Hamlet's interjections (his "O
wormewood, wormewood!" and "If she should breake now") would
furnish important clues for determining the lines he inserted for her.

With the traps set and ready to be sprung, Hamlet chooses to sit by Ofelia. She will provide his cover. But as always when Hamlet is playing a part, the byplay has many overtones.

Ofelia is the successor of the foster-sister in Saxo. As we have said, one of the probes of Amleth's sanity involved luring him to a secluded spot and having him come on a beautiful girl who appeared to be alone with him, although in fact courtiers would be hidden among the trees, watching. Warned of the trap by a courtier who was friendly to him, Amleth abstained from intercourse with her then, but later, in an impenetrable fen with no one watching, they had intercourse. She gladly acceded, having known him since childhood.

The two scenes Hamlet has with Ofelia are clearly derived from this sequence in Saxo. In the first, the scene in the gallery (II.ii, pp. 24-27), he discovers they are being spied upon and, as in Saxo, plays indifference to the girl there and then. He heaps upon her his disillusionment with womankind; bids her go to a nunnery rather than be a mother of sinners; predicts she will be slandered no matter how virtuous she is; and tells her, if she must marry, to marry a fool, for wise men know what monsters (cuckolds) women make of them. He works himself up to a final threat: there will be no more marriages; all that are married but one shall live; the rest are to keep as they are (unmarried).

So much for the scene in the woods, as it were, with the courtiers (here the King and Corambis) listening and watching. As for the scene in the fen, in this case it takes place at the play, in full view (though perhaps not in hearing) of the Court. There cannot be intercourse here; nonetheless intercourse is the subject which Hamlet, ambiguously, broaches to Ofelia: "Lady will you give me leave... / To lay my head in your lappe?" "No my Lord." And he pretends she mistook his question: "Upon your lap, what do you thinke I meant contrary matters?" And when, after more interplay between them, she says, "Your jests are keene my Lord," he answers,

> It would cost you a groning to take them off.
> *Ofel.* Still better and worse.
> *Ham.* So you must take your husband....

The dialogue has come full circle. At the beginning, "lay my head in your lappe" and "contrary matters" implied intercourse between a lewd fellow and a whore. But now the intercourse is between a virgin and her husband. And where the earlier Hamlet-Ofelia scene ended with "Ile no more marriages," rejecting, *inter alia,* any marriage between Hamlet and Ofelia, the second scene ends with a virgin on her marriage night with her husband. As it is Hamlet's jests whose keenness she, a virgin, is to take off, the wedding night here prefigured is with Hamlet as her husband.

There are some facts that should be kept in mind when considering the implications of this scene. Hamlet loves Ofelia (although we are not to know that until she is dead). In his view, she has jilted him though she loved him dearly before. Therefore when, after the Prologue has delivered his speech, Hamlet comments on its brevity, asking, "I'st a prologue, or a poesie for a ring?" which elicits Ofelia's acquiescent "T'is short my Lord," Hamlet's riposte "As womens love" may be more than idle banter, more than a dig at the Queen. It may come from the heart.

In the meantime, while we have been looking behind the scenes, the Court sits assembled; the Queen has invited Hamlet to sit beside her, but he has chosen Ofelia, and has begun his suggestive byplay with her.

The dumb show enters. The Duke, the Duchess,[1] and lastly the murderer go through their brief pantomime in the orchard.

As I read it, Hamlet does not expect the dumb show and worries that the King will be forewarned before the trap can be sprung. So when Ofelia asks, "What meanes this my Lord?," Hamlet shows his anxiety by answering, "This is myching Mallico, that meanes mischiefe."[2]

At the entrance of the Prologue, Ofelia again asks, "What doth this meane my lord?" and Hamlet, again fearful that the Prologue

[1]In Q1, the characters are *King* and *Queene* in the stage directions denoting their entrance; thereafter they are *Duke* and *Dutchesse*. In Q2 the characters are *King* and *Queene* throughout.

[2]In Q1 misprinted "my chiefe"; in Q2 (III.ii, p. 50) corrected to "mischiefe."

will prematurely put into words the meaning of the dumb show (the argument of the play) answers:

> You shall heare anone, this fellow will tell you all.
> *Ofe.* Will he tell us what this shew meanes?
> *Ham.* I, or any shew you'le shew him,
> Be not afeard to shew, hee'le not be afeard to tell:
> O these Players cannot keepe counsell [cunsell], thei'le tell
>   all.

The double meaning is plain: if a maid unmasks her beauty to them, the Players will blazon her forth,[1] and the Prologue will blazon forth the meaning of the dumb show.

The Prologue now speaks:

> For us, and for our Tragedie,
> Heere stowping to your clemencie,
> We begge your hearing patiently.

And this is where Hamlet, relieved of his anxiety, expostulates, "T'st a prologue, or a poesie for a ring?"

The Play-Duke and Play-Duchess enter. Hamlet is all attention now. The "Lady" among the Players will soon speak the Duchess's lines, the lines that are to test the Queen. Listen to her and to Hamlet when the lines are spoken. Will the Queen not blench at them?

> *Duke* Full fortie yeares are past, their date is gone,
> Since happy time joyn'd both our hearts as one:
> And now the blood that fill'd my youthfull veines,
> Runnes weakely in their pipes, and all the straines
> Of musicke, which whilome pleasde mine eare,
> Is now a burthen that Age cannot beare:
> And therefore sweete Nature must pay his due,
> To heaven must I, and leave the earth with you.

---

[1]Compare Leartes's earlier warning to Ofelia: "The Chariest maide is prodigall enough, / If she unmaske hir beautie to the Moone. / Vertue it selfe scapes not calumnious thoughts" (I.iii, p. 11).

1. *Dutchesse* **O say not so, lest that you kill my heart,**
2. **When death takes you, let life from me depart.**
   Duke Content thy selfe, when ended is my date,
   Thou maist (perchance) have a more noble mate,
   More wise, more youthfull, and one.
3. *Dutchesse* **O speake no more, for then I am accurst,**
4. **None weds the second, but she kils the first:**
5. **A second time I kill my Lord that's dead,**
6. **When second husband kisses me in bed.**
   Ham. O wormewood, wormewood!
   Duke I doe beleeve you sweete, what now you speake,
   But what we doe determine oft we breake,
   For our devises[1] stil are overthrowne,
   Our thoughts are ours, their ends[2] none of our owne:
   So thinke you will no second husband wed,
   But die thy thoughts, when thy first Lord is dead.
7. *Dutchesse* **Both here and there pursue me lasting strife,**
8. **If once a widdow, ever I be wife.**
   Ham. If she should breake (it)[3] now.
   Duke T'is deepely sworne, sweete leave me here a while,
   My spirites growe dull, and faine I would beguile the tedious
   time with sleepe.
9. *Dutchesse* **Sleepe rock thy braine,**
10. **And never come mischance beteene us twaine.**
    Exit Lady.

As the Duke lies sleeping, Hamlet breaks in:

Madam, how do you like this play?
   Queene The Lady protests too much.
   Ham. O but **shee'le** keepe her word.
   King Have you heard the argument, is there no offence in it?
   Ham. No offence in the world, poyson in jest, poison in jest.

By "offence," the King means matter that is offensive (objectionable)
to him or to the Queen. Already the dumb show has put suspicions

[1] In Q1 "demises"; corrected in Q2 (III.ii, p. 52) to "devises."
[2] In Q1 misprinted "end's"; corrected to "ends" in Q2 (ibid.).
[3] In Q1 "it" is omitted; corrected by insertion in Q2 (ibid.).

in his mind. Already second marriages and the wife's killing her first husband have been mentioned. Hamlet, on the other hand, treats "offence" as though it meant "crime" and denies the poisoning was a crime, because the act was done in jest. Poisoning in jest is no offense. (And this reference to jest begins the sequence on that subject which is to end with Ofelia's "Your jests are keene my Lord.")

The King changes the subject. He has led Hamlet too near the suspicious question—the poisoning—and wishes to sheer off. He asks what Hamlet calls the name of the play. But Hamlet, as always at whatever cost, cannot resist pressing the taunt (and thus risk doing just what he feared the dumb show and the Prologue might have done, viz., scare the King into rising before Lucianus has played his part):

> *Ham.* Mouse-trap: mary how trapically: this play is
> The image of a murder done in *guyana, Albertus*
> Was the Dukes name, his wife *Baptista,*
> Father, it is a knavish peece a worke: but what
> A that, it toucheth not us, you and I that have free
> Soules, let the galld jade wince, this is one
> *Lucianus* nephew to the King.

Hamlet, in carrying his taunt so far, finds himself indeed playing Chorus. For suddenly the man has entered who will set the trap. If his soul be not free, will not the King wince? If it is his sin being re-enacted, will he not bleach? ("And if he doe not bleach, and change at that, / It is a damned ghost that we have seene.") The murderer will be tested. Lucianus is onstage.

Hamlet cannot say "this is one / *Lucianus* brother to the King" without giving too much away. But his mind is so centered on changing "brother" to "nephew" that he forgets that he has just told the King the play concerns a Duke and his wife, not a King and Queen.

At this point the innocent Ofelia intervenes: "Ya're as good as a *Chorus* my lord." The Chorus she speaks of "interpreted" a dumb show. (This is what Hamlet did in *Der BB* when only a dumb show was enacted.) Here Hamlet is doing what in his anxiety he told Ofelia the Prologue would do: "thei'le tell all."

But choruses interpreted puppet shows as well as dumb shows. Hamlet answers Ofelia's praise with "I could interpret the love you beare, if I sawe the poopies[1] dallying." The poopies are Ofelia and a lover, but as in all his talk with her in this scene, there is a *double entendre*. The poopies are also the King and Queen, whom Hamlet is watching. Presumably they are showing each other affection in some way—"dallying." Ofelia responds to the talk about poopies with,

> Y'are very pleasant my lord.
> *Ham.* Who I, your onlie jig-maker, why what shoulde a man do but be merry? for looke how cheerefully my mother lookes, my father died within these two houres.

There are reasons why the Queen could be looking cheerful, each with its own significance:

1. She has been dallying with the King.
2. She has come to the play "joy'd at the soule" that Hamlet "is inclin'd to any kinde of mirth," and Hamlet has discussed the play with her quite rationally.
3. She is innocent of any part in, or indeed any knowledge of the murder. This will become clear in her scene with Hamlet after the play. Hamlet's lines, contrived to make her blench if guilty, have left her quite unmoved. Hamlet, watching her, has seen her cheerfully dallying, neither blenching nor disturbed by his carefully contrived lines.

The literal-minded Ofelia corrects Hamlet as to his father's death with, "Nay, t'is twice two months, my Lord," and Hamlet cries:

> Two months, nay then let the divell weare blacke,
> For i'le have a sute of Sables: Jesus, two months dead,
> And not forgotten yet?

---

[1] "Poopies": puppets.

The irony is in the contrast between this "two months"—taken as so long a time that young Hamlet has become old enough for a "sute of Sables," age's apparel, to be appropriate to him—and, in his first soliloquy, the two months between the death of his mother's first husband and her marriage to a second, taken as so short a time "a beast / Devoid of reason would not have made / Such speede" (I.ii, p. 7).

Hamlet continues:

> ...nay then there's some
> Likelyhood, a gentlemans memorie may outlive death,[1]
> But by my faith hee must build churches then,
> Or els hee must follow the old Epitythe,
> With hoh, with ho, the hobi-horse is forgot.

And then follows the dialogue already quoted:

> *Ofel.* Your jests are keene my Lord.
> *Ham.* It would cost you a groning to take them off.
> *Ofel.* Still better and worse.
> *Ham.* So you must take your husband....

These are Hamlet's last words to Ofelia alive.

The time has come for the trap to be sprung. Lucianus, the Play-Murderer, is evidently indulging in some melodramatic acting. Hamlet cries out to him:

> Begin, a poxe, leave thy damnable faces and begin,
> Come, the croking raven doth bellow for revenge.

He is calling for the speech that will test the King. And now at last the murderer speaks his six lines:

---

[1]Due to a printer's error, in Q1 this line reads, "a gentlemans death may outlive memorie." In Q2 (III.ii, p. 49): "then there's hope a great mans memorie may out-live his life halfe a yeere."

1. **Thoughts blacke, hands apt, drugs fit, and time agreeing,**
2. **Confederate season, else no creature seeing:**
3. **Thou mixture rancke, of midnight weedes collected,**
4. **With *Hecates* bane thrise blasted, thrise infected,**
5. **Thy naturall magicke, and dire propertie,**
6. **On[1] wholesome life usurps immediately.**

Exit.

> *Ham.* He poysons him for his estate.
> *King* Lights, I will to bed.
> *Cor.* The king rises, lights hoe.

Exeunt King and Lordes.

Horatio and Hamlet agree the King is guilty:

> *Hor.* The king is mooved my lord.
> *Ham.* I *Horatio,* i'le take the Ghosts word
> For more than all the coyne in *Denmarke.*

Rossencraft and Gilderstone report that Hamlet's mother craves to speak to him. Hamlet abuses them, claiming they try to play him like a pipe, and that they, like sponges, soak up orders and rewards from the King. As they leave, Corambis enters, as usual coming right after Rossencraft and Gilderstone and bringing the same news: his mother would speak with him. Hamlet gibes at him by pointing out a cloud which Corambis agrees looks first like a camel, then like a weasel ("T'is back't like a weasell"), and finally like a whale. Only when the old man has given his assent to each likeness, does he receive an answer to his message: "Why then tell my mother i'le come by and by." *Exit Corambis.*

Hamlet says good night to Horatio, who leaves.[2] Then, in the first explicit reference to his mother since his bitter soliloquy in act I ("O that this too much griev'd and sallied flesh"), Hamlet expresses his pent-up anxiety, not yet wholly allayed even by her evidently innocent response to the Duchess's lines.

---

[1]In Q1, "one"; changed in Q2 (III.ii, p. 53) to "on."

[2]Most readers will have forgotten Horatio was there. This is another instance in which the presence of Rossencraft and Gilderstone moves Horatio into the background.

> My mother she hath sent to speake with me:
> O God, let ne're the heart of *Nero* enter
> This soft bosome.
> Let me be cruell, not unnaturall.
> I will speake daggers, those sharp wordes being spent,
> To doe her wrong my soule shall ne're consent.

But that he is not sure of this restraint, the prayer makes evident. If he finds she was an accessory, there is no telling. The Ghost, too, fearing Hamlet may lose control, will appear (somewhat tardily) to protect her.

As we have said, until Hamlet knows whether the Queen was an accomplice, he cannot kill the King. If she was an accomplice, and he kills the King, she will afford him (Hamlet) no protection against the courtiers, who will do away with him as a regicide. The courtiers do not know the King murdered his brother. They think the late King died of a serpent's sting. And this mad young Prince will have no way of proving the Ghost's story as true, or even that the Ghost told such a story. With the Queen's aid and protection and with her to back up his story, the situation changes radically.

But more important than these practical matters is the ideological view. The wreaking of vengeance is bestial. No matter how just the punishment, executing it is brutal: the executioner performs a filthy task. Hamlet's reason recognizes this. He is, as a rational being, reluctant to kill the King. So, unless and until his mother joins him in this bestial function as a means of redeeming herself, he will postpone it—indefinitely. That he was born to carry it out is indeed a cursed spite.

III.iii, pp. 42-43 (Q2)[1] On his way to this fateful interview—and he knows that it is fateful—Hamlet happens on the King, kneeling before an altar. The King has entered with a soliloquy that shows the play has touched his conscience and he has knelt to try to pray Heaven for pardon.

[1]In Q2 Rosencraus and Guyldensterne enter with the King and are told they will be accompanying Hamlet to England. When they go out, Polonius (Corambis) enters and reports that Hamlet is on his way to his mother's chamber. All this, before the King tries to repent.

It is the doom of Hamlet—who hates outward semblance and believes only in the truth within—always to take outward semblance as truth. He does so in Corambis's case and in Ofelia's case. Corambis, in planning the Hamlet-Ofelia eavesdropped-on interview, is trying to prove what he believes: that Hamlet is mad from thwarted love for Ofelia; if so, he can be cured by their marriage. Ofelia, as the decoy, is trying to prove the same thing. They are working for, not against, Hamlet. But Hamlet, seeing the eaves-dropping, assumes that they are conspiring against him. Similarly, Rossencraft and Gilderstone. They are for him. He assumes they are against him. (Ultimately he will assume Leartes is his friend, who is in fact his mortal enemy.)

So here, he comes upon the King, kneeling, apparently praying. Hamlet assumes he *is* praying, and acts accordingly. In fact the King is not praying. He cannot pray: "My wordes fly up, my sinnes remaine below. / No King on earth is safe, if Gods his foe." True prayer carries the sins, not just the words describing them, up. "Aske grace of heaven"——he bids himself—"to keepe thee from despaire." But he can't. Like Macbeth, after his primal murder, the King cannot pray. Hamlet takes the semblance, the kneeling, for truth and sees him as praying.

Hamlet thinks aloud. It is in the soliloquies that we learn how his mind works, and through them we see it is—as we have said   a characteristic of his to start in one direction, and then, reason taking over, to turn in another.

One such reversal came at the beginning of the scene in the gallery where Hamlet and Ofelia were spied on by the King and Corambis—and where, in Q1, the audience was seeing Hamlet for the first time after he had decided to put on the antic disposition. He came in, "poring uppon a booke."

> *Ham.* To be, or not to be, I there's the point,
> To Die, to sleepe, is that all? I all:
> **No,** to sleepe, to dreame, I mary there it goes.
> II.ii, p. 24

Another abrupt change in direction came at the end of his soliloquy when he was left alone onstage after the Player had given the passionate speech about the fall of Troy. The Player's emotions stirred Hamlet's, and he berated himself for having been so passive in the face of real—not fictional—calamities. But suddenly he bid his brain to turn about:

> Why this is brave, that I the sonne of my deare father,
> Should like a scalion, like a very drabbe
> Thus raile in wordes. **About my braine,**
>
> II.ii, p. 33

and after this abrupt reversal he concocted action—the play—to catch the conscience of the King.

So now again: the King is kneeling, defenseless and unaware. Hamlet's impulse is to seize the moment and carry out his revenge. He draws his sword:

> I so, come forth and worke thy last,
> And thus hee dies: and so am I revenged:
> **No, not so....**

He desists, ostensibly because he reasons that if he kills the King at prayer, the penitent will make his way to Heaven. But we know there is a less theological reason for his restraint. He must see the Queen and win her confession of guilt, or her revelation of innocence and agreement to assist in punishing the King. Reason expressed and unexpressed thus postpones the killing of the King.

III.iv, pp. 43-46   He puts up his sword and moves on to his mother's chamber. There he finds her apparently alone. He locks the door. They bicker. She moves to leave him. He evidently takes hold of her and drags her toward a seat.

> *Ham.*.... come here, sit downe, for you shall heare me speake.
> *Queene* What wilt thou doe? Thou wilt not murder me:
> Helpe hoe.

> *Cor.* [from behind the arras] Helpe for the Queene.
> *Ham.* I a Rat, dead for a Duckat.
> Rash intruding foole, farewell,
> I took thee for thy better.
> *Queene* Hamlet, what has thou done?
> *Ham.* **Not so much harme, good mother,**
> **As to kill a king, and marry with his brother.**
> *Queene* How! Kill a king!

Alone with his mother, the suspicion (so long kept secret) is expressed; the charge is made. At last Hamlet has said to the Queen, "You killed my father and married his brother." It must be remembered that up to this point the audience has not been told whether the Queen knows her first husband has been murdered, or whether she thinks he died—as the whole of Denmark believed—from a snakebite.

> *Queene* How! Kill a king!
> *Ham.* I a King....

And he tells her to sit down, and he'll make her look into her heart and see how black it shows.

> *Queene* Hamlet, what mean'st thou by these **killing words?**[1]
> *Ham.* Why this I meane....

He has at hand portraits of her two husbands. He describes her first husband in noble terms, continuing,

> ...and he is dead.
> **Murdred, damnably murdred,** this was your husband,
> Looke you now, here is your husband...

and he describes her second husband in ignoble, indeed villainous terms, concluding:

---

[1]Probably she means "words about killing" rather than "words that kill." Thus this line is part of Q1's emphasis on murder in this scene.

A! have you eyes and can you looke on him
That slew my father, and your deere husband,
To live in the incestuous pleasure of his bed?
   Queene O Hamlet, speake no more.
   Ham. To leave him that bare a Monarkes minde,
For a king of clowts, of very shreads.
   Queene Sweet Hamlet cease.
   Ham. Nay but still to persist and dwelle in sinne,
To sweate under the yoke of infamie,
To make increase of shame, **to seale damnation.**
   Queene Hamlet, no more.
   Ham. Why appetite with you is in the waine,
Your blood runnes backeward now from whence it came,
Who'le chide hote blood within a Virgins heart,
When lust shall dwell within a matrons breast?
   Queene Hamlet, thou cleaves my heart in twaine.
   Ham. O throw away the worser part of it, and keepe the
     better.
                Enter the ghost in his night gowne.[1]

Hamlet speaks to the Ghost, which, of course, the Queen
hears. The Ghost answers Hamlet, which the Queen does not
hear. The Ghost (his honesty now proven) says to Hamlet, "Doe
not neglect, nor long time put it [the vengeance] off," and then:

> But I perceive by thy distracted lookes,
> Thy mother's fearefull, and she stands amazde:
> Speake to her Hamlet, for her sex is weake,
> Comfort thy mother, Hamlet, thinke on me.

The Queen neither hears nor sees the Ghost. So she thinks it is
Hamlet's madness that conjures up this Ghost to see, to talk to, to
listen to:

> *Queene* Alas, it is the weakenesse of thy braine,
> Which makes thy tongue to blazon thy hearts griefe,

---

[1]"For owners of draughty castles the night gown was the thick wrap which was
removed before getting into bed." D. Hartley, *Lost Country Life,* p. 268.

i.e., "which makes you talk as if to your dead father," and at the thought of his dead father, the Queen suddenly realizes it is not just his dead father, but his *murdered* father, and that he has accused her of participating in that murder: "As to kill a king, and marry with his brother." She cries out:

> **But as I have a soule, I sweare by heaven,**
> **I never knew of this most horride murder:**
> But Hamlet, this is onely fantasie,
> And for my love forget these idle fits.

She has the skepticism natural to those who have not seen the Ghost.[1]

The Queen's reaction, coupled with her declaration of innocence, leads Hamlet to an important revelation.

> Idle, no mother, my pulse doth beate like yours,
> **It is not madnesse that possesseth Hamlet.**

He then asks her to forbear the adulterous bed tonight and win herself little by little to "lothe him [the King] quite:"

> **And mother, but assist mee in revenge,**
> **And in his death your infamy shall die.**
>   *Queene Hamlet,* I vow by that majesty,
> That knowes our thoughts, and lookes into our hearts,
> **I will conceale, consent, and doe my best,**
> **What stratagem soe're thou shalt devise.**
>   *Ham.* It is enough,[2] mother good night:
> Come sir, I'le provide for you a grave,
> Who was in life a foolish prating knave.
>   *Exit Hamlet with the*
>   *dead body.*

[1]Earlier, in the first platform scene, Marcellus, who had seen the apparition, said of Horatio, who had not, *"Horatio sayes tis but our fantasie"* (I.i, p. 1).

[2]Hamlet's response to the Queen's oath parallels the conclusion to his own oath after his first scene with the Ghost, when he vowed that, in the tables of his memory, remembrance of the Ghost "all alone shall sit… / Soe t'is enough I have sworne" (I.v, pp. 16-17).

Act IV

There is no impediment left to Hamlet's execution of the punishment of his father's murderer. Indeed the Queen has vowed to help him wreak the revenge, and in doing so, as Hamlet foretells, her "infamy shall die." She will redeem herself from the infamy that her seduction by, and hasty incestuous marriage to, the King have placed her under.

Mortal, nevertheless, is the Queen. Hamlet has told her of the murder, and she believes him. Hamlet has asked her to join him in executing his revenge, in meting out just punishment to the criminal, and she has vowed, "I will conceale, consent, and doe my best, / What stratagem soe're thou shalt devise." But, as the Play-Duke so plainly warned his copiously professing Play-Duchess:

> I doe beleeve you sweete, what now you speake,
> But what we doe determine oft we breake,
> For our devises stil are overthrowne,
> Our thoughts are ours, their ends none of our owne:
> So thinke you will no second husband wed,
> But die thy thoughts, when thy first Lord is dead.
>
> III.ii, p. 38

In spite of her oath to help Hamlet, the Queen's behavior is not freed from the King's influence. There is nothing to suggest that she forbears his bed; she still believes his lies as, under his spell, she evidently has done since her seduction. At the same time, it is evident that she believes Hamlet and the disclosures he has made. So when she tells the King that her son was "as raging as the sea / ...and in his rage / The goode olde man he killes" (IV.i, p. 46), she is keeping her word; she is protecting Hamlet. But in fact it was in real but temporary madness that Hamlet killed Corambis; he was acting on impulse, without reason. It proves to be a fatal error, for Corambis's death will beget his own, as well as that of Ofelia and the others.

In this play there are several sorts of madness: the feigned madness of the antic disposition; the temporary madness that overtakes Hamlet when impulse prevails over reason; the true madness of the bereaved Ophelia; and the mad passion of rage which characterizes Leartes after his father's death and that also characterizes Hamlet at the moment when he kills the King. Hamlet has as much cause for rage as Leartes; in fact he has more cause. But in the early part of the play, reason restrains him. Reason demands that the Ghost's charges against the King be verified. And even after the King has proved himself guilty, reason prompts Hamlet to spare a would-be penitent, and move on to his mother's chamber. There, however, when he hears the voice from behind the arras, he stabs without stopping to look. This impulse, this un-reasoning violence, begins the sequence of events that will destroy him. He has given the King proof that he is dangerous. In later scenes he will yield again to impulse when he leaps into Ofelia's grave to out-rant Leartes. Again the impulse will be fateful; in trying to atone for his rashness, he will trust Leartes too far. Hamlet is being quite truthful in his apology to Leartes when he says both these acts (the killing of Corambis and the leap into Ofelia's grave) were due to his madness. Finally, his revenge upon the King—are we to consider that another instance in which the sovereignty of reason has abandoned him? It is true that the double-death, by rapier and poison, is what the King himself had planned. Thus Hamlet is following the theme developed in Saxo and Belleforest, of Amleth's killing his foe with his foe's own weapon. It may also be true that regicide, fratricide and incest were considered such heinous crimes by the contemporary audience that no punishment meted out to the King would have seemed too severe. Nevertheless, forcing poison down a dying man's throat comes across as a savage act, motivated by frenzy more than by justice.

At this point recall the incident described in both Saxo and Belleforest: Amleth, after killing the courtier—hidden under the mattress to eavesdrop on the Queen's and Amleth's "private" interview—disposed of the body by cutting it up, boiling it, and putting it down the privy where the pigs, wallowing in the filth, ate the flesh and scattered the bones. King Feng, on returning from his trip (which was planned to induce Amleth and his mother to think they could meet secretly) sought out the eavesdropping courtier, could not find him, and asked Amleth what had happened to him. Amleth replied that he had fallen down the privy and been eaten by the pigs. This report of devoured flesh and scattered bones provides the emblematic themes for two Q1 scenes we will be dealing with: the scene which follows immediately between Hamlet and the King, in the presence of the Queen and Rossencraft and Gilderstone (the flesh scene, IV.i, pp. 46-48); and, later, the scene between the gravedigger and Hamlet, with Horatio present (the bones scene, V.i, pp. 55-58).

IV.i,   The first of these two scenes continues the action that
pp. 46-48   ended Act III. The King, attended by Rossencraft and
(Q2)[1]   Gilderstone, has joined the Queen, apparently in a room adjacent to her bedchamber. Rossencraft and Gilderstone are sent to find Hamlet and the body of Corambis, and while they are offstage the King tells the Queen that Hamlet will be sent to England. Hamlet enters with Rossencraft and Gilderstone.

> *Gil.* My lord, we can by no meanes
> Know of him where the body is.
>   *King* Now **sonne** Hamlet, where is this dead body?
>   *Ham.* At supper, not where he is eating, but
> Where he is eaten, a certaine company of politicke wormes
>   are even now at him.
> **Father,** your fatte King, and your leane Beggar
> Are but variable services, two dishes to one messe:
> Looke you, a man may fish with that worme
> That hath eaten of a King,
> And a Beggar eate that fish,

---

[1]Act IV, scene i of Q1 is in Q2 divided into three short scenes. In the first the King sends Rosencraus and Guyldensterne to find Hamlet. They find Hamlet in another part of the castle but cannot get him to tell where the body is (scene ii). In the third scene they bring Hamlet before the King in some unspecified part of the castle. This makes three scenes in Q2 where, in Q1, there is only one.

Which that worme hath caught.
   King What of this?
   Ham. Nothing **father,** but to tell you, how a King
May go a progresse through the guttes of a Beggar.
   King But **sonne** *Hamlet,* where is this body?
   Ham. In heav'n, if you chance to misse him there,
Father, you had best looke in the other partes below
For him, and if you cannot finde him there,
You may chance to nose him as you go up the lobby.
   King Make haste and finde him out.
   Ham. Nay doe you heare? do not make too much haste,
I'le warrant you hee'le stay till you come.
   King Well **sonne** *Hamlet,* we in care of you: but specially
in tender preservation of your health,
The which we price even as our proper selfe,
It is our minde you forthwith goe for *England,*
The winde sits faire, you shall aboorde to night,
Lord *Rossencraft* and *Gilderstone* shall goe along with you.
   Ham. O with all my heart: **farewel mother.**
   King **Your loving father,** *Hamlet.*
   Ham. **My mother** I say: you married my mother,
My mother is your wife, man and wife is one flesh,
And so (my mother) farewel: for England hoe.
                      exeunt all but the king
                      [*and Queene*].

   King Gertred, leave me,
And take your leave of *Hamlet,*
                 [*She exits.*]
To England is he gone, ne're to returne.

That is the flesh scene: the flesh aspect of death, who, *vice*
worms, feeds upon the flesh of the dead; the flesh aspect of the
beggar eating the fish caught by the worm that ate of the King—i.e.,
the flesh of the live lean beggar becoming the dead fat king by
feeding on him; the flesh aspect of marriage: the husband and wife
becoming one in flesh. The Queen, as flesh, is the King's, but, as
spirit, is her son's. Hamlet counters the King's conspicuous "sonne"s
with equally unctuous "father"s, but it is the Queen he is addressing.
His farewell is to the part allied to him, her spirit. He is telling her,

in effect, that he knows what he is doing: he will return. When he returns she has sworn she will help him with this King, this satanic flesh; and the implication is that by so doing she will redeem herself to salvation. Heaven will be her destination, and her son's, and her first husband's. Her second husband's will be hell.

IV.ii, Hamlet has gone. And now the dramatization departs from pp. 48 its sources. In the prose stories the hero returns for a (Q2, IV.iv) triumphant coronation. In the play too he triumphs; he fulfills his mission. But in doing so he must die. Since he must die and since in the end it will be necessary to restore order to the State, some preparation for the finale is needed at this point. The First Quarto dispatches it in six lines. The stage directions read: *Enter Fortenbrasse, Drumme and Souldiers.* The drum and soldiers doubtless afforded some pageantry to make the scene more telling, but all Fortenbrasse does is to send a Captain to the King of Denmark to ask for "a free passe and conduct over his land, / According to the Articles agreed on." With that, he bids his army "goe march away." *Exeunt all.* Still, the audience is reminded of his existence, and his proximity is explained, preparatory to his turning up at the crucial moment when the play is ending.

The stage directions give us neither the timing nor the locale of the Fortenbrasse scene, but the action that now follows evidently takes place in the palace after an indeterminate lapse of time.

Enter King and Queene.

IV.iii,   *King* Hamlet is ship't for England, fare him well.
pp. 48-52   I hope to heare good news from thence ere long,
(Q2, IV.v)   If every thing fall out to our content,
            As I doe make no doubt but so it shall.
        Queene God grant it may, heav'ns keep my *Hamlet* safe.

Again, mortal is the Queen. She has been told her second husband was the murderer of her first. Yet, when the King tells her Hamlet is being sent to England for his health, she evidently believes him. When the King says he hopes to hear good news from England, she believes him to mean "good" news in her sense of "good."

The Queen then announces that Ofelia is "quite bereft her wittes." The King responds that Ofelia's brother has come from France:

> And he hath halfe the heart of all our Land,
> And hardly hee'le forget his fathers death,
> Unless by some meanes he be pacified.

This preparation shows that Hamlet in England is in the thoughts of the King and Queen: never to return in the King's hope and belief, and safe in the Queen's. Also in their thoughts is Corambis's death, and its effect on both of his children: the Queen reporting on his daughter ("quite bereft her wittes"), the King on his son (mad with rage and in rebellion). We see them, in those conditions, in that order, first the piteous girl and then the raging man.

Enter Ofelia playing on a Lute and her haire downe, singing. She wears her hair as a bride, and no doubt her costume accords.

(A word on the songs in this play: Ofelia, mad, sings, and the subject and language of her songs betray a loss of reason, a topsy-turviness, which logic in a sane person excludes. The only other singer will be the gravedigger. His song is of an old man bidding farewell to love, and the grave he is digging is—as in the song—for such a guest as love, most meet. The parallels will coalesce when one realizes with Hamlet that the grave being dug is for Ofelia: "The faire *Ofelia* dead!")

Now Ofelia sings: the subject of her song is a farewell to her true love gone on a pilgrimage, never to return, and an elegy for her father, dead and gone and in his grave.

> *Ofelia* How should I your true love know
> From another man?
> By his cockle hatte, and his staffe,
> And his sandall shoone.

Who is this true love? He is on a journey (Hamlet)

> White his shrowde as mountaine snowe,
> Larded with sweete flowers,
> That bewept to the grave did not goe
> With true lovers showers:

Whose is this shrouded corpse? Who went to his grave without true lovers' showers? (Her father)

> He is dead and gone Lady, he is dead and gone,
> At his head a grasse greene turffe,
> At his heeles a stone.

Who is this buried topsy-turvy with his headstone at his heels, a grass lump at his head? This is the shrouded corpse (her father) in his grave

> *King* How i'st with you sweete *Ofelia?*
> *Ofelia* Well God yeeld you.
> It grieves me to see how they laid him in the cold ground,
> I could not chuse but weepe:

Again, the shrouded corpse (her father)

> And will he not come againe?
> And will he not come againe?
> No, no, hee's gone, and we cast away mone,
> And he never will come againe.

The true love on a journey (Hamlet)

> His beard as white as snowe:

The shrouded corpse (her father)

> All flaxen was his pole,

The true love on a journey (Hamlet, the golden haired)

> He is dead,

(Her father)

> he is gone,

The true love on a journey (Hamlet)

> And we cast away moane:
> God a mercy on his soule.
> And of all christen soules I pray God.
> God be with you Ladies, God be with you.
>
> exit Ofelia.

For whose soul is she praying? Here again in her final prayer she confuses the two souls, before merging them with all Christian souls. She also confuses the King's sex. Her "God be with you Ladies" parallels Hamlet's "farewel mother," when, on the verge of his departure for England, he is conversing with his "father" (IV.i, p. 47). To Hamlet (sane) and to Ofelia (mad), in the presence of the King and Queen, only the Queen has spiritual existence. The Ghost has no flesh or bones; it is all spirit. The King has no spirit. He is all flesh and bones.

"This is a change indeede,"[1] exclaims the King. And now this King—who shortly before tried to ask Heaven's grace to keep him from despair, but couldn't pray—continues:

> O Time, how swiftly runnes our joyes away?
> Content on earth was never certaine bred,
> To day we laugh and live, to morrow dead.

Hedonism has failed. Already deep in sin for the murder of his brother, he has nevertheless contrived for his own safety the murder of his nephew. He cannot any more pray to Heaven. He cannot any more laugh on earth. No power he can reach now can keep him from despair. "Never to hope again" is Lucifer's doom.[2] But, as in Lucifer's case, and as in Macbeth's case, so in the King's: despair has no conscience and no fear.

---

[1]There is irony in the parallel between this exclamation and Ofelia's about Hamlet, after her scene with him while the King and Corambis are eavesdropping: "Great God of heaven, what a quicke change is this?" (II.ii, p. 27).

[2]"And when he falls he falls like Lucifer, / Never to hope again."
Henry VIII, III.ii

King How now, what noyse is that?

> *A noyse within.*

Rebellion breaks in upon the King and Queen in the person of Leartes. Whereas his sister is "bereft her wittes" by reason of her father's death and her true love's departure, Leartes is mad with rage, his reason overcome by his passion.

> *Lear.* [To his mob offstage.] Stay there untill I come,
> O thou vile[1] king, give me my father:
> Speake, say, where's my father?
>   *King* Dead.
>   *Lear.* Who hath murdred him? Speake, i'le not
> Be juggled with, for he is murdred.
>   *Que.* True, but not by him.
>
> > [*And she grabs the raging rebel.*]

Nothing could show more clearly the spell cast over the Queen when she is with the King. True, Leartes represents a threat to the rule of the King *and* the Queen. The Queen, in physically seeking to protect the King, is seeking to protect sovereignty. But in being the one to declare that the King did not kill Corambis, which is the first step in saying who did, she forgets her son in her concentration on the safety of her husband.

> *Lear.* By whome, by heav'n I'le be resolved.
>   *King* Let him goe *Gertred,* away, I feare him not,
> There's such divinitie doth wall a king,
> That treason dares not looke on.
> Let him goe *Gertred,* that your father is murdred,
> T'is true, and we most sory for it,
> Being the chiefest piller of our state:
> Therefore will you like a most desperate gamster,
> Swoop-stake-like, draw at friend, and foe, and all?
>   *Lear.* To his good friends thus wide I'le ope mine arms.
> And locke them in my hart, but to his foes,
> I will no reconcilement but by bloud.
>   *King* Why now you speake like a most loving sonne:
> And that in soule we sorrow for his death,

---

[1]"Vilde" in Q1; corrected in Q2 (IV.v, p. 73) to "vile."

Your selfe ere long shall be a witnesse,
Meane while be patient, and content your selfe.
                        Enter Ofelia as before.
    Lear. Who's this, *Ofelia?* O my deere sister!
I'st possible a yong maides wits[1]
Should be as mortall as an olde mans life?[2]
O heav'ns themselves! how now *Ofelia?*
    Ofel. Wel God a mercy, I a bin gathering of floures:
Here [to the Queen], here is rew [for sorrow, remorse] for you,
You may call it hearb a grace [for repentance] a Sundayes,
Heere's some for me too: you must weare your rew
With a difference, there's a dazie [for light of love].
Here Love [to Leartes, whom she takes for her true love,
        Hamlet] there's rosemary for you
For remembrance: I pray Love remember,
And there's pansey for thoughts.
    Lear. [Hearing the words, ignoring—maybe ignorant of—
        the flower language[3]] A document in madnes, thoughts,
        remembrance:
O God, O God!
    Ofelia [To the King] There is fennell [for flattery?] for
        you, I would a giv'n you
Some violets [for loyalty], but they all withered, when
My father died:

Death enters her mind. To whom does she address her next remark?
Perhaps to the Queen?

                        alas, they say the owle was
A Bakers daughter [a loose woman], we see what we are,
But can not tell what we shall be.
For bonny sweete Robin is all my joy.
    Lear. Thoughts and afflictions, torments worse than hell.
    Ofel. Nay Love, I pray you make no words of this now:
I pray now you shall sing a downe,
And you a downe a, t'is a the Kings daughter
And the false steward....

[1]Q1; misprinted "life," corrected in Q2 (IV.v, p. 75) to "wits."
[2]Q1 misprinted "sawe," corrected in Q2 (ibid.) to "life."
[3]For a discussion of the flower language, see the notes on this scene in *A New Variorum Edition of Shakespeare,* ed. H. H. Furness, vol. 1 of *Hamlet,* pp. 346-349.

Ofelia again confuses the identities. It is, of course, of the steward's daughter and the false King (Prince). This part of the scene must be read in conjunction with the first Leartes-Ofelia scene, the only other scene between them. There Leartes warned Ofelia against Hamlet's suit.

> *Lear.* But ere I part, marke what I say to thee:
> I see Prince *Hamlet* makes a shew of love
> Beware *Ofelia,* do not trust his vowes,
> Perhaps he loves you now, and now his tongue
> Speakes from his heart, but yet take heed my sister,
> The Chariest maide is prodigall enough,
> If she unmaske hir beautie to the Moone.
> Vertue it selfe scapes not calumnious thoughts,
> Believ't *Ofelia,* therefore keepe aloofe
> Lest that he trip thy honor and thy fame.
>   *Ofel.* Brother, to this I have lent attentive eare,
> And doubt not but to keepe my honour firme,
> But my deere brother, do not you
> Like to a cunning Sophister,
> Teach me the path and ready way to heaven,
> While you forgetting what is said to me,
> Your selfe, like to a carelesse libertine
> Doth give his heart, his appetite at ful,
> And little recks how that his honour dies.
>   *Lear.* No, feare it not my deere *Ofelia.*
>
> I.iii, pp. 10-11

And Corambis in the same scene repeated with more definiteness these warnings, saying that Hamlet's vows were springs to catch woodcocks, his letters snares to entrap, his gifts "keyes / To unlocke Chastitie unto Desire" (I.iii, p. 12).

Now in her madness, Ofelia follows her reference to the daughter and the false King (Prince) by singing the valentine song,[1] but she topsy-turvies the valentine legend in which the man seeks the girl (the first girl he sees on Valentine's Day) rather than, as Ofelia has

---

[1]In Q2, Ophelia sings the valentine song during her first, not her second, mad scene. As Laertes has not yet entered, this passage has lost the poignancy of having his presence remind the audience of the brother's and sister's former scene together.

it, the girl seeking the man. The song turns the warnings she has received from her brother and father into facts. The false King (Prince) has tripped her honor. His vows have been springs and have caught her, the woodcock. He has promised to marry her. This promise was his key to unlock her chastity to his desire, which, in the song, it does. But after she gives herself to him, and he tumbles her, he does not keep his promise to marry her. When she reminds him of this promise, he replies, "So would I a done, by yonder Sunne / If thou hadst not come to my bed." The song is thus Ofelia's condemnation of young men ("Yong men will doo't when they come too't / By cocke they are too blame"), her retort to Hamlet's condemnation of women in the Hamlet-Ofelia (King and Corambis) gallery scene.

When Ofelia has concluded her song, she bids them farewell and leaves them, again confusing the King's sex and confusing Leartes with Hamlet: "So God be with you all, God bwy Ladies" (to the King and Queen). "God bwy you Love" (to Leartes). *Exit Ofelia* (forever).

> *Lear.* Griefe upon griefe, my father murdered,
> My sister thus distracted:
> Cursed be his soule that wrought this wicked act.[1]
>> *King* [Though the Queen is onstage, it is clear that she
>> does not hear the King and Leartes.] Content you good
>> Leartes for a time,
> Although I know your griefe is as a floud,
> Brimme full of sorrow, but forbeare a while,
> And thinke already the revenge is done
> On him that makes you such a haplesse sonne.
>> *Lear.* You have prevail'd my Lord, a while I'll strive,
> To bury griefe within a tombe of wrath,
> Which once unhearsed, then the world shall heare
> Leartes had a father he held deere.

Grief and wrath are to be buried together: we would say to bury (temporarily) grief and wrath in one tomb, and when they (grief and wrath) are unhearsed, the world shall learn that Leartes loved

---

[1]Inexplicably no one has yet identified to Leartes this accursed.

his father. It is his grief that begets his wrath, his rage, the passion that defines Leartes.

> *King* No more of that, ere many dayes be done,
> You shall heare that you do not dreame upon.
> > *Exeunt om.*

IV, iv, As the previous scene ended with *Exeunt om.* the stage
pp. 52-53
  (Q2)[1] may have remained empty long enough to denote a lapse of time. Then, *Enter Horatio and the Queene.* Before we consider this scene, it should be noted that, although Hamlet had entreated his mother to "forbeare the adulterous bed" (III.iv, p. 45) there is nothing to suggest that she has carried out any change in her domestic arrangements. The King and Queen have appeared together as usual, before and during Ofelia's mad scenes. Now, however, Horatio has found her alone.

> *Hor.* Madame, your sonne is safe arriv'de in *Denmarke,*
> This letter I even now receiv'd of him,
> Whereas he writes how he escap't the danger,
> And subtle treason that the king had plotted,
> Being crossed by the contention of the windes,
> He found the Packet sent to the king of *England,*
> Wherein he saw himselfe betray'd to death,
> As at his next conversion with your grace,
> He will relate the circumstance at full.

Before Hamlet left for England, the Queen had learned that her husband was a murderer. Now she knows the King likewise tried to betray Hamlet to death.

> *Queene* Then I perceive there's treason in his lookes
> That seem'd to sugar o're his villanie:
> But I will soothe and please him for a time,

(Which is surely what she has been doing)

[1]This scene is excised in the later versions. It occurs only in Q1.

For murderous mindes are always jealous,
But know not you *Horatio* where he [Hamlet] is?

Horatio says yes, he does, and that he is to meet Hamlet tomorrow
morning in the east part of the city.

> *Queene* O faile not, good *Horatio,* and withall, commend me
> A mothers care to him, bid him a while
> Be wary of his presence, lest that he
> Faile in that he goes about.
> *Hor.* Madam, never make doubt of that.

Obviously, the Queen believes Horatio knows that Hamlet
intends to kill the King, and she trusts Horatio completely.

Horatio says he thinks the news of Hamlet's return has come
to Court already and suggests the Queen observe the King:

> …and you shall
> Quickely finde, *Hamlet* being here,
> Things fell not to his minde.
> *Queene* But what became of *Gilderstone* and *Rossencraft?*
> *Hor.* He being set ashore, they went for *England,*
> And in the Packet there writ down that doome
> To be perform'd on them poynted for him:
> And by great chance he had his father's Seale
> So all was done without discoverie.

This is all that is disclosed in Q1 of Hamlet's voyage and return:
the ship was crossed by the contention of the winds; Hamlet was set
ashore in Denmark; Rossencraft and Gilderstone went on to their death.

IV.v,
pp. 53-54
(Q2)[1]
The King and Leartes enter. This is their second scene.
The first began with Leartes bursting in at the head of
a mob—who at his command stayed without—demanding
to know what had happened to his father. It ended with the King's
promise that "ere many dayes be done, / You shall heare that you

---

[1]In Q2, a scene (vi) intervenes here in which Horatio receives sailors bringing
letters from Hamlet. There is no such scene in Q1.

For differences in the way Q2 handles the exposition of the thwarting of the
King's treacherous plan and Hamlet's safe return to Denmark, see Appendix B.

do not dreame upon" (IV.iii, p. 52). But now the King instead has heard what he did not dream upon. The news has reached the King (Q1 does not tell us how) that Hamlet, far from being executed as the King had planned, has returned to Denmark.

> *King* Hamlet from *England!* is it possible?
> What chance is this? They are gone, and he come home.
>   *Lear.* [Who has evidently learned by now that it was
>   Hamlet who killed Corambis] O he is welcome, by my
>   soule he is:
> At it my jocund heart doth leape for joy,
> That I shall live to tell him, thus he dies.
>   *King* Leartes, content your selfe, be rulde by me,
> And you shall have no let for your revenge.
>   *Lear.* My will, not all the world.
>   *King* Nay but Leartes, marke the plot I have layde.

And here the play creaks. It would seem that the plot the King is concocting depends on an assessment of Hamlet's character which comes as a complete surprise to us. Nothing we have seen or heard prepares us for the assurance the King gives that Hamlet will agree to the duel because he is jealous of Leartes's prowess.

>   *King* I have heard him often with a greedy wish,
> Upon some praise that he hath heard of you
> Touching your weapon, which with all his heart,
> He might be once tasked for to try your cunning.

And after he has disclosed his plot of the poisoned rapier:

>   *Lear.* My lord, I like it well:
> But say lord *Hamlet* should refuse this match.
>   *King* I'le warrant you, wee'le put on you
> Such a report of singularitie,
> Will bring him on, although against his will.

The King appears to be reassuring Leartes with promises that are basically unsound, and they mislead the audience as well, for no scene will follow in which Hamlet will be "brought on" by hearing

Leartes praised. When the time comes it will be conscience, not emulation, which moves Hamlet to accept the challenge. However, the King succeeds in his immediate purpose; he convinces Leartes that the duel will occur, and adds, as a guaranty of its success:

> And lest that all should misse,
> I'le have a potion that shall ready stand,
> In all his heate when that he calles for drinke,
> Shall be his period and our happinesse.

The former scene between the King and Leartes was interrupted by Ofelia's final mad scene. And now this, their second scene, is interrupted by the Queen's entrance and announcement of Ofelia's death by drowning. In each case, the result is an aggravation of Leartes's thirst for vengeance.

> *Queene* Sitting upon a willow by a brooke,
> The envious sprig broke, into the brooke she fell,
> And for awhile her clothes spread wide abroade,
> Borc the yong Lady up: and there she sate smiling,
> Even Mermaide-like, twixt heaven and earth,
> Chaunting olde sundry tunes uncapable
> As it were of her distresse, but long it could not be,
> Till that her clothes, being heavy with their drinke,
> Dragg'd the sweete wretch to death.
>   *Lear.* So, she is drownde:
> Too much of water hast thou *Ofelia;*
> Therefore I will not drowne thee in my teares,
> Revenge it is must yeeld this heart releefe,
> For woe begets woe, and griefe hangs on griefe.
> *Exeunt.*

ACT V

V.i,
pp. 54-
59

As we have heard earlier, Horatio is to meet Hamlet in the east part of the city (IV.iv, p. 52). Evidently there is a graveyard there. It is to this graveyard that the Clown and "an other" now enter. Following so closely the Queen's description

of Ofelia's drowning, the talk of the Clown and "2" must have been
recognized by the audience as referring to Ofelia.

> *Clowne* I say no, she ought not to be buried
> In christian buriall.
> 2 Why sir?
> *Clowne* Mary because she's drownd.
> 2 But she did not drowne her selfe.

The Clown, however, argues that because the water did not come to
her, and therefore she went to the water, she drowned herself.

> 2 I but see, she hath a christian buriall,
> Because she is a great woman.
> *Clowne* Mary more's the pitty, that great folke
> Should have more authoritie to hang or drowne
> Themselves, more than other people:
> Goe fetch me a stope of drinke.

But before 2 goes, the Clown propounds a riddle of who builds
strongest, a mason, a shipwright, or a carpenter. The Clown's answer
to his own riddle turns out to be:

> A Grave-maker, for the houses he buildes
> Last till Doomes-day. Fetch me a stope of beere, goe.

The gravediggers are clowns; they provide a comic interlude.
But when one clown departs and Hamlet and Horatio enter, we are
in the midst of an emblematic passage, having little to do with the
action of the play, but much to do with one of the play's major
themes. We are in Death's country. And Death in the form of the
Clown, busily digging Ofelia's grave and singing mangled fragments
of a song,[1] will be host to these two transients.

> *Enter Hamlet and Horatio.*
> *Clowne* A picke-axe and a spade,
> A spade for and a winding sheete,

[1]The Clown's song is a garbled version of "An Aged Lover Renounceth Love,"
a poem printed in Tottel's *Miscellany,* 1557.

Most fit it is, for t'will be made,
For such a ghest most meet.

> *He throws up a shovel.*

   Ham. Hath this fellow any feeling of himselfe,
That is thus merry in making of a grave?
See how the slave joles their heads against the earth.
   Hor. My lord, Custome hath made it in him seeme nothing.
   Clowne A pick-axe and a spade, a spade,
For and a winding sheete,
Most fit it is for to be made,
For such a ghest most meet.
   Ham. Looke you, there's another *Horatio.*
Why mai't not be the scull of some Lawyer?
. . . .
...why that same boxe there will scarse
Holde the conveiance of his land, and must
The honor lie there? O pittifull transformance!
I prethee tell me *Horatio,*
Is parchment made of sheep-skinnes?
   Hor. I my Lorde and of calves-skinnes too.
   Ham. I'faith they proove themselves sheepe and calves
That deale with them, or put their trust in them.

Skin is thus brought into the conversation as well as skulls, and another skull is dug up.

>   *Ham.* ...why may not that be such a ones
> Scull, that praised my Lord such a ones horse,
> When he meant to beg him? *Horatio,* I prethee
> Lets question yonder fellow,
> Now my friend, whose grave is this?

And the Clown banters with the Prince till finally he designates the grave as for "one that was a woman," and Hamlet, noting the fellow's insistence on precision, comments that,

> This seaven yeares have I noted it: the toe of the pesant,
> Comes so neere the heele of the courtier,
> That he gawles his kibe....

Then he questions the Clown as to how long a man will lie in the ground before he rots. The Clown says three years for a tanner, whose hide is so tanned it will hold out water longer than others, and then:

> *Clowne* Looke you, heres a scull hath bin here this dozen
>   yeare,
> Let me see, I ever since our last King *Hamlet*
> Slew *Fortenbrasse* in combat, yong *Hamlets* father,
> Hee that's mad.

There is more banter about how Hamlet came to be mad and on what ground and why he was sent to England, where the men are as mad as he. Then:

> *Ham.* Whose scull was this?

Death knows his people. Here, the Clown has said, is a skull that has lain here a dozen years. When Hamlet asks whose skull it was the Clown is not at a loss for an answer.

> *Clowne* This, a plague on him, a madde rogue it was,
> He powred once a whole flagon of Rhenish on[1] my head.

And then the devastating question by Death to the living:

> *Clowne* Why, do not you know him?

The anonymity of the dead. This is the poignant preparation for the burial to be. All skulls are anonymous: a lawyer, a flatterer, a jester, Alexander, Caesar, my Lady who now paints herself an inch thick, all golden lads and girls. Only Death knows them apart. The fair Ofelia, dead, will have no more identity than they.

> *Clowne* Why, do you not know him? This was one *Yorickes*
>   scull.
> *Ham.* Was this? I prethee let me see it, alas poor *Yoricke*
> I knew him *Horatio,*
> A fellow of infinite mirth, he hath carried mee twenty times

[1]Misprinted "of" in Q1; corrected to "on" in Q2 (V.i, p. 86).

upon his backe, here hung those lippes that I have Kissed a hundred times, and to see, now they abhorre me: Wheres your jests now *Yoricke?* your flashes of meriment; now go to my Ladies chamber, and bid her paint her selfe an inch thicke, to this she must come *Yoricke. Horatio,* I prethee tell me one thing, doost thou thinke that *Alexander* looked thus?

Hor. Even so my Lord.

Ham. And smelt thus?

Hor. I my lord, no otherwise.

Ham. No, why might not imagination worke, as thus of *Alexander, Alexander* died, *Alexander* was buried, *Alexander* became earth, of earth we make clay, and *Alexander* being but clay, why might not time bring to passe, that he might stoppe the bounghole of a beere barrell?

Imperious *Caesar* dead and turned to clay,

Might stoppe a hole, to keepe the winde away.

> *Enter King and Queene, Leartes, and other lordes, with a Priest after the coffin.*

Yorick's nasty skull has polluted Hamlet's memory of his childhood, when Yorick was such fun for the very young Prince to play with and so dear to him. To escape that sense of pollution, he removes his thought from the jester, his playmate, to the remote great: Caesar and Alexander—What is Hecuba to him? Or Caesar or Alexander to me?—and renders them trivial by describing them as usable and useful clay. *Sic transit gloria mundi,* as enter the King and Queen and the Court for the end of Ofelia's maimed rites. Hamlet has no knowledge of Ofelia's death. He has been "wary of his presence" and has kept aloof, rambling with Horatio in Death's country. Now suddenly the Court bursts in on him.

Ham. What funerall's this that all the Court laments?

It shews to be some noble parentage:

Stand by a while.

Lear. What ceremony else? say, what ceremony else?

Priest My Lord, we have done all that lies in us,

And more than well the church can tolerate,

She hath had a Dirge sung for her maiden soule:

And but for favour of the king, and you,
She had beene buried in the open fieldes,
Where now she is allowed christian buriall.
    Lear. So, I tell thee churlish Priest, a ministring Angell
shall my sister be, when thou liest howling.
    Ham. The faire *Ofelia* dead!
    Queene Sweetes to the sweete, farewell:
I had thought to adorne thy bridale bed, faire maide,
And not to follow thee unto thy grave.
    Lear. Forbeare the earth a while: sister farewell.

Leartes leapes into the
grave.

Now powre your earth on, *Olympus* hie,
And make a hill to o're top olde *Pelion.*[1]

Hamlet leapes in after
Leartes.

    Ham. What's he that conjures so?[2]
Beholde tis I, *Hamlet* the Dane.
    Lear. The divell take thy soule.
    Ham. O thou praiest not well,
I prethee take thy hand from off my throate,
For there is something in me dangerous,
Which let thy wisdome feare, holde off thy hand.

The rebellious Leartes—here, as when he burst in upon the King
and Queen—comes face to face with sovereignty.

The King had said:
    Let him goe *Gertred,* away, I feare him not,
    There's such divinitie doth wall a king,
    That treason dares not looke on.
    Let him goe *Gertred.*...

IV.iii, p. 50

Now Hamlet, in disclosing himself, proclaims himself royal, as
"*Hamlet* the Dane"; his "take thy hand from off my throate," repeated

---

[1]Misprinted in Q1 *"Pellon,"* corrected to *"Pelion"* in Q2 (V.i, p. 88).

[2]Mistakenly given to Leartes in Q1; the corresponding line correctly given to
Hamlet in Q2 (ibid.).

in "holde off thy hand," is a royal command, like the King's repeated "Let him goe *Gertred.*" It is again sovereignty confronting rebellion. Facing Leartes in the open grave, Hamlet makes his declaration:

> I lov'de *Ofelia* as deere as twenty brothers could:
> Shew me what thou wilt doe for her:
> Wilt fight, wilt fast, wilt pray,
> Wilt drinke up Esill,[1] eate a crocadile? Ile doot:
> Com'st thou here to whine?
> And where thou talk'st of burying thee alive,
> Here let us stand; and let them throw on us,
> Whole hills of earth, till with the heighth thereof,
> Make Ossa[2] as a Wart.

Reason no longer controls Hamlet; for the moment he is truly mad and speaks his feelings without the constraint of thought or logic. He is treating Leartes as if the brother (poor intruding fool) were trying to displace Ofelia's true love at her spiritual bridal bed; he is treating Leartes as, in Juliet's tomb, Romeo treats Paris. Hamlet, in his passion, sees Leartes trying to usurp—as a rebel—not only Hamlet's sovereignty, but his true love as well. And he challenges Leartes as if he were challenging a rival. The King, who has been a silent bystander, now fearing the struggle will interfere with his plotted fencing match, either by injury to one or the other, or perhaps by the arousal of such animosity in Hamlet that he will not entertain a friendly swordplay with Leartes, breaks in:

> Forbeare *Leartes,* now is hee mad, as is the sea,
> Anone as milde and gentle as a Dove:
> Therefore a while give his wilde humour scope.

But Hamlet, far from dove-like, still speaks to Leartes as a sovereign to a subject:

> What is the reason sir that you wrong mee thus?
> I never gave you cause: but stand away,
> A Cat will meaw, a Dog will have a day.

[1]Misprinted as "vessels" in Q1; corrected to "Esill" (vinegar) in Q2 (V.i, p. 88).
[2]Misprinted "Oosell" in Q1; corrected to "Ossa" in Q2 (V.i, p. 89).

Perhaps a rebel (a cat) will cry out rebellion (meaw),[1] but nonetheless the sovereign (a dog) will have a reign (a day). With this speech, Hamlet and Horatio exit. The Queen, who has not spoken since Hamlet disclosed himself, now intercedes:

> Alas, it is his madnes makes him thus,
> And not his heart, *Leartes.*

The Queen's designation of Hamlet as mad is similar to her designation of Hamlet as mad when he killed Corambis; it is Hamlet acting without the restraint of reason. The King agrees: "My lord, t'is so." But then, just as earlier, when he was expecting news of Hamlet's death from England, and calmed Leartes with "thinke already the revenge is done" (IV.iii, p. 51), he speaks to Leartes for his ear alone, although the Queen is still onstage.

> ...but wee'le no longer trifle,
> This very day shall *Hamlet* drinke his last,
> For presently we meane to send to him,
> Therfore *Leartes* be in readynes.
>   *Lear.* My lord, till then my soule will not bee quiet.
>   *King* Come *Gertred,* wee'l have *Leartes,* and our sonne,
> Made friends and Lovers as befittes them both,
> Even as they tender us, and love their countrie.
>   *Queene* God grant they may.
> *Exeunt omnes.*

Here, though Hamlet has convinced his mother that the King murdered her first husband, and Horatio has convinced her that the King plotted to have Hamlet killed, she still does not suspect the King when he says he is going to have Hamlet and Leartes made friends. The King always arranges things so that he seems to be on the same side as the Queen vis-à-vis Hamlet. He said he was sending Hamlet to England for his health; he now says the fencing match will make Hamlet and Leartes friends. Since she is in accord with the ends, she apparently puts her faith in the means, even

[1]For the cat as a symbol of rebellion, see L. Hotson, *Mr W. H.,* pp. 207-208.

though she knows the truth about the past. She believes the fencing match to be an honest sporting event until she drinks the poisoned wine. The reason her son falls into the same trap becomes clear at the beginning of the following scene.

V.ii, The action now shifts back to the castle.
pp. 59-
63

> *Enter Hamlet and Horatio.*
> *Ham.* beleeve mee, it greeves mee much *Horatio,*
> That to *Leartes* I forgot my selfe:
> For by my selfe me thinkes I feele his griefe,
> Though there's a difference in each others wrong.

These lines have dropped out of Q2 but reappear in the Folio (V.ii, 2nd p. 259) and in subsequent versions. They provide an important clue to Hamlet's motive in acceding to the duel. His pangs of conscience for having wronged Leartes serve to dull his usual suspicions of the King and all who surround the King.

Enter a Braggart Gentleman. This is the embassage of Death. In *Der Bestrafte Brudermord* (act V, p. 286) the message is brought by the jester Phantasmo. When he announces to Hamlet and Horatio that there is to be a fencing match between Hamlet and Leonhardus for a wager, Hamlet says to Horatio that somebody has been fooling Phantasmo, and to show how easy it is to make Phantasmo say anything you want him to, Hamlet uses the cold-temperate, hot-temperate alternation, as in Q1 Hamlet will now use cold and hot to make a fool of the Braggart Gentleman. It is a device similar to the banter he had already used in act III, scene ii (p. 41) when Corambis came in with a message that Hamlet's mother wanted to see him. Then Hamlet induced Corambis to describe a cloud as first a camel, then a weasel, then a whale. Now, like Phantasmo and Corambis, the Braggart Gentleman corroborates each of Hamlet's changing suggestions, and what with this banter, and the Gentleman's "sweete Prince"'s, and the comments on the Gentleman's perfume, much fancy language surrounds the message, which is that the

King has laid a wager on Hamlet's side of six Barbary horses against six French rapiers with all their accoutrements. Hamlet asks for more particulars.

> *Gent.* Mary sir, that yong Leartes in twelve venies
> At Rapier and Dagger do not get three oddes of you,
> And on your side the King hath laide,
> And desires you to be in readinesse.
> *Ham.* Very well, if the King dare venture his wager,
> I dare venture my skull:[1] when must this be?
> *Gent.* My Lord, presently, the king and her majesty
> With the rest of the best judgement in the Court,
> Are comming downe into the outward pallace.
> *Ham.* Goe tell his majestie I wil attend him.

There is no hesitation here. The only qualm is due to a sudden foreboding after the messenger has left.

> *Ham.* Beleeve me *Horatio,* my hart is on the sodaine
> Very sore all hereabout.
> *Hor.* My lord, forbeare the challenge then.
> *Ham.* No *Horatio,* not I, if danger be now,
> Why then it is not to come, there's a predestinate providence
> in the fall of a sparrow; heere comes the King.

But danger now does not necessarily foreclose danger to come. Only death will do that. Danger here is a synonym for death. Though Horatio suggests Hamlet forbear the challenge, Hamlet will have none of it. Fatalism rejects foreboding. The King has told Leartes that Hamlet could be "brought on" if his competitiveness were aroused (IV.v, p. 54). But, as we have said, the King's foresight is misleading; no such reluctance shows itself. Hamlet, in his present mood of contrition, accepts the challenge as a matter of course. He rejects the foreboding as a matter of philosophy.

---

[1] Is "skull" a misspelling for "skill"? As far as Hamlet knows, the proposed duel is merely a test of skill, not a fight to the death. The line does not occur in Q2 or in subsequent versions and so cannot be verified.

> *Enter King, Queene, Leartes, Lordes.*
> *King* Now sonne *Hamlet,* we have laid upon your head,
> And make no question but to have the best.
> *Ham.* Your majestie hath laide a the weaker side.
> *King* We doubt it not, deliver them the foiles.

Feeling that he has wronged Leartes, as well as Leartes's father, Hamlet approaches the fencing match with an apology on his lips. He has not the slightest thought that Leartes is the King's man, the Devil's man, ruthless in his treasonous revenge.

> *Ham.* ...therefore lets be at peace,
> And thinke I have shot mine arrow o're the house,
> And hurt my brother.

But it was no aimless thrust of a dagger that killed Corambis. It was one aimed at what Hamlet thought was someone other than Corambis (viz., the King). Leartes says he's satisfied in nature, "but in termes of honor"—honor of Leartes, who is about to effect as dishonorable a plot as could be devised!

> *Lear.* . . . I'le stand aloofe,
> And will no reconcilement,
> Till by some elder maisters of our time
> I may be satisfied.
> *King* Give them the foyles.
> *Ham.* I'le be your foyle *Leartes,* these foyles,
> Have all a length,[1] come on sir.

As there is no mention in this scene of preparing the wine, something is clearly left out of Q1 here. In *Der BB* it is with a diamond that the drink is made lethal. In Q2, we have the following explicit passage:

> *King* Give them the foiles young *Ostricke...*
> . . . .
> *Laer.* This is to heavy: let me see another.
> *Ham.* This likes me well, these foiles have all a length.

[1]Misprinted in Q1 as "laught," corrected to "length" in Q2 (V.ii, p. 95).

> *Ostr.* I my good Lord.
> *King* Set me the stoopes of wine upon that table,
> If *Hamlet* give the first or second hit,
> Or quit in answere of the third exchange,[1]
> Let all the battlements their ordnance fire.
> The King shall drinke to *Hamlets* better breath,
> And in the cup an Unice shall he throwe,
> Richer then that which foure successive Kings
> In Denmarkes Crowne have worne: give me the cups,
> And let the kettle to the trumpet speake,
> The trumpet to the Cannoneere without,
> The Cannons to the heavens, the heaven to earth,
> Now the King drinkes to *Hamlet,* come beginne.
> > *The trumpets the while.*
> And you the Judges beare a wary eye.
> > V.ii, pp. 95-96

If the "Unice" ("pearl") had been included in Q1, judging by Q2, it would have come between Hamlet's "these foyles, / Have all a length" and his "come on sir." Just as surely, it would not have been described with such elaborate detail as in Q2.

As things stand in Quarto One, the contestants now choose their foils, and without more ado the match begins. The wager seems to be that in twelve "venies" Leartes will not exceed Hamlet by three hits. A venue may end with a hit for Leartes or for Hamlet or with no hit either way. Because of the odds, Leartes's losses count more heavily than Hamlet's. Hence the Court's mounting tension as Leartes loses the opening venues.

> *Ham.* …come on sir: a hit.
> *Lear.* No none.
> > *Heere they play.*
> *Ham.* Judgement.
> *Gent.* A hit, a most palpable hit.
> *Lear.* Well, come againe.
> > *They play againe.*

[1]Kittredge says this means "repay Laertes (score a hit) in the third bout." Notes to act V, scene ii, lines 278-280 in *The Tragedy of Hamlet Prince of Denmark,* ed. G. L. Kittredge, p. 295.

Ham. Another. Judgement.
Lear. I, I grant, a tuch, a tuch.
King Here *Hamlet,* the King doth drinke a health to thee.
Queene Here *Hamlet,* take my napkin, wipe thy face.

The King, prepared for any eventuality, brings forward the poisoned cup. But it is as though divine intervention ("predestinate providence") takes charge of the fatal drink. What happens now is not in accordance with any human plan. Hamlet brushes the cup aside saying he will down it later. The Queen intercepts it and, not to be outdone by the King, drinks to Hamlet. In doing so, she meets her death, but her eyes are opened at last. She gives her great redeeming cry. Satan (the King) is foiled. His treason is made manifest. Hamlet is free at last to execute his revenge, and with the King's own weapons.

King Give him the wine.
Ham. Set it by. I'le have another bowt first,
I'le drinke anone.
Queene Here *Hamlet,* thy mother drinkes to thee.
                              Shee drinkes.
King Do not drinke *Gertred:* O t'is the poysned cup!
Ham. Leartes come, you dally with me,
I pray you passe with your most cunningst play.
Lear. I! say you so? have at you.
Ile hit you now my Lord:
And yet it goes almost against my conscience.
Ham. Come on sir.

And divine intervention, as though evoked by that reference to conscience, interferes with the plot of the poisoned sword (as it has frustrated the plot of the poisoned wine); but here, to bring the play to its tragic end, it allows the mortal wounding of the hero, before intervening to put the poisoned foil in his unwitting hand. He, thinking it an honest foil, buttoned and, of course, unpoisoned, wins another hit and mortally wounds Leartes.

They catch one anothers Rapiers, and both are wounded.
Leartes falles downe, the Queen falles downe and dies.

At this moment the King, by exclaiming "Looke to the Queene," makes her the focus of attention. She gives her dying words, a cry from a heart no longer divided.

> *Queene* O the drinke, the drinke, *Hamlet,* the drinke.
> *Ham.* Treason, ho, keepe the gates.

Hamlet has taken command and the courtiers will make no move to restrain him. They know at last there has been foul play; something is rotten in the state of Denmark. But Hamlet, though he now knows the wine was poisoned, does not yet know that in his hand is an unbuttoned and poisoned foil. This news will come to him only from Leartes, repentant. The King will not confess.

> *Lords* How ist my Lord *Leartes?*
> *Lear.* Even as a coxcombe should,
> Foolishly slaine with my owne weapon:
> *Hamlet,* thou has not in thee half an hour of life,
> The fatall Instrument is in thy hand.
> Unbated and invenomed: thy mother's poysned
> That drinke was made for thee.
> *Ham.* The poysned Instrument within my hand?

The moment has arrived. Satan is doomed.

> Then venome to thy venome, die damn'd villaine:
> Come drinke, here lies thy union here.
>   *The king dies.*

The Divine Will sees to it that Leartes's vengeful rage is stilled. The Queen has already—in my view—redeemed herself. Now Leartes.

> *Lear.* O he is justly served:
> *Hamlet* before I die, here take my hand,
> And withall, my love: I doe forgive thee.
>   *Leartes dies.*
> *Ham.* And I thee,

And here the pagan glory of devoted suicide—considered and rejected as God-forbidden by the Danish (Christian) Hamlet—bursts forth:

> O I am dead, *Horatio,* fare thee well.
> *Hor.* No, I am more an antike Roman,
> Then a Dane, here is some poison left.

The nobility of Horatio's attempted suicide cannot be overemphasized. The slaughter preceding it is not noble. The Queen's cry is, with its relish of salvation, a relief; Leartes's confession and repentance another relief. The killing of the King, however, has no glory in it. It is like a hanging, an execution, or any death administered as justice: brutal. Its manner: stabbing a defenseless man with a poisoned sword and then forcibly pouring poisoned wine down his throat: brutal. And Hamlet—as the hangman, the executioner—is cruel, ruthless, pitiless. The play ending on such a note would have been ignoble, beastly. The audience's sympathy would have gone out to the hanged, the executed. They would have weighed the scourge and not the offense, converting "his Gyves to graces."

But as the Divine Will is manifested in the ultimate punishment of the transgressor, suddenly a light breaks forth at the natural level illuminating the doom (supernatural): Horatio, in utter disregard of the Everlasting's canon against self-slaughter (Christian), ocizcs the drink to commit the glorious and noble suicide of a Roman (pagan), and die with his friend. With his last strength the dying Hamlet forestalls this generous act, not to save Horatio from the consequences in the afterlife of violating the Everlasting's ban—for a moment we are in the pagan cosmogony—but to request that, as a superior act of friendship, Horatio tell Hamlet's story so that his name may be cleared of the scandal it would suffer from the events left unexplained.

> *Ham.* Upon my love I charge thee let it goe,
> O fie *Horatio,* and if thou shouldst die,
> What a scandale wouldst thou leave behinde?
> What tongue should tell the story of our deaths,

If not from thee?
O my heart sinckes *Horatio,*
Mine eyes have lost their sight, my tongue his use:
Farewel *Horatio,* heaven receive my soule.

Hamlet dies.

The ending, like the rest of the play, moves fast. The future must be secured, and the stage cleared of the dead bodies. Fortenbrasse has long been waiting in the wings. It is time now for him to enter and, as Fortenbrasse II, to replace the tyrant who usurped the Hamlet I/Hamlet II line. The ambassadors must come from England bringing word of Rossencraft's and Gilderstone's death. In the end, the roles of the two erstwhile schoolfellows have reverted to the vestigial roles of the old stories, and they have died as the King's henchmen and Hamlet's foes.

Horatio orders a scaffold to be reared up in the marketplace and bids "the State of the world" to assemble there. He does not summarize the speech he will make, merely promising that he will "shew to all... / The first beginning of this Tragedy" and that there will be "such a sad story tolde / That never mortal man could more unfolde." It is left for Fortenbrasse to speak the play's last lines, restoring order to the disordered realm. His final words are brief, but they depict a fallen hero, an image of nobility for the audience to depart with:

I have some rights of memory to this kingdome,
Which now to claime my leisure doth invite mee:
Let foure of our chiefest Captaines
Bear *Hamlet* like a souldier to his grave:
For he was likely, had he lived,
To a prov'd most royall.
Take up the bodie, such a sight as this
Becomes the fieldes, but here doth much amisse.

Finis

CHAPTER THREE

THE VARYING *HAMLETS*

According to its title page, the 1604 Q2 is an enlarged text of an earlier version. Below is a selection of the notes Foster made while he was coming to the conclusion that the 1603 Q1 represents that earlier version and can therefore serve as a guide to the interpretation of Q2 and thence to the 1623 Folio and the "Hamlet"s we have today. I (Shiras) am responsible for the selection of the notes printed below, and, in fact, some were written by me during discussions of the play with Foster. But the ideas and opinions expressed are all his.

HAMLET AS IT WAS

"Newly imprinted and enlarged to almost as much againe as it was, according to the true and perfect Coppie." This is the statement that appears on the title page of the Second Quarto. Besides claiming authenticity, it implies a preceding version roughly half as long, the play "as it was." The question is, does the First Quarto represent that earlier version, antecedent to Q2, or (as some scholars claim), is Q1 an offshoot, unauthorized and somehow rushed earlier into print?

Q1 is 2160 lines long. Q2 is 3732.[1] If Q1 is indeed the play "as it was" mentioned on the title page of Q2, the statement that Q2 has been enlarged to almost as much again is somewhat, but not wildly, exaggerated.

Seven years after Shakespeare's death, two surviving members of his troop, Heminge and Condell, had thirty-six of his plays printed in what is now known as the Folio (1623). The Folio texts

---

[1]In order to avoid the irregularities of broken lines, run-over lines, long and short prose lines, etc., every line along which the printer has placed words to be spoken, whether few words or many, is counted as a full line. Stage directions are not counted, except those describing the action of the dumb show.

are thought to represent the acting versions. In general the Folio *Hamlet* follows Q2, but there are passages in which it differs, and in some of those passages it more closely resembles Q1, so the script from which Q1 was printed was apparently available to the editors of the Folio. The Folio excises about 200 lines that appear in Q2 but are not in Q1. For instance, the fourth act scene in which Fortenbrasse, his Captain, and his army cross the stage on the way to war in Poland, is 6 lines long in Q1, but is 66 lines long in Q2, where Hamlet is introduced into the scene, talks with the Captain, and delivers his soliloquy "How all occasions doe informe against me." The scene in the Folio—reduced to 7 lines—reads much as it does in Q1. Hamlet has been eliminated.

The Folio's elimination of Hamlet from the scene with the Captain is a significant change. But many of the 50-plus instances in which the Folio departs from Q2 and coincides with Q1 are brief, involving one line at most.[1] For example, in Q1 Hamlet has a way of repeating himself when he is deep in thought. In act I, scene ii (pp. 9, 10), when he has heard Horatio's disturbing news about the apparition of the Ghost, he says: "Indeed, indeed sirs, but this troubles me"; and a few lines further down he answers Horatio's "It would a much amazed you" with "Yea very like, very like." In the same passage, Q2 has only one "indeed" and one "very like." But apparently the trick of gaining time by repetition had entered into the contemporary way of acting *Hamlet*. At any rate, the Folio maintains it.

All three versions of *Hamlet*—Q1, Q2, and the Folio—have a nearly identical cast of principal characters. There is only one important change: the name of the Lord Chamberlain is Corambis in Q1 (and, parenthetically, his servant is Montano); in Q2 and subsequent versions the Chamberlain is Polonius (with a servant named

---

[1]For a comprehensive list of the agreements and disagreements of the early texts (1603-1664), see "Textual Notes," in *The Tragedy of Hamlet Prince of Denmark,* ed. G. L. Kittredge, pp. 299-320.

Reynaldo). Interestingly, the parallel character in the German *Der Bestrafte Brudermord* is Corambus. It is surely credible to suggest that Corambis or Corambus was the name in the lost English "Ur-Hamlet" and that it survived in both Q1 and *Der BB* but became Polonius as one of the many changes Shakespeare made when he was lengthening and revising the play.

The process of revision may have occurred in two stages.

As in *Julius Caesar* and *Macbeth,* the first act of *Hamlet* is intense. We are prepared for fateful things to come. The first act in Q1 is 272 lines shorter than that act in Q2. Q1, therefore, lacks some of the poetry in the longer version, but it lacks none of the dramatic artistry with which the act is constructed. In fact, in this one act the two versions are so nearly equal in skillful exposition and dramatic suspense that it seems as though Shakespeare had already started to revise Q1, and had reworked the first act, before dropping the Q1 version and going on to a wholly rewritten version, Q2.

But the question arises: why rewrite so wholly? If Q1 had been revised once and only needed to be lengthened and have its poetic imagery heightened, why change it in a multitude of ways, some of which have no bearing on the dramatic or literary quality? The first act in Q1—the very act that is nearest in quality to Q2—is 634 lines long. In Q2 the first act is 906 lines. Of the 600-plus lines in Q1, roughly half appear in Q2 unchanged. The other half are reworded, reordered, or relocated. For example:

Q1:

> *Marcellus* Question it *Horatio.*
>
> I.i, p.2

Q2:

> *Marcellus* Speake to it *Horatio.*
>
> I.i, p.2

❡

Q1:

> *Horatio* Our late King, who as you know was by Forten-Brasse of *Norway,*

Thereto prickt on by a most emulous cause...

I.i, p. 3

Q2:

Horatio...our last King,
Whose image even but now appear'd to us,
Was as you knowe by *Fortinbrasse* of *Norway,*
Thereto prickt on by a most emulate pride

I.i, p. 3

❡

Q1:

Hamlet...O let me not thinke of it,
My fathers brother: but no more like
My father, then I to *Hercules.*
Within two months, ere yet the salt of most
Unrighteous teares had left their flushing
In her galled eyes: she married, O God, a beast
Devoyd of reason would not have made
Such speede: Frailtie, thy name is Woman,
Why she would hang on him, as if increase
Of appetite had growne by what it looked on.
O wicked wicked speede, to make such
Dexteritie to incestuous sheetes,
Ere yet the shooes were olde,
The which she followed my dead fathers corse
Like *Nyobe,* all teares: married, well it is not,
Nor it cannot come to good.

I.ii, p. 7

Q2:

Hamlet Must I remember, why she should hang on him
As if increase of appetite had growne
By what it fed on, and yet within a month,
Let me not thinke on't; frailty thy name is woman
A little month or ere those shooes were old
With which she followed my poore fathers bodie
Like *Niobe* all teares, why she
O God, a beast that wants discourse of reason
Would have mourn'd longer, married with my Uncle,
My fathers brother, but no more like my father
Then I to *Hercules,* within a month,
Ere yet the salt of most unrighteous teares,

Had left the flushing in her gauled eyes
She married, o most wicked speede; to post
With such dexteritie to incestuous sheets,
It is not, nor it cannot come to good.

I.ii, p. 10

Many of the changes could, in themselves, seem adventitious, the sort of word-evolution that occurs during the life of a dramatic script. But taking them all in all, they are too numerous; they proceed on and on throughout the play. Mostly they remain unimportant, but we have to be on our guard against thinking that every change that is brief is insignificant. Sometimes, amid the trivial changes, come words that are not merely said differently, but are thought differently. Consider the lines quoted above about the Queen's increase of appetite. In Q1 it grows by what it *looked on;* in Q2—a totally different image—by what it *fed on.* This change from a benign to a ravening appetite darkens the character of the Queen, and the darker concept is reinforced by the imagery which the Ghost uses in a following scene: "So lust, though to a radiant angel linckt / Will sate itself in a celestiall bed / And prey on garbage" (Q2, I.v, p. 21). "Looked" was not changed to "fed" by a forgetful actor or a careless scribe. To my way of thinking, "fed" is the word of a revising author whose poetic concepts have come clearer.

Throughout Q2, this change of concept can be seen: Shakespeare is thinking along different lines. The tone is darker: metaphors linked to disease are used where none existed in Q1; Hamlet is more despondent about this world, and the next; the King's satanic power is greater (the Queen never escapes his clutches; Laertes is inflamed to a greater villainy; Rosencraus and Guyldensterne are more subservient). At the same time Q2 is more given to hyperbole. The King's rowses are on a grander scale. When Laertes returns from Paris with a band of followers, his entrance is threatening but quite orderly in Q1, whereas in Q2 a messenger announces his stormy arrival as though the end of the world were coming. Hamlet, in the funeral scene, says he loved Ophelia, not as dear as twenty brothers could, as in Q1, but dearer than forty thousand brothers.

Then too, destiny is personified in a different way in Q2. Though both Quartos speak of a special Providence even in the fall of a sparrow, there is no mention in Q1 of Fortune as the arbiter of man's lot in life. Yet this Goddess, the emblematic dispenser of weal and woe, is prevalent in Q2. She is mentioned some fourteen times.

If an author is revising a work, perhaps some years later, it is not surprising that his concepts and his way of poetizing them should change. The superiority of the verse in Q2 is plain for all to see. But we are still faced with changes that are harder to explain, the ones that apparently have no dramatic or literary significance. Why, when Q1 and Q2 are overall the same play, is Q2 written so differently, page for page? We have no positive answer, but one recurring difference may provide a clue. It concerns a change that seems trivial now, but perhaps the times gave it importance.

In the old prose stories, in *Der BB,* and in Q1 a customary title for Hamlet is "Prince." He may be either Lord Hamlet or Prince Hamlet when he is addressed, but is usually Prince Hamlet when he is being referred to. In Q1 the title is applied to him eighteen times. In Q2 it is given him only twice: when he is being referred to—Polonius tells the King, as he does in Q1, that he has bidden Ophelia to reject Hamlet's advances and quotes himself as having said to her, "Lord *Hamlet* is a Prince out of thy star" (II.ii, p. 32); and again when Horatio bids Hamlet farewell in the new and beautiful speech "Now cracks a noble hart, good night sweete Prince" (V.ii, p. 98). Aside from these two instances, it is evident that, as a title for Hamlet, the word is avoided in Q2 and the surrounding dialogue differs accordingly. Here are some examples of parallel passages:

Q1:
> *King* And now **princely** Sonne *Hamlet*
> What meanes these sad and melancholy moodes?
> . . . .
> *Ham.* My lord, ti's not the sable sute I weare:
> No nor the teares that still stand in my eyes,
>
> I.ii, p. 6

Q2:

> *King* But now my Cosin *Hamlet,* and my sonne.
> *Ham.* A little more than kin and lesse than kind.
> I.ii, p. 8

❡

Q1:

> *King* Spoke like a kinde and a most loving Sonne,
> And there's no health the King shall drinke to day,
> But the great Canon to the clowdes shall tell
> The rowse the King shall drinke unto **Prince** *Hamlet.*
> I.ii, pp. 6-7

Q2:

> *King* This gentle and unforc'd accord of *Hamlet*
> Sits smiling to my hart, in grace whereof,
> No jocond health that Denmarke drinkes to day,
> But the great Cannon to the cloudes shall tell,
> And the Kings rowse the heaven shall brute again,
> Respeaking earthly thunder; come away.
> I.ii, p. 9

❡

Q1:

> *Leartes* I see **Prince** *Hamlet* makes a shew of love
> Beware *Ofelia,* do not trust his vowes.
> I.iii, p. 10

Q2:

> *Laertes* For *Hamlet,* and the trifling of his favour,
> Hold it a fashion, and a toy in blood.
> I.iii, p. 13

❡

Q1:

> *Ofelia* O my deare father, such a change in nature,
> So great an alteration in a **Prince,**
>
> . . . .
>
> *Corambis* Why what's the matter my *Ofelia?*

Ofelia O yong **Prince** *Hamlet,* the only floure of *Denmark,*
Hee is bereft of all the wealth he had.

                                                    II.i, p. 20

Q2:

Ophelia O my Lord, my Lord, I have been so affrighted.
Polonius With what i'th name of God?
Ophelia My Lord, as I was sowing in my closset,
Lord *Hamlet* with his doublet all unbrac'd,
No hat upon his head, his stockins fouled,

                                                    II.i, p. 27

In searching the text for these "Prince"'s, the reader is also struck by the fact that the sardonic "father" which Hamlet uses five times in Q1 is not used in Q2. The word occurs in Q1 (III.ii, pp. 36, 37, 39) when the King asks "How now son *Hamlet,…* shall we have a play?" and Hamlet answers, "I father," and again when, in giving the King the name of the play, Hamlet adds, "Father, it is a knavish peece a worke." Later when the King is trying to locate Corambis's corpse, his "Now sonne Hamlet, where is this dead body?" provokes a "father" not once but three times in Hamlet's baffling answers (IV.i, pp. 46, 47). The "father"'s have disappeared in Q2.

Were these words—the usual royal title and the customary familiar term—shunned so that no analogy might be suggested between the corrupt court at Hamlet's Elsinore and the situation at court in England? The idea seems far-fetched now, but it must be remembered that at the time Q2 was written, probably in the earliest years of the seventeenth century, the question of Elizabeth's successor had become a divisive issue. There were fears that her death might occasion disorders, even civil war. The likeliest contender was King James VI of Scotland. If he were successful, England would have what it had lacked for many years, a King on the throne and a young Prince in direct line of succession. But the members of the Privy Council—and/or the players themselves—may have decided that, as a matter of policy, it would be better not to remind the audience of the Scottish royal lineage and of the King's infamous stepfather. For King James was the son—and the Prince was a grandson—of the widowed Queen of Scots who had contracted a hasty marriage with the man believed to have murdered her husband.

The Hamlet story was well-known and had been acted before. Apparently Shakespeare's Q2 version could be granted a license and could be staged but any seditious material would have caused it to be censored or even rejected. It is my belief, for the reason I have suggested or for some reason unknown to us, that Shakespeare removed some words as a matter of policy, and that while he was about it he made numerous other small changes so that, with its added poetry and changed wording, Q2 represented a whole new manuscript. A re-created Q2 would explain the statement on the title page that the play presented there was enlarged to almost as much as it was, according to the true and perfect copy. This claim of being "according to the true and perfect Coppie," unusual for a Shakespearean title page, sounds very much like a repudiation of some earlier, shorter *Hamlet,* formerly acted.

I see no reason to doubt that Q1 represents that earlier, shorter *Hamlet.* I think that it had been written wholly or mostly by Shakespeare, who then revised it (perhaps revising the first act twice); and that when he revised it he adhered to practically the same plot and cast of characters, but altered the script throughout, so that when it was licensed it could be performed as a new play and could be regarded from that day onward as the authentic *Hamlet.*

"TO BE, OR NOT TO BE," THE TWO VERSIONS

People who know nothing else about the play know that Hamlet says "To be, or not to be." The soliloquy as it appears in Quarto Two (III.i, pp. 43-44)—and reappears virtually unchanged in all later editions—is one of the most famous of all the famous passages in Shakespeare. The speech also occurs in Quarto One (II.ii, pp. 24-25), but there it is in a different form and is quite differently regarded. The first few lines, in fact, have been cited by critics as evidence that Q1 is a pirated version, and cannot be the work of Shakespeare. In Q1, the soliloquy begins:

> To be, or not to be, I there's the point,
> To Die, to sleepe, is that all? I all:
> No, to sleepe, to dreame, I mary there it goes,
> For in that dreame of death, when wee awake,
> And borne before an everlasting Judge,
> From whence no passenger ever retur'nd,
> The undiscovered country, at whose sight
> The happy smile, and the accursed damn'd.

At this point the critics are apt to break off. "The dullest poetaster could not have been guilty of this nonsense" proclaims Israel Gollancz in his preface to *Hamlet*.[1] If a poetaster could not be guilty, a printer could be, and I think was. It appears that five important lines have been scrambled in the printing and two words are missing. When the lines are rearranged and the words are added, the speech reads:

> To be, or not to be, I there's the point,
> To Die, to sleepe, is that all? I all:
> No, to sleepe, to dreame, I mary there it goes,
> **For in that dreame of death, when wee awake,**
> **[In] the undiscovered country**
> **From whence no passenger ever retur'nd,**
> **And borne before an everlasting Judge**
> **At whose sight the happy smile, and the accursed**
>   **[are] damn'd,**
> But for this, the joyfull hope of this,
> Whol'd beare the scornes and flattery of the world,
> Scorned by the right rich, the rich curssed of the poore?
> The widow being oppressed, the orphan wrong'd,
> The taste of hunger, or a tirants raigne,
> And thousand more calamities besides,
> To grunt and sweate under this weary life,
> When that he may his full *Quietus* make,

---

[1] *The Tragedy of Hamlet, Prince of Denmark,* vol. 5 of *The Works of William Shakespeare,* De Luxe ed., E. Burdick, ix.

> With a bare bodkin, who would this indure,
> But for a hope of something after death?
> Which pusles the braine, and doth confound the sence,
> Which makes us rather beare those evilles we have,
> Than flie to others that we know not of.
> I that, O this conscience makes cowardes of us all,
> Lady in thy orizons, be all my sinnes remembred.

This speech in Q1 has a simple theme: that in view of the ills of the world no reasonable man would fail to commit suicide were it not that the hope—the "joyfull hope"—of salvation would be lost by self-slaughter. It is the fear of losing salvation that makes cowards of us all, i.e., makes us unwilling to act.

The ills Hamlet enumerates could be those being experienced in the out-of-joint society and in the unnatural conditions he was born to set right:

1. The scorns and flattery of the world: the rich scorn the poor; Hamlet says, "so poore a man as *Hamlet*" (Q1, I.v, p. 19). The poor curse the rich; Hamlet curses the King, "Murderous, bawdy, smiling damned villaine" (Q1, I.v, p. 16).
2. The widow oppressed: the Queen, oppressed by the King because he has seduced her to his wicked will.
3. The orphan wronged: Hamlet, the orphan, wronged by the murder of his father, the marriage of his mother, and the theft of a crown.
4. The taste of hunger: *King* "How now son *Hamlet,* how fare you...?" *Hamlet* "Y'faith the Camelions dish, not capon cramm'd, / feede a the ayre" (Q1, III.ii, pp. 36-37).
5. A tyrant's reign: the reign of Hamlet's incestuous, usurping uncle.

He is describing his world for the eavesdropping ears of the King and the Chamberlain. But in Q2, the ills enumerated in the latter half of this soliloquy are more generalized.

> For who would beare the whips and scornes of time,
> Th'oppressors wrong, the proude mans contumely,
> The pangs of despiz'd love, the lawes delay,

> The insolence of office, and the spurnes
> That patient merrit of th'unworthy takes,
> When he himselfe might his quietas make
> With a bare bodkin; who would fardels beare,
> To grunt and sweat under a wearie life.

These wrongs are not related to any particular situation at Elsinore; and when we come to "who would fardels beare" we are in a porter's world, far from the court.

The philosophy too is different in Q2, and darker. The "joyfull hope" of Q1 is gone. Q2 substitutes dread, "the dread of something after death," and eliminates the Q1 awakening before a just Judge who will bless the happy and damn the accursed. Indeed there is no sure awakening in Q2. Though there is still the undiscovered country "from whose borne / No traviler returnes," it exists only in death's dream.

> For in that sleepe of death what dreames my come
> When we have shuffled off this mortall coyle
> Must give us pause, there's the respect
> That makes calamitie of so long life.

In both Quartos suicide is presented as travelling from known evils to worse, but in Q1 not committing suicide leaves one with a hope of better things to come, whereas in Q2 it leads only to the avoidance of worse ills. Both Quartos conclude that "conscience dooes make cowards," but Q2 appends a further thought:

> And thus the native hiew of resolution
> Is sickled ore with the pale cast of thought,
> And enterprises of great pitch and moment,
> With this regard theyr currents turne awry,
> And loose the name of action.

These lines are often quoted in analyses of Hamlet's character. They are among the best known in the play, but famous though they are, it must be admitted that they have little to do with suicide, the subject of this soliloquy. They are more akin to

"Bestiall oblivion, or some craven scruple / Of thinking too precisely on th'event," which allows our "capabilitie and god-like reason / To fust in us unusd," lines which occur later (Q2, IV.iv, p. 70), when Hamlet, on his way to England, is blaming himself for his inaction (although then he is blaming himself not because he is still alive in this weary world, but because his enemy, the King, is still alive).

It seems as though the need to embellish and alter the play, and the press of ideas in Shakespeare's mind, led to the insertion of line that are often magnificent but not always apposite. The soliloquy in the First Quarto is simple, more direct, more optimistic. It is shorter by a dozen lines and is badly printed. But we recognize some of its imagery. The phrase "his full *Quietus* make, / With a bare bodkin" is there. It will be echoed in Quarto Two and may have suggested the thought, added in Q2, that death, if it could be final, is "a consumation / Devoutly to be wisht." But the possibility of "something after death" (in Q1 it is a hope, in Q2 a dread) leads to similar results in both Quartos. It "makes us rather beare those ills we have / Than flie to others that we know not of." Though the Q1 version seems crude, it points toward the superb poetry that will eventuate.

THE POETRY OF Q2 AND THE DRAMA OF Q1

Hamlet is poetic drama steeped in its tragic subject, death: the death of the first Fortenbrasse, the first Hamlet, Polonius, Ophelia, the schoolfellows, the Queen, the King, Laertes, Hamlet (Alexander, Caesar, the lawyer, the flatterer, the jester). The genius that immortalizes that theme comes to us from Quarto Two. It is Quarto Two that lifts doom into the realm of poetry—not merely the magnificent rhetoric of certain passages, nor even the fascination of Hamlet's philosophic quandaries, but also quite simply the surge and rhythm of the (sometimes imperfect) blank verse. To find an example of how its poetry enhances Q2, one has only to compare the transformation of a thought which in Quarto One is given to the Duke in the play-within-a-play, but which is taken over by Hamlet and rephrased in the last act of Q2.

Q1:

> *Duke* I doe beleeve you sweete, what now you speake,
> But what we doe determine oft we breake,
> For our demises[1] stil are overthrowne,
> Our thoughts are ours, their end's none of our owne.
>
> III.ii, p. 38

Q2:

> *Ham.* …rashly,
> And praysd be rashness for it: let us knowe,
> Our indiscretion sometime serves us well
> When our deepe plots doe pall, & that should learne us
> Ther's a divinity that shapes our ends,
> Rough hew them how we will.
>
> V.ii, p. 89

This is Shakespeare at his top. It is as though, when the time came to write Q2, he was working *tête-en-feu*. Neither the formalities of the verse nor the limitations of the language seemed to hamper him. If he could not find words to fit his thoughts to the line, he invented new ones. In a single speech (I.i, p. 4) "palmy," "sheeted," and "gibber" all appear for the first time in the English language with the meaning given them here. He fitted words together with so fine an ear that it has seemed natural to link them ever since. The dialogue has been expanded; soliloquies have been added; the characters express themselves in new poetic imagery. As a result the play has been enormously improved. It has also been impaired.

Leaving aside considerations of *Hamlet* as a literary masterpiece, the Q1 version proves to be ingeniously crafted as drama. The Ghost reveals his secret; Hamlet assumes the antic disposition and this action results in the probes that are made to determine the cause of his strange behavior. The first probe is (as in the old stories) a seemingly chance encounter with a beautiful woman. Hamlet realizes the meeting is a trap, and so is on his guard against subsequent probes; in Q1 the subsequent probes are, first, by the

[1]Devices. See p. 45n.

Lord Chamberlain, and then by two schoolfellows. With the arrival of the Players Hamlet takes the initiative; he devises a probe of his own and the stage is given over to the preparations for, and the production of, the *Murder of Gonzago.* The *Murder* rises to a climax: will the King blench and the Ghost be proved honest? These are still open questions and we are all on the jury. The King does blench; his secret is in the open. He tries—and fails—to repent, and then it is kill or be killed for him and Hamlet. Hamlet kills the King (only it turns out to be Corambis). The King kills Hamlet (only it turns out to be Rossencraft and Gilderstone). Hamlet perforce accedes to exile, but before leaving he has received his mother's oath that she is innocent of her first husband's murder and her vow to help him in his revenge. He thwarts the King's treacherous plan and makes his way back to Elsinore. The King, with Leartes as his tool, devises a final fatal trap. But Fate provides Hamlet with the poisoned foil, and after the Queen gives her expiring cry about the lethal drink, Hamlet survives long enough to kill the King with the King's own poisons.

T. S. Eliot's criticism of *Hamlet* as an artistic failure, lacking in "objective correlative,"[1] does not apply to Q1. This play moves, and the characters' emotions are fully sustained by motivations that are in turn sustained by the course of events. The hero, even in this laconic version, is not a simple character. He is melancholy but witty; introspective but impulsive. Unlike Leartes, he has no stomach for the revenge Fate has thrust upon him, yet he achieves it. And the shorter, simpler script of Q1 makes his delay seem less protracted. Also, since his speeches are shorter and fewer, we have less of his self-criticism. The way that others view him takes on more weight. He is obviously honored and respected by the sentries and the Players; to Horatio, he is a chief worth dying for; Ofelia has loved him as the only flower of Denmark, a courtier, scholar, soldier; he is the half-heart of his mother; and in the end he rises to the occasion and out-duels a stronger opponent. All these facts, though

[1]"Hamlet and His Problems," in *Twentieth Century Interpretations of Hamlet: A Collection of Critical Essays,* ed. D. Bevington, pp. 22-26.

proportionately less important, still obtain in Q2 and all subsequent Shakespearean versions. Amleth, in the tales, is a legendary superhero; Hamlet is a human Elizabethan courtier and intellectual. Nevertheless he is a direct descendant of the Amleth depicted in the first few episodes of the prose stories, the episodes chosen for dramatization.

It seems obvious that Q1 would be a prize possession for a stock company in need of scripts. Here were foul deeds rising; ingenuity pitted against corruption; suspense, awe, humor, action. True, the script needed to be amplified. A mature Burbage and an experienced troop could handle a more ambitious play. But the material had proved popular over the centuries, and essentially, the play was already there.

Apparently, as the revision progressed, some play-doctoring was considered necessary. Shakespeare must have decided—probably with the concurrence of his troop—that the King's enmity for Hamlet develops too suddenly. In Q1, the King seems to have no evil intentions until after the play-within-a-play; and after the stabbing of Corambis furnishes a pretext for exiling Hamlet. When the Queen discloses the murder done by Hamlet, the King tells her that her son "shall presently to England" (Q1, IV.i, p. 46) and presently indeed her son goes, that very night, to remain offstage for the rest of act IV. By the time we next see Hamlet, the King has perfected his plot with Leartes and the climax comes swiftly. A longer confrontation was evidently deemed desirable.

The solution chosen was to postpone the overheard scene (beginning with "To be, or not to be" and continuing with the "Get thee to a Nunnery" passage) from the position it held in Q1 (II.ii, pp. 24-27), to the next act in Q2 (III.i, pp. 43-45). The veiled threats Hamlet utters during this scene in Q1 are reiterated in Q2 ("I am very proude, revengefull, ambitious" and "I say we will have no mo marriage, those that are married alreadie, all but one shall live") and become reasons for the King's decision that Hamlet is dangerous and must be dealt with. It would have been too early for

the King to make this decision if the scene had been left in its act
II location, because then the theme of the antic disposition is just
getting underway. So it was moved to the only other place in which
Polonius is having an audience with the King and Queen, the
first scene of act III. And, perhaps to add plausibility to the
King's reaction to Hamlet's threats, a passage was inserted which
shows that the King is already in a troubled state before Hamlet
enters. Polonius, preparing Ophelia for the part she is to play,
sententiously remarks:

> ...reade on this booke,
> That show of such an exercise may cullour
> Your lowliness; we are oft too blame in this,
> Tis too much proov'd, that with devotions visage
> And pious action, we doe sugar ore
> The devill himselfe.

These words prompt the King to say, evidently in an aside:

> O tis too true,
> How smart a lash that speech doth give my conscience
> The harlots cheeke beautied with plastring art,
> Is not more ougly to the thing that helps it,
> Then is my deede to my most painted word:
> O heavy burthen.
>> *Enter Hamlet.*
>> Q2, III.i, p. 43

Immediately after the Hamlet-Ophelia scene, the King tells Polonius
that it is not love, nor even madness that troubles Hamlet, but
something in his soul that may prove dangerous, and then and
there he (the King) voices his determination that Hamlet "shall
with speede to *England"* (Q2, III.i, p. 46). And so the battle line
between the mighty opposites is already drawn, and the English
scheme is taking shape in the King's mind.

This is an important change, and it is not the only one.
Further play-doctoring takes place when Hamlet has a scene alone
with his mother. In the First Quarto this scene (III.iv) follows along

the lines of the meetings Amleth has with his mother in the prose stories. Amleth kills the eavesdropping courtier; then reproaches his mother for her incestuous marriage, drawing unflattering comparisons between her first and second husbands; admits that he is sane; and later (on the eve of his departure for England) evolves a plan with her whereby she can help him toward his revenge. The scene between Hamlet and his mother in Q1 is comparable to the above except that, unlike Amleth, Hamlet proposes no plan, even though the Queen, having sworn that she did not know of her husband's murder, accedes to Hamlet' mission of revenge and vows that she will help in any stratagem he may devise. She becomes his ally, but the truth is Hamlet has no stratagem to share with her, and never will have. He departs for England with no deep plot in mind and when he returns readiness will be his all. In effect, he puts himself in the hands of Divine Providence and ultimately the most the Queen does is to give a warning cry, "the drinke, the drinke."

The playwright, and perhaps his troop, may have felt that the talk about stratagems raised false expectations. They evidently decided not to make the Queen an ally of Hamlet's in any capacity except that of a fond but erring mother. The purport of the Hamlet-Queen scene is much changed in Quarto Two (III.iv). He hints at the murder of the late King but not so explicitly that the Queen is moved to claim innocence. Revenge is never mentioned. Hamlet's main purpose seems to be to make his mother see the degradation of her present marriage with a usurping "vice of Kings" compared to her honorable estate with her late royal husband. He does indeed "speake daggers" to her (his words are threatening enough to alarm the Ghost) and her conscience is touched, but her aroused emotions are not put to any use in support of Hamlet's cause. He confides to her that he is mad in craft, not in fact; and she swears not to reveal what he has said. But we have no way of knowing, either from what she says to Hamlet or from her future actions, what she really believes. This policy of adhering to a more neutral Queen is evident again in act IV. The Q1 scene (IV.iv) in which Horatio informs the

Queen that Hamlet has returned to Elsinore, safe from the King's treacherous English plan, has been excised. In Q2 (IV.vi, vii) news of Hamlet's return is brought by sailors and messengers; we do not know that the Queen ever learned of her husband's murderous plot against her son.

As play-doctors sometimes discover, changes to effect some improvement in a drama may have produced unintended effects elsewhere in the script. The revisions discussed above alter other aspects of the play in the following ways.

The play-within-a-play is less of a climax. Since the King has already told us that his conscience is troubling him and that he means to exile Hamlet, the mousetrap does no more than prove to Hamlet what we already know. The trap, being less suspenseful, also seems less necessary. The question then arises: does Hamlet himself believe it to be necessary, or is it merely an excuse for prolonging his inaction?

Furthermore, it is hard to reconcile this enterprising Hamlet—managing the *Murder of Gonzago,* instructing the Players, allaying the King's suspicions, exchanging repartee with Ophelia, keeping a watchful eye on the King *and* the Queen—with the Hamlet who was so savagely on the defensive in the immediately preceding "nunnery" scene with Ophelia. And when he goes to his mother's chamber, after the play, his revised scene with her is so unproductive in terms of the ongoing action, yet so highly emotional that, in order to give it validity, some modern interpreters hinge his whole character on it. They consider that is shows him to be a victim of the Oedipus complex, whose true obsession is his mother's marriage, not his father's death.[1]

And there is a new bit of dialogue, a sort of coda, tacked on to the end of Hamlet's scene with his mother in Q2. He suddenly says "I must to England, you knowe that." She answers "Alack I had

---

[1]The psychiatrist Ernest Jones proposes this theory in his book *Hamlet and Oedipus.* Sir Laurence Olivier describes his introduction to the theory during a meeting with Professor Jones, as recorded in *Laurence Olivier on Acting,* pp. 77-79.

forgot. / Tis so concluded on." Hamlet continues:

> Ther's letters seald, and my two Schoolefellowes,
> Whom I will trust as I will Adders fang'd,
> They beare the mandat, they must sweep my way
> And marshall me to knavery: let it worke,
> For tis the sport to have the enginer
> Hoist with his owne petar, an't shall goe hard
> But I will delve one yard belowe their mines,
> And blowe them at the Moone: o tis most sweete
> When in one line two crafts directly meete.
>
> Q2, III.iv, pp. 64-65

How he learned the details of a plan the King had formulated only that afternoon, we do not know. But he seems to be telling his mother indirectly (as in this scene, all information is indirect) that treason is at work. Moreover, he appears to welcome the challenge. His mood is one of confidence.

Yet the contradictions continue, for when we see him in the next act, in a passage which is also new in Q2, he seems a different person. He is bitterly self-reproachful. On his way to England he has chanced upon the Captain who is leading Fortenbrasse's army to war in Poland. The sight of these brave men, going "to their graves like beds," brings on the soliloquy "How all occasions doe informe against me, / And spur my dull revenge." He accuses himself of bestial oblivion

> ...or some craven scruple
> Of thinking too precisely on th'event,
> A thought which quarterd hath but one part wisedom,
> And ever three parts coward...

and he ends with resolution:

> ...o from this time forth,
> My thoughts be bloody, or be nothing worth.
>
> Q2, IV.iv, pp. 69-70

But this rhymed couplet is not very convincing coming from a man who has switched moods so often, and who is going tamely off to England, apparently with no thoughts, bloody or otherwise, of how he is going to achieve his revenge.

The Hamlet that is the product of the changes and revisions found in Q2 is eloquent in thought but ineffectual in action. And yet the Hamlet that is preponderant in Q1—the hero who has had a difficult mission imposed on him but who means to achieve it—is still there. In fact Q2 emphasizes the admiration and loyalty that he inspires. The adjective noble, meaning noble in mind or nature,[1] is newly attached to him four times: the Ghost uses it ("thou noble Youth," I.v, p. 20); Ophelia mourns, "O what a noble mind is heere orethrowne!" and "Now see that noble and most soveraigne reason / Like sweet bells jangled out of time" (III.i, p. 45); and even Laertes, in his dying moment, says "Exchange forgivenesse with me noble *Hamlet*" (V.ii, p. 97). Q2 also makes the point that he is the idol of the populace. The King explains to Laertes that he could not proceed against Hamlet after Polonius's death because of

> ...the great love the generall gender beare him
> Who dipping all his faults in theyr affection,
> Worke like the spring that turneth wood to stone,
> Convert his Gyves to graces....
>
> IV.vii, p. 77

And in the end, although Hamlet must die, he fences with a stronger opponent and, like a true popular hero, wins at the odds. Crazy as he seems when masked by the antic disposition, the deeper flaws in his character—cowardice and "thinking too precisely on th'event"—are attributed to him only by himself, and do not exist for the other characters in the play.

---

[1]This use of the word appears frequently in *Julius Caesar,* culminating in Anthony's famous tribute to Brutus: "This was the noblest Roman of them all" (V.v).

What did Shakespeare intend? How did his troop, the King's Men, play this enigmatic script? The answer is forever hidden from us, but there are some clues available. For one thing, the play the troop put on the boards was apparently not precisely the *Hamlet* that is printed today. The Folio version edited by two of Shakespeare's actors, is thought to be based on a prompter's copy. It therefore probably represents the acting version. If so, its excisions represent cuts made by the actors. Among the passages that appear in Q2 but that do not appear in the Folio (nor in Q1), the following are notable because they have a bearing on the interpretation of the play:

1. Hamlet's "dram of eale" speech about the "vicious mole of nature" that chances in particular men (I.iv, pp. 17-18).
2. Hamlet's speech to his mother at the end of their scene together, beginning with the lines "Ther's letters seald, and my two Schoolefellowes, / Whom I will trust as I will Adders fang'd" showing his suspicion of treachery behind the English trip (III.iv, pp. 64-65).
3. Hamlet's meeting with Fortenbrasse's Captain, and the ensuing soliloquy "How all occasions doe informe against me" (IV.iv, pp. 69-70).

These passages are considered to be authentically Shakespeare's and all are included in the canon, but apparently they were not seen on the contemporary stage. That audience did not hear about the fatal flaw, the "vicious mole of nature"—now often suggested as a clue to Hamlet's character—and they did not witness the wild swing in Hamlet's character which occurs in Q2 when, soon after the self-confident speech about hoisting his enemies with their own petard, he bitterly accuses himself of cowardice in the soliloquy "How all occasions doe informe against me." These excisions result in a more consistent Hamlet. They may not have been made for that reason; perhaps the actors never viewed their hero as inconsistent. The script may have been cut simply with a view to getting on with the action. But the Folio *Hamlet* is, without a doubt, closer to the more coherent version of Q1.

Quandaries still exist, though, in revisions first introduced in
Q2; revisions that are carried over into the Folio and subsequently
into the canon *Hamlet*. In the revised versions, the postponement of
"To be, or not to be" and the overheard passage produces an
inconsistent third act. At the end of act II Hamlet was moving
resolutely ahead with plans for the play-within-a-play. Now he
enters act III with talk of suicide, and proceeds, in his bitter repulsion
of Ophelia, to utter threats against the life of the man he is trying to
trap unaware. The risk he takes, in arousing the King's suspicions
just at this crucial moment, seems insane. It makes no sense.

There are textual indications that, as originally planned, the
scenario of Q2 was more like that of Q1. It has been widely noted
that the first act develops almost identically in both versions; it
seems as though the second act was also meant to have a corresponding sequence of events. Ophelia would tell her father about
Hamlet's wild behavior; he would jump to the conclusion that the
cause was rejected love and he would bid Ophelia go with him to
the court. They would go; the King would ask how the love theory
could be tested; the encounter between Hamlet and Ophelia would
be planned and, Hamlet conveniently entering, the encounter would
take place then and there. Hamlet would sense that he was being
watched, and therefore he would be on his guard during the next
two tests—the interview alone with Polonius and then the visit from
his schoolfellows. The schoolfellows would announce the coming of
the Players; with the arrival of the Players, Hamlet would take
command, and the stage would then be given over to preparations
for the play.

All this happens in both Quartos except that, although Polonius
bids Ophelia go with him to the King and they go out together, for
some reason (never explained) Polonius arrives at court alone in Q2.
This difference between the two Quartos is important because in
spite of the fact that Hamlet's meeting with Ophelia—planned by
the King and Polonius as a test of Hamlet's sanity—is decided on
then and there, in Q2 the meeting itself cannot take place until
Ophelia is available. For this reason the test that serves as the

second probe   in Q1—Polonius "boarding" Hamlet—becomes the
first probe in Q2, after which the act proceeds exactly as though the
Hamlet-Ophelia meeting had taken place. Hamlet calls Polonius a
"fishmonger" (i.e., a pander[1]) and later "Jepthah," quite as though
the old man had already loosed his daughter to him, and he is as
immediately suspicious of Rosencraus and Guyldensterne as he was
in Q1. Apparently the Hamlet-Ophelia episode was simply wrenched
from its place in act II, with no replanning of the scenes surrounding
it. The episode was then inserted into the only other scene where
Polonius and Ophelia are onstage alone with the King: act III, scene i.
By this transfer the troop gained the advantage discussed pre-
viously of having Hamlet's veiled threats to the King alert the King
to danger. And perhaps too, they preferred the first sight of the antic
disposition to be humorous (Hamlet discomfiting Polonius) rather
than serious and highly emotional ("To be, or not to be" and Hamlet
victimizing Ophelia). But they paid a price. The hallmark of the antic
disposition consists of the barbs that underlie the apparently zany
remarks. These are quite lost in the fishmonger and Jepthah dialogue
of Q2 because the preceding action is missing. And, far more serious,
in the next act the momentum of the action leading to the play-
within-a-play is disrupted and Hamlet's behavior becomes irrational.

The play has turned enigmatic. Is it a study of a man doomed
by a cursed spite to undertake a mission he has no ready way of
achieving?   Or does it show, not Fate, but the man's very nature
holding him back? Either point of view can be corroborated by
analysis of the canon *Hamlet.* The psychologically oriented twentieth
century takes more interest in the latter view. But remember that
the early seventeenth century is nearly four hundred years removed.

Shakespeare had a model for his hero. Anyone with a knowledge
of that model has clues to the intrinsic Hamlet. Amleth, the Danish
Prince, is faced with a dilemma. He tells his mother that the desire
of revenging his father's death is engraven on his heart.

---

[1]J. Foster, *A Shakespeare Word-Book,* p. 232; M. R. Martin and R. C. Harrier,
The Concise Encyclopedic Guide to Shakespeare, p. 124.

> Nevertheless, I must stay the time, meanes, and occasion,
> lest by making over great hast, I be now the cause of mine
> owne sodaine ruine and overthrow, and by that meanes end
> before I beginne to effect my hearts desire. . . . for seeing
> that by force I cannot effect my desire, reason alloweth me
> by dissimulation, subtiltie, and secret practises to proceed
> therein[1].

This situation provides the playwright with a conflict that must
sustain five acts of drama. Shakespeare, and apparently the author
of the "Ur-Hamlet" earlier, use the early episodes of the Amleth
story as mainstays for their plots. It is not until Hamlet leaves for
England in the fourth act that Shakespeare departs entirely from
the story's framework, in order to bring about the duel with Laertes,
the revenge, and Hamlet's death. And even then the Hamlet that
emerges to effect his revenge is very much the Amleth that declares
himself and is acclaimed by his people. But he resembles that
victorious Amleth for a brief moment only.

"It may be observed," Dr. Johnson writes of Shakespeare, "that
in many of his plays the latter part is evidently neglected. When he
found himself near the end of his work, and in view of his reward,
he shortened the labor to snatch his profit. He therefore remits
his efforts where he should most vigorously exert them and his
catastrophe is improbably produced or imperfectly presented."[2]
Hamlet has his moment, in the duel and in the accomplishment of
his revenge; and in Q2 Shakespeare has provided him and Horatio
with a beautiful farewell. But Hamlet never has the opportunity that
Amleth has to declare himself and to come entirely clear of the
mask he has had to assume. With his dying breath, he bids Horatio
to tell his story and Horatio intends to comply, promising that there
is much to tell. But it is left to Fortenbrasse, chancing upon the scene,
to do for Hamlet what Amleth so prolifically does for himself.
There is nothing in the script to indicate that Fortenbrasse ever saw

[1]"The History of Hamblet, by F. De Belleforest," in *The Sources of "Hamlet":
With Essay on the Legend by Sir Israel Gollancz,* ed. I. Gollancz, p. 217.

[2]*Samuel Johnson on Shakespeare,* ed. W. K. Wimsatt, Jr., pp. 33-34.

or spoke to Hamlet in his life, but now this heir to the kingdom assumes authority. In nine lines, he winds up the play and eulogizes a Hamlet that "was likely, had he beene put on, / To have prooved most royall." And most probably, the audience departed satisfied. For after all, it is the play itself that tells Hamlet's story, and that story has shown a hero that inherently was, and would have proved, most royal. At least so the hero appears in Quarto One. And in spite of all the ambiguities introduced by the additions and revisions of Quarto Two, I believe the outcome was the same when the longer script was played by Shakespeare's troop, with the author onstage.

ACKNOWLEDGMENTS

Passages from *The Sources of "Hamlet": With Essay on the Legend by Sir Israel Gollancz* (London, 1926) are quoted by permission of the Oxford University Press.

Quotations from *Der Bestrafte Brudermord, oder Prinz Hamlet aus Dänemarck* are from *Shakespeare in Germany, 1590–1700, With Translations of Five Early Plays,* edited and translated by Ernest Brennecke (1964), by permission of the University of Chicago Press.

The Henry E. Huntington Library, San Marino, California, has given us permission to quote from its facsimile editions of *Shakespeare's Hamlet, The First Quarto, 1603,* printed in 1931, and *Shakespeare's Hamlet, The Second Quarto, 1604,* printed in 1938. Besides quoting from the First quarto we have reproduced that early version in its entirety, again with the kind permission of the Huntington Library.

With permission from the Oxford and Yale University Presses, we refer at times to the Folio collection of Shakespeare's plays, *Mr. William Shakespeares Comedies, Histories, and Tragedies,* brought out by John Heminge and Henry Condell, and printed by Isaac Jaggard and Ed. Blount in London, 1623 (facsimile edition prepared by Helga Kokeritz, 1954).

All quotations from *A New Variorum Edition of Shakespeare,* ed. H. H. Furness, as well as any reference to that work, are given by permission of Dover Publications, New York, NY. The Dover edition, first published in 1963, is an unabridged republication of the 10th edition of the work first published by J. B. Lippincott and Company in 1877, Philadelphia, PA.

APPENDIX A

Some Textual Puzzles

Quarto Two and the Folio are basically the two texts used in conflating authorized editions of *Hamlet*. Quarto One is seldom referred to, except as having a few stage directions lacking in the other two versions. Yet the First Quarto can be a useful addition in establishing the text of the play. Though each of the texts originates errors of its own, Q2 corrects most of the misprints in Q1 and the Folio corrects many of Q2's misprints, sometimes by reinstating the text as it appears in Q1. Since the editors of the Folio apparently were willing to rely on Q1 to correct mistakes originating in Q2, we will follow their example and use Q1 as well as the other two texts in an effort to interpret four of the verbal difficulties in the canon *Hamlet* that have challenged commentators over the years.

We start with two of Hamlet's speeches, each of which is limited to one of our texts. His "dram of eale" speech appears only in Q2; his speech "the *interim's* mine" only in the Folio. Both contain difficulties, but both are considered authentic and so are included in the canon. Since they have no variant versions to enlighten us, we will try to clarify the difficulties by examining the meaning of corresponding words or phrases in other passages of the texts.

Although the lines relating to the "dram of eale" appear only in Q2, the situation leading up to them is the same in all three texts. On the platform where the sentries have been keeping watch, Hamlet, Horatio, and the officer Marcellus are awaiting the appearance of the Ghost. They have had a conversation about the sounds of revelry coming from the castle. Hamlet has explained that "The King doth wake to night and takes his rowse," calling it "a custome / More honourd in the breach, than the observance." At that point, both in Q1 and the Folio, their talk is broken off by the entrance of the Ghost. But in Q2 the Ghost holds off; Hamlet has time for a further speech about the rowse taking place in the castle,[1] and in that speech he will speak the lines which we wish to examine. He is addressing his contemporary audience when he deplores the fact that:

> This heavy headed reveale east and west
> Makes us tradust, and taxed of other nations,
> They clip us drunkards, and with Swinish phrase
> Soyle our addition, and indeede it takes
> From our atchievements, though perform'd at height
> The pith and marrow of our attribute.

Then the thought of that flaw which has soiled the reputation of the nation suggests its parallel effect on a flawed individual:

> So oft it chaunces in particuler men,
> That for some vicious mole of nature in them
> As in their birth wherein they are not guilty,
> (Since nature cannot choose his origin)
> By their ore-grow'th of some complextion
> Oft breaking downe the pales and forts of reason,
> Or by some habit, that too much ore-leavens
> The forme of plausive manners, that these men
> Carrying I say the stamp of one defect
> Being Natures livery, or Fortunes starre,
> His vertues els be they as pure as grace,
> As infinite as man may undergoe,
> Shall in the generall censure take corruption
> From that particular fault: **the dram of eale**
> **Doth all the noble substance of a doubt**
> **To his owne scandle.**
>
> Q2, I.iv, pp. 17-18

For an Elizabethan piece of rhetoric, all is clear up to the last three lines, and even in those, the sense can be grasped if one does not linger over them. But in post-Elizabethan times a literal transla-

---

[1]It should be noted as background to this passage that the Danes were drinkers and they had come to England (King James's wife was a Dane) and made nuisances of themselves in public places, as heavy drinkers do.

tion has been, and still is, a source of disagreement in each successive edition of the play.

The nub of the problem is "of a doubt." The words just preceding it, the "dram of eale," are not difficult. "Eale" is for "evil," as elsewhere "deale" is used for "devil."[1] "Dram" is a liquid measure, here used as an expression meaning a small amount, as we find it used in Q1.[2] The small amount, the "dram," is the subject of "doth" (i.e., "does"). So far the meaning is "the dram of evil does...." But what is "of a doubt" and how does it fit in? The "a" seems to be an article preceding a noun, thus "a doubt" would have the sense of "an uncertainty." So we would understand the words today. But 17th-century audiences might have heard both words differently.

Often, though not always, where Q1 and the Folio print the pronoun "he," Q2 uses "a." The most famous quotation offering an example occurs in the dialogue between Hamlet and Horatio about the late King, Hamlet's father.

> *Hora.* I saw him once, **a** was a goodly King.
> *Ham.* Λ was a man take him for all in all
> I shall not looke upon his like againe.
>
> Q2, I.ii, p. 11

Now consider "of a doubt" again, with the understanding that "a" may be a pronoun. In that case it could be the subject of a verb following it, and "doubt" could be that verb. If a verb, the meaning of "doubt" is not immediately apparent, but this is a case where other passages in the texts prove helpful. For instance, in the fourth act, Laertes is on fire to avenge his father, but is temporarily softened and, against his will, moved to tears by the death of his sister. In Q2, he says to the King:

---

[1] See Hamlet's soliloquy after his scene with the Players: "The spirit that I have seene / May be a deale, and the deale hath power / T'assume a pleasing shape" (Q2, II.ii, p. 41).

[2] The King is plotting Hamlet's death by means of a rapier "Steeped in a mixture of deadly poyson, / That if it drawes but the least dramme of blood, / In any part of him, he cannot live" (Q1, IV.v, p. 53).

I have a speech a fire that faine would blase,
But that this folly **drownes** it.

IV.vii, p. 82

The Folio, though keeping the sense the same, offers a variant. There the lines read:

I have a speech of fire, that faine would blaze,
But that this folly **doubts** it.

IV.vii, p. 276

Thus in both texts Laertes's tears for Ophelia temporarily quench the rage for revenge that consumes him. The Folio's "doubt" is a contracted verb for "do out," as "doff" and "don" are still used for "do off" and "do on." And, in Q2, "do out" is what our dram of eale does; literally: "the dram of eale" / Does all the noble substance of him do out / "To his own scandle." In modern prose: "To his shame the dram of evil quenches all his noble substance."

We may be dealing with a printer's error in the use of "a" for the pronoun "him" since its usual meaning is "he," but I believe the sense of the passage requires the above meanings for the much contested words. This passage, added by Q2, the Folio excises, perhaps because of the downgrading of the Danes as drunks. But it is reinstated in most texts and the lines relating to an individual—"So oft it chaunces in particuler men…" *ff.*—have been honored as pointing up an unavoidable trait which will cause the downfall of the tragic hero: a fatal flaw.

Our second enigma, Hamlet's "the *interim's* mine" speech, occurs only in the last of our three texts, the Folio. In the Folio's final scene, Horatio utters a veiled warning that Hamlet's dooming of Rosincrance and Guildensterne, by his alteration of the King's death-mandate, means imminent trouble with the King.

Hor. It must be shortly knowne to him from England
What is the issue of the businesse there.

Hamlet answers:

> It will be short,
> **The *interim's* mine, and a mans life's no more**
> **Then to say one:** but I am very sorry good *Horatio,*
> That to *Laertes* I forgot my selfe;
> For by the image of my Cause, I see
> The Portraiture of his; Ile count[1] his favours:
> But sure the bravery of his griefe did put me
> Into a Towring passion.
>
> Folio, V.ii, 2nd p. 259

Our difficulty is confined to the second and third lines of this speech. In this case, the words are not obscure. The question is whether, as printed, they convey the meaning that the author intended. "The interim's mine and a mans life's no more" is poetry and one of the play's famous thoughts; its conclusion, "Then to say one," descends to the prosaic and besides makes little sense. Later editors have emended it by substituting "than" for "then"; quite permissible since "then" and "than" were interchangeable in contemporary usage when used as a conjunction of comparison.[2] But "Than to say one" still does nothing but detract from the line preceding it. Scholars have suggested that "to say one" was an expression referring to some game or activity well known in Shakespeare's day. If so, familiarity might have given the words meaning but could do little to make them less insipid. "A man's life's no more than to say one"? No! I question whether this passage was written the way the Folio has printed it.

Again, this is a case where another version of this speech in a different text would be useful for comparison, but it does not exist. Q1, because its scenario is not the same, opens its final scene quite differently. In that version, Hamlet has already described his sea

---

[1]Presumably a misprint for "court."

[2]Q1 is apt to use the form "than" for this conjunction; Q2 and the Folio, "then." For example, in the second scene of act I:
  Q1, p. 9: "A countenance more in sorrow than in anger."
  Q2, p. 12 and Folio, p. 155: "A countenance more in sorrow then in anger."

voyage and the King's traitorous mandate to England in a letter to
Horatio, and Horatio has passed the information on to the Queen
(and to the audience) in the preceding act (IV.iv, pp. 52-53). All that
remains to be clarified in the final scene is Hamlet's motive for
acceding to a duel proposed by his bitter enemy, and this motive
Q1, laconic as always, supplies in the four opening lines:

> *Ham.* beleeve mee, it greeves mee much *Horatio,*
> That to *Leartes* I forgot my selfe:
> For by my selfe me thinkes I feele his griefe,
> Though there's a difference in each others wrong.
>   V.ii, p. 59

Thus it is in order to make amends to Leartes that Hamlet will
accept the King's summons to a duel. But in Q2 and succeeding
texts, Horatio has no scene alone with the Queen, and Hamlet's
letters have been less informative. Therefore there is more exposition to be dealt with in the final scene (V.ii). Hamlet must tell
Horatio about the King's treacherous decree of death, and about his
(Hamlet's) forgery of a new royal mandate dooming Rosencraus and
Guyldensterne. He is then in the process of enumerating the King's
crimes against him, when a courtier enters with the King's proposal
of a duel. So his grievances are expounded, but, in Q2, the remorse
for his treatment of Laertes is omitted. I believe the omission was
inadvertent; a prompter's script was incomplete, or a printer was
careless. For surely to have Hamlet fall into the King's trap, just as
he is detailing the King's treacherous acts, is unconvincing. It
advances the plot at the cost of credibility.

   We are left with the Folio as the only early text in which the
final scene includes both themes: Hamlet's case against the King and
his desire to make his peace with Laertes. The scene begins with
his grievances and leads up to the speech we are examining, where
after admitting that the time left to him is short, he declares his
intention to act, and goes on to apologize for his behavior to Laertes.
I believe that originally the opening lines to this speech were:

> It will be short,
> The *interim's* mine, and a mans life's no more.
> Then to say on——but I am very sorry good *Horatio,*
> That to *Laertes* I forgot my selfe;

The emendations required for this reading are slight. They entail:

1. The insertion of a period after the second line, no unusual requirement in the printing of that time.[1]

2. At the beginning of the third line, the retention of "then" as originally printed; "then" in its adverbial sense instead of as an alternative to the conjunction "than."[2]

3. "One" interpreted as "on," a word for which "one" was sometimes substituted.[3] And, still in the third line, a dash substituted for the colon, showing that Hamlet is interrupting himself.

If read in this way, the thought of life as an interim is complete in itself. The concept appears again in "our little life / is rounded by a sleep" *(Tempest,* IV.i). And the phrase "to say on" is familiar; Hamlet has used it twice when he was urging the Player to continue with his passionate speech: "Prythee say on, . . . say on, come to *Hecuba*" (Folio, II.ii, p. 264). Now, Hamlet is about to "say on" when he breaks off to deplore his conduct with Laertes and to declare his intention of making amends. He has just concluded this speech when a courtier enters to propose the duel with Laertes, and

[1] The preceding scene has ended without punctuation of any sort.
> *King* An houre of quiet shortly shall we see,
> Till then, in patience our proceeding be
> Folio, V.i, 2nd p. 259

[2] See p. 119(n).

[3] For an example of "one" used for "on," see Q1, III.ii, p. 39. The murderer in the play-within-a-play says of the poison he is injecting in his victim's ear:
> Thy naturall magicke, and dire propertie,
> One wholesome life usurps immediately.
Q2 and the Folio print this line: "On wholsome life..." (Q2, III.ii, p. 53; Folio, III.ii, p. 268).

Hamlet accepts the challenge. This is a readable and believable version. To be bemused by a transcriber's or a printer's error into thinking the lines were written:

> The *interim's* mine, and a mans life's no more
> Then to say one:

is in my view indefensible. Yet this reading has been a blot on every *Hamlet* from the Folio to the present day.

Now comes a different situation. We will cite two passages; some version of each appears in all three texts, Q1, Q2, and the Folio. But the meaning is not the same in each text. Our object will be to show how variations in the choice or the order of the words affect the meaning.

The first example concerns a speech of Hamlet's that alludes to conditions in the Elizabethan theatre, but which, in its Q1 version, is still meaningful to us. Q2 amends it in a way that conveys less to modern audiences. The Folio restores some of the Q1 version but still leaves the final meaning indeterminate.

Rosencraus and Guyldensterne have announced that the Players are approaching Elsinore. Hamlet describes the greeting they will have from him. Although they have not yet arrived, it is, in effect, his welcoming speech. Here it is, as it appears in Q1:

> ...they shall be welcome,
> He that playes the King shall have tribute of me,
> The ventrous Knight shall use his foyle and target,
> The lover shall sigh gratis,
> The clowne shall make them laugh
> That are tickled in the lungs, or the blanke verse shall halt
>   for't,
> And the Lady shall have leave to speake her minde freely.
>   II.ii, p. 29

Thus, all the Players shall act their appointed roles, including the Clown who will get his laugh or hold up the play. It might be noted here that Shakespeare seems to have had clowns on his mind in Q1. Their ad-libbing will be denounced again in the following act when Hamlet is giving instructions to the Players about performing the play-within-a-play. There he devotes 18 lines—a long speech for this brief Quarto—to describing how clowns interrupt "some necessary point in the Play"; perhaps to display "one sute / Of jeasts, as a man is knowne by one sute of / Apparell" (III.ii, pp. 35-36). This emphasis on the bad habit of clowns may have been aimed at Will Kempe, a famous comedian who had been a member of Shakespeare's company, but had left it at about the turn of the century to play elsewhere. In the Q2 edition, emphasis on this subject has diminished, perhaps because Kempe's defection was no longer topical. No clown is mentioned in Hamlet's welcoming speech, and later in his instructions to the Players, the 18 lines of Q1 have decreased to 6 lines.

In Q2, then, the parallel to the welcoming speech reads:

> He that playes the King shal be welcome, his Majestie shal have tribute on me, the adventerous Knight shall use his foyle and target, the Lover shall not sigh gratis, the humorus Man shall end his part in peace, and the Lady shall say her minde freely: or the black verse shall hault for't.
>
> II.ii, p. 35

In this version the Lover is *not* to sigh gratis; the humorous Man (i.e., the man of humours) is introduced, and all that remains from the lines about the Clown—"or the black [blanke] verse shall hault for't"—is tagged onto the Lady.

The Folio corrects the printing error (substituting "blanke" for "black" verse) and gives still another version:

> He that playes the King shall be welcome; his Majesty shall have Tribute of mee: the adventurous Knight shal use his Foyle and Target: the Lover shall not sigh *gratu,* the humorous man shall end his part in peace: the Clowne shall make those laugh whose lungs are tickled a'th'sere: and the Lady shall say her minde freely; or the blanke Verse shall halt for't.
>
> II.ii, p. 262

So the Clown is back, in a middling sort of way, but the words that are his in Q1—"or the blanke verse shall halt for't"—are still tagged onto the Lady, as they are in Q2. The loss is real, because, applied to the Lady, they convey no definite image. We have no clue as to what would cause the Lady to be unfree about speaking, and so to halt the verse. But we do know scene-stealers, they are still among us. So when Q1 gives us the Clown taking center stage and ad-libbing or pantomiming until he gets his laugh, we know precisely what is happening.

Our final passage shows that a misprint in Q2, if it remains uncorrected in the Folio, may persist in later editions, even if the correct printing appears in Q1. In the byplay between Hamlet and Ophelia during the play-within-a-play, Ophelia comments on Hamlet's jests. Below is the dialogue as printed in Q1:

> *Ofel.* Your jests are keene my Lord.
> *Ham.* It would cost you a groning to take them off.
> *Ofel.* Still better and worse.
> *Ham.* **So you must take your husband....**
>   III.ii, p. 39

In Q2 the final line is misprinted: "So you mistake your husbands" (III.ii, p. 53). The Folio perpetuates this error by printing "So you mistake Husbands" (III.ii, p. 268). If it were not for the Q1 version, "mistake" might be considered the correct verb, though meaningless. Indeed, the line has been printed as "So you mistake your husband" in a recent edition,[1] so little respect is given to Quarto One.

---

[1]Act III, scene ii, line 246 in *Hamlet,* vol. 12 of *The Arden Shakespeare,* ed. Harold Jenkins (1981), p. 303.

APPENDIX B

Major Differences in the Scenarios of the First and Second Quartos

When the action of Quarto Two differs from that of Quarto One, the Quarto One activity is shown in the column on the left, and Quarto Two on the right.

ACT I

Q1, five scenes: pp. 1-19   Q2, five scenes: pp. 1-25

The five scenes cover essentially the same action in both Quartos.

ACT II

Q1, two scenes: pp. 19-33   Q2, two scenes: pp. 25-41

The main difference occurs in the second scene. Hamlet's soliloquy, "To be, or not to be," and his "Get thee to a nunnery" passage with Ophelia (Q1, II. ii, pp. 24-27) are deferred in Q2 to act III, scene i (pp. 43-45). Aside from this difference, Q2 follows the action of Q1.

ACT III

Q1, four scenes: pp. 33-46   Q2, four scenes: pp. 41-65

Q1, scene i: Q2, scene i:

Rosencraus issues Hamlet's invitation for the Court to attend a play that night. The King accepts.

Corambis suggests an interview between the Queen and Hamlet after the play, to be overheard by him. The King and Queen agree.	The King and Polonius prepare Ophelia for her encounter with Hamlet. The King, in an aside, deplores the heavy burden that his hidden guilt imposes on his conscience.

125

Deferred soliloquy, "To be, or not to be," and "Get thee to a nunnery" passage between Hamlet and Ophelia inserted here.

The King tells Polonius of the decision to send Hamlet to England for his health.

The King agrees that Polonius shall overhear an interview between the Queen and Hamlet after the play.

Q1, scene ii: Q2, scene ii:

In both Quartos, scene ii covers the preparations for the play-within-a-play, the enactment of the play, the King's abrupt departure, Hamlet's conviction that the Ghost spoke the truth, and the summons for Hamlet to go to his mother's chamber.

Q1, scene iii: Q2, scene iii:

The King tells Rosencraus and Guyldensterne that they will be making a speedy departure with Hamlet to England. Polonius enters and reports to the King that Hamlet is on his way to his mother's room.

The King has a soliloquy and prays. Hamlet passes by, draws his sword, but decides against killing the King at prayer.

Q1, scene iv: Q2, scene iv:

In both versions the murder of Polonius comes early in this scene, but the two versions then develop differently.

In the ensuing dialogue between the Queen and Hamlet, Hamlet names the King as the murderer of his father and receives his mother's vow of innocence. He reveals that he is sane and she swears to assist in his revenge.

Hamlet dwells mainly on his mother's incestuous marriage, and does no more than hint that the King is a murderer. He reveals that he is sane, and the Queen vows to keep his secret, but is given no opportunity to declare her innocence of the murder or to promise assistance in any plan of revenge.

Act IV

Q1, five scenes: pp. 46-54

Q2, seven scenes: pp. 65-82

Q1, scene i:

Q2, scene i:

The Queen reports that Hamlet, mad, killed Polonius. The King sends Rosencraus and Guyldensterne to find Hamlet and to find the body of Polonius.

The King tells the Queen that Hamlet will be shipped to England: Rossencraft and Gilderstone return with Hamlet.

Q2, scene ii:

Rosencraus and Guyldensterne find Hamlet; he calls them "sponges" of the King and doesn't disclose where the body is.

Q2, scene iii:

The King, entering with two or three attendants, reaffirms his reasons for sending Hamlet abroad; Rosencraus and Guyldensterne return bringing in Hamlet.

Hamlet, under the mask of the antic disposition, parries the King's questions; then reveals that the body is in the lobby. The King sends Hamlet to England; Hamlet departs with Rosencraus and Guyldensterne.

Q1, scene ii:	Q2, scene iv:

Fortinbrasse sends a Captain of his army to the King for free pass and conduct over the land.

This scene continues with Hamlet and Rosencraus and Guyldensterne meeting the Captain. Hamlet's talk with the Captain inspires Hamlet's soliloquy, "How all occasions due informe against me."

Q1, scene iii:	Q2, scene v:

Horatio and a Gentleman persuade the Queen to give an audience to Ophelia.

Ophelia enters, mad, then departs; Laertes, back from France, confronts the King; Ophelia enters a second time.

Q1, scene iv:

Horatio, alone with the Queen, tells of a letter received from Hamlet revealing his safe return after foiling the King's death-plot against him by replacing his name with the names of Rossencraft and Gilderstone.

Q2, scene vi:

Sailors bring letters from Hamlet announcing his return; Horatio, who receives the letters, reads his aloud, describing Hamlet's encounter with the pirates but making no mention of his escape from the King's death-plot.

Q1, scene v: Q2, scene vii:

The King has been told of   A Messenger delivers Hamlet's
Hamlet's return offstage.   letter to the King announcing
                                    Hamlet's return.

The King and Laertes plot a duel against Hamlet; the Queen
reports Ophelia's death.

ACT V

Q1, two scenes: pp. 54-63   Q2, two scenes: pp. 82-99

Q1, scene i: Q2, scene i:

The structure of scene i in the graveyard is essentially the
same in both Quartos.

Q1, scene ii: Q2, scene ii:

Hamlet tells Horatio of his   Hamlet describes to Horatio
contrition for his treatment   how he foiled the King's death-
of Leartes.   plot during his voyage to
                                    England (but omits any mention
                                    of his treatment of Laertes).

A courtier enters with news of the King's wager with Laertes,
and from there on there is no important difference in the
structure of the two Quartos, although, at the end, the state of
the Queen's soul remains more ambiguous in Q2.

FACSIMILE OF THE
1603 FIRST QUARTO

Pagination of the First Quarto [pp. 1-63]
is shown in brackets at the bottom of each page.

THE
Tragicall Historie of
HAMLET
Prince of Denmarke

By William Shake-speare.

As it hath beene diuerse times acted by his Highnesse seruants in the Cittie of London : as also in the two Vniuersities of Cambridge and Oxford, and else-where

At London printed for N.L. and Iohn Trundell.
1603.

The Tragicall Historie of

HAMLET
Prince of Denmarke.

Enter two Centinels.

1. STand : who is that?
2. STis I.
1. O you come most carefully vpon your watch,
2. And if you meete *Marcellus* and *Horatio,*
The partners of my watch, bid them make haste.
1. I will : See who goes there.
              Enter Horatio and Marcellus.
Hor. Friends to this ground.
Mar. And leegemen to the Dane,
O farewell honest souldier, who hath releeued you?
1. *Barnardo* hath my place, giue you good night.
Mar. Holla, *Barnardo.*
2. Say, is *Horatio* there?
Hor. A peece of him.
2. Welcome *Horatio,* welcome good *Marcellus.*
Mar. What hath this thing appear'd againe to night.
2. I haue seene nothing.
Mar. *Horatio* sayes tis but our fantasie,
And wil not let beliefe take hold of him,
Touching this dreaded sight twice seene by vs,
            B   There-

Therefore I haue intreated him a long with vs
To watch the minutes of this night,
That if againe this apparition come,
He may approoue our eyes,and speake to it.

    Hor. Tut, t'will not appeare.

    2. Sit downe I pray, and let vs once againe
Assaile your eares that are so fortified,
What we haue two nights seene.

    Hor. Wel,sit we downe,and let vs heare *Bernardo* speake
of this.

    2. Last night of al,when yonder starre that's west-
ward from the pole,had made his course to
Illumine that part of heauen. Where now it burnes,
The bell then towling one.

Enter Ghost.

    Mar. Breake off your talke, see where it comes againe.

    2. In the same figure like the King that's dead,

    Mar. Thou art a scholler, speake to it *Horatio.*

    2. Lookes it not like the king?

    Hor. Most like, it horrors mee with feare and wonder.

    2. It would be spoke to.

    Mar. Question it *Horatio.*

    Hor. What art thou that thus vsurps the state,in
Which the Maiestie of buried *Denmarke* did sometimes
Walke?By heauen I charge thee speake.

    Mar. It is offended.   *exit Ghost.*

    2. See,it stalkes away.

    Hor. Stay, speake, speake, by heauen I charge thee
speake.

    Mar. Tis gone and makes no answer.

    2. How now *Horatio*,you tremble and looke pale,
Is not this something more than fantasie?
What thinke you on't?

    Hor. Afore my God, I might not this beleeue, without
the sensible and true auouch of my owne eyes.

Mar.

[2]

Prince of Denmarke.

Mar. Is it not like the King?

Hor. As thou art to thy selfe,
Such was the very armor he had on,
When he the ambitious *Norway* combated.
So frownd he once, when in an angry parle
He smot the sleaded pollax on the yce,
Tis strange.

Mar. Thus twice before, and iump at this dead hower,
With Marshall stalke he passed through our watch.

Hor. In what particular to worke, I know not,
But in the thought and scope of my opinion,
This bodes some strange eruption to the state.

Mar. Good, now sit downe, and tell me he that knowes
Why this same strikt and most obseruant watch,
So nightly toyles the subiect of the land,
And why such dayly cost of brazen Cannon
And forraine marte, for implements of warre,
Why such impresse of ship-writes, whose sore taske
Does not diuide the sunday from the weeke:
What might be toward that this sweaty march
Doth make the night ioynt labourer with the day,
Who is't that can informe me?

Hor. Mary that can I, at least the whisper goes so,
Our late King, who as you know was by Forten-
Brasse of *Norway*,
Thereto prickt on by a most emulous cause, dared to
The combate, in which our valiant *Hamlet*,
For so this side of our knowne world esteemed him,
Did slay this Fortenbrasse,
Who by a seale compact well ratified, by law
And heraldrie, did forfeit with his life all those
His lands which he stoode seazed of by the conqueror,
Against the which a moity competent,
Was gaged by our King:
Now sir, yong Fortenbrasse,
Of inapproued mettle hot and full,

B 2   Hath

The Tragedy of Hamlet

Hath in the skirts of *Norway* here and there,
Sharkt vp a fight of lawleffe Refolutes
For food and diet to fome enterprife,
That hath a ftomacke in't : and this (I take it) is the
Chiefe head and ground of this our watch.
                              Enter the Ghoft.
But loe,behold, fee where it comes againe,
Ile croffe it,though it blaft me : ftay illufion,
If there be any good thing to be done,
That may doe eafe to thee,and grace to mee,
Speake to mee.
If thou art priuy to thy countries fate,
Which happly foreknowing may preuent, O fpeake to me,
Or if thou haft extorted in thy life,
Or hoorded treafure in the wombe of earth,
For which they fay you Spirites oft walke in death, fpeake
to me, ftay and fpeake, fpeake,ftoppe it *Marcellus.*
     2.   Tis heere.   *exit Ghoft.*
     Hor.   Tis heere.
     Marc.   Tis gone, O we doe it wrong, being fo maiefti-
call, to offer it the fhew of violence,
For it is as the ayre invelmorable,
And our vaine blowes malitious mockery.
     2.   It was about to fpeake when the Cocke crew.
     Hor.   And then it faded like a guilty thing,
Vpon a fearefull fummons : I haue heard
The Cocke,that is the trumpet to the morning,
Doth with his earely and fhrill crowing throate,
Awake the god of day, and at his found,
Whether in earth or ayre, in fea or fire,
The ftrauagant and erring fpirite hies
To his confines, and of the trueth heere of
This prefent obiect made probation.
     Marc.   It faded on the crowing of the Cocke,
Some fay, that euer gainft that feafon comes,
Wherein our Sauiours birth is celebrated,

                                                  The

Prince of Denmarke.

The bird of dawning fingeth all night long,
And then they fay, no fpirite dare walke abroade,
The nights are wholefome, then no planet frikes,
No Fairie takes, nor Witch hath powre to charme,
So gratious, and fo hallowed is that time.

   Hor. So haue I heard, and doe in parte beleeue it:
But fee the Sunne in ruffet mantle clad,
Walkes ore the deaw of yon hie mountaine top,
Breake we our watch vp, and by my aduife,
Let vs impart what wee haue feene to night
Vnto yong Hamlet: for vpon my life
This Spirite dumbe to vs will fpeake to him:
Do you confent, wee fhall acquaint him with it,
As needefull in our loue, fitting our duetie?

   Marc. Lets doo't I pray, and I this morning know,
Where we fhall finde him moft conueniently.

Enter King, Queene, Hamlet, Leartes, Corambis,
and the two Ambaffadors, with Attendants.

   King Lordes, we here haue writ to *Fortenbraffe,*
Nephew to olde *Norway,* who impudent
And bed-rid, fcarcely heares of this his
Nephews purpofe : and Wee heere difpatch
Yong good *Cornelia,* and you *Veltemar*
For bearers of thefe greetings to olde
Norway, giuing to you no further perfonall power
To bufineffe with the King,
Then thofe related articles do fhew:
Farewell, and let your hafte commend your dutie.

   Gent. In this and all things will wee fhew our dutie.

   King. Wee doubt nothing, hartily farewel:
And now *Leartes* what's the newes with you?
You faid you had a fute what i'ft *Leartes?*

   Lea: My gratious Lord, your fauorable licence,
Now that the funerall rites are all performed,

B 3

I

[5]

The Tragedie of Hamlet

I may haue leaue to go againe to *France*,
For though the fauour of your grace might ſtay mee,
Yet ſomething is there whiſpers in my hart,
Which makes my minde and ſpirits bend all for *France*.

   King ı Haue you your fathers leaue, *Leartes?*
   Cor. He hath, my lord, wrung from me a forced graunt,
And I beſeech you grant your Highneſſe leaue.
   Kiug   With all our heart, *Leartes* fare thee well.
   Lear. I in all loue and dutie take my leaue.
   King. And now princely Sonne *Hamlet*,   *Exit.*
What meanes theſe ſad and melancholy moodes?
For your intent going to *Wittenberg*,
Wee hold it moſt vnmeet and vnconuenient,
Being the Ioy and halfe heart of your mother.
Therefore let mee intreat you ſtay in Court,
All *Denmarkes* hope our cooſin and deareſt Sonne.
   Ham. My lord, ti's not the ſable ſute I weare:
No nor the teares that ſtill ſtand in my eyes,
Nor the diſtracted hauiour in the viſage,
Nor all together mixt with outward ſemblance,
Is equall to the ſorrow of my heart,
Him haue I loſt I muſt of force forgoe,
Theſe but the ornaments and ſutes of woe.
   King This ſhewes a louing care in you, Sonne *Hamlet*,
But you muſt thinke your father loſt a father,
That father dead, loſt his, and ſo ſhalbe vntill the
Generall ending. Therefore ceaſe laments,
It is a fault gainſt heauen, fault gainſt the dead,
A fault gainſt nature, and in reaſons
Common courſe moſt certaine,
None liues on earth, but hee is borne to die.
   Que. Let not thy mother looſe her praiers *Hamlet*,
Stay here with vs, go not to *Wittenberg.*
   Ham. I ſhall in all my beſt obay you madam.
   King Spoke like a kinde and a moſt louing Sonne,
And there's no health the King ſhall drinke to day,

                                    But

Prince of Denmarke.

But the great Canon to the clowdes shall tell
The rowse the King shall drinke vnto Prince Hamlet.

Exeunt all but Hamlet.

Ham. O that this too much grieu'd and sallied flesh
Would melt to nothing, or that the vniuersall
Globe of heauen would turne al to a Chaos!
O God within two moneths; no not two : maried,
Mine vncle : O let me not thinke of it,
My fathers brother : but no more like
My father, then I to *Hercules.*
Within two months, ere yet the salt of most
Vnrighteous teates had left their flushing
In her galled eyes : she married, O God, a beast
Deuoyd of reason would not haue made
Such speede: Frailtie, thy name is Woman,
Why she would hang on him, as if increase
Of appetite had growne by what it looked on.
O wicked wicked speede, to make such
Dexteritie to incestuous sheetes,
Ere yet the shooes were olde,
The which she followed my dead fathers corse
Like *Nyobe,* all teares : married, well it is not,
Nor it cannot come to good:
But breake my heart, for I must holde my tongue.

Enter Horatio *and* Marcellus.

Hor. Health to your Lordship.
Ham. I am very glad to see you, (Horatio) or I much
forget my selfe.
Hor. The same my Lord,and your poore seruant euer.
Ham. O my good friend, I change that name with you:
but what make you from *Wittenberg* Horatio?
Marcellus.
Marc. My good Lord.
Ham. I am very glad to see you, good euen sirs:
But what is your affaire in *Elsenoure?*
Weele teach you to drinke deepe ere you depart.

Hor.

[7]

The Tragedy of Hamlet

Hor. A trowant difpofition, my good Lord.

Ham. Nor fhall you make mee trufter
Of your owne report againſt your felfe:
Sir, I know you are no trowant:
But what is your affaire in *Elſenoure?*

    Hor. My good Lord, I came to fee your fathers funerall.

    Ham. O I pre thee do not mocke mee fellow ftudient,
I thinke it was to fee my mothers wedding.

    Hor. Indeede my Lord, it followed hard vpon.

    Ham. Thrift, thrift, *Horatio*, the funerall bak't meates
Did coldly furnifh forth the marriage tables,
Would I had met my deereft foe in heauen
Ere euer I had feene that day *Horatio*;
O my father, my father, me thinks I fee my father,

    Hor. Where my Lord?

    Ham. Why, in my mindes eye *Horatio*.

    Hor. I faw him once, he was a gallant King.

    Ham. He was a man, take him for all in all,
I fhall not looke vpon his like againe.

    Hor. My Lord, I thinke I faw him yefternight,

    Ham. Saw, who?

    Hor. My Lord, the King your father.

    Ham. Ha, ha, the King my father ke you.

    Hor. Ceafen your admiration for a while
With an attentiue eare, till I may deliuer,
Vpon the witneſſe of thefe Gentlemen
This wonder to you.

    Ham. For Gods loue let me heare it.

    Hor. Two nights together had thefe Gentlemen,
Marcellus and *Bernardo*, on their watch,
In the dead vaſt and middle of the night.
Beene thus incountered by a figure like your father,
Armed to poynt, exactly *Capapea*
Appeeres before them thrife, he walkes
Before their weake and feare oppreſſed eies.
Within his tronchions length,

                     While

Prince of Denmarke

While they diſtilled almoſt to gelly.
With the act of feare ſtands dumbe,
And ſpeake not to him: this to mee
In dreadfull ſecreſie impart they did.
And I with them the third night kept the watch,
Where as they had deliuered forme of the thing.
Each part made true and good,
The Apparition comes : I knew your father,
Theſe handes are not more like.

    Ham. Tis very ſtrange.

    Hor. As I do liue, my honord lord, tis true,
And wee did thinke it right done,
In our dutie to let you know it.

    Ham. Where was this?

    Mar. My Lord, vpon the platforme where we watched.

    Ham. Did you not ſpeake to it?

    Hor. My Lord we did, but anſwere made it none,
Yet once me thought it was about to ſpeake,
And lifted vp his head to motion,
Like as he would ſpeake, but euen then
The morning cocke crew lowd, and in all haſte,
It ſhruncke in haſte away, and vaniſhed
Our ſight.

    Ham. Indeed, indeed ſirs, but this troubles me:
Hold you the watch to night?

    All We do my Lord.

    Ham. Armed ſay ye?

    All Armed my good Lord.

    Ham. From top to toe?

    All. My good Lord, from head to foote.

    Ham. Why then ſaw you not his face?

    Hor. O yes my Lord, he wore his beuer vp.

    Ham. How look't he, frowningly?

    Hor. A countenance more in ſorrow than in anger.

    Ham. Pale, or red?

    Hor. Nay, verie pal

              C   *Ham.*

Ham. And fixt his eies vpon you.

Hor. Moſt conſtantly.

Ham. I would I had beene there.

Hor. It would a much amazed you.

Ham. Yea very like,very like,ſtaid it long?

Hor. While one with moderate pace
Might tell a hundred.

Mar. O longer, longer.

Ham. His beard was griſleld, no.

Hor. It was as I haue ſeene it in his life,
A ſable ſiluer.

Ham. I wil watch to night, perchance t'wil walke againe.

Hor. I warrant it will.

Ham. If it aſſume my noble fathers perſon,
Ile ſpeake to it, if hell it ſelfe ſhould gape,
And bid me hold my peace, Gentlemen,
If you haue hither conſealed this ſight,
Let it be tenible in your ſilence ſtill,
And whatſoeuer elſe ſhall chance to night,
Giue it an vnderſtanding,but no tongue,
I will requit your loues,ſo fare you well,
Vpon the platforme, twixt eleuen and twelue,
Ile viſit you.

All. Our duties to your honor.   *exeunt.*

Ham. O your loues,your loues, as mine to you,
Farewell, my fathers ſpirit in Armes,
Well, all's not well. I doubt ſome foule play,
Would the night were come,
Till then,ſit ſtill my ſoule, foule deeds will riſe
Though all the world orewhelme them to mens eies. *Exit.*

       -Enter Leartes and *Ofelia.*

Leart. My neceſſaries are inbarkt, I muſt aboord,
But ere I part, marke what I ſay to thee:
I ſee Prince *Hamlet* makes a ſhew of loue
Beware *Ofelia,* do not truſt his vowes,
Perhaps he loues you now, and now his tongue,

                        Speakes

Prince of Denmarke.

Speakes from his heart, but yet take heed my sister,
The Charieſt maide is prodigall enough,
If ſhe vnmaske hir beautie to the Moone.
Vertue it ſelfe ſcapes not calumnious thoughts,
Belieu't *Ofelia*,therefore keepe a looſe
Leſt that he trip thy honor and thy fame.

  Ofel. Brother, to this I haue lent attentiue eare,
And doubt not but te keepe my honour firme,
But my deere brother, do not you
Like to a cunning Sophiſter,
Teach me the path and ready way to heauen,
While you forgetting what is ſaid to me,
Your ſelfe, like to a careleſſe libertine
Doth giue his heart, his appetite at ful,
And little recks how that his honour dies.

  Lear. No, feare it not my deere *Ofelia*,
Here comes my father, occaſion ſmiles vpon a ſecond leaue.

Enter Corambis.

  Cor. Yet here *Leartes?* aboord, aboord, for ſhame,
The winde ſits in the ſhoulder of your ſaile,
And you are ſtaid for, there my bleſſing with thee
And theſe few precepts in thy memory.
" Be thou familiar, but by no meanes vulgare;
" Thoſe friends thou haſt, and their adoptions tried,
'· Graple them to thee with a hoope of ſteele,
" But do not dull the palme with entertaine,
" Of euery new vnfleg'd courage,
" Beware of entrance into a quarrell; but being in,
" Beare it that the oppoſed may beware of thee,
" Coſtly thy apparrell, as thy purſe can buy.
" But not expreſt in faſhion,
" For the apparell oft proclaimes the man.
And they of *France* of the chiefe rancke and ſtation
Are of a moſt ſelect and generall chiefe in that:
" This aboue all, to thy owne ſelfe be true,
And it muſt follow as the night the day,

C 2

Thou

The Tragedy of Hamlet

Thou canſt not then be falſe to any one,
Farewel, my bleſſing with thee.

   Lear. I humbly take my leaue, farewell *Ofelia*,
And remember well what I haue ſaid to you.   *exit.*

   Ofel. It is already lock't within my hart,
And you your ſelfe ſhall keepe the key of it.

   Cor. What i'ſt *Ofelia* he hath ſaide to you?

   Ofel. Somthing touching the prince *Hamlet*.

   Cor. Mary wel thought on, t'is giuen me to vnderſtand,
That you haue bin too prodigall of your maiden preſence
Vnto Prince Hamlet, if it be ſo,
As ſo tis giuen to mee, and that in waie of caution
I muſt tell you; you do not vnderſtand your ſelfe
So well as befits my honor, and your credite.

   Ofel. My lord, he hath made many tenders of his loue
to me.

   Cor. Tenders, I, I, tenders you may call them.

   Ofel. And withall, ſuch earneſt vowes.

   Cor. Springes to catch woodcocks,
What, do not I know when the blood doth burne,
How prodigall the tongue lends the heart vowes,
In briefe, be more ſcanter of your maiden preſence,
Or tendring thus you'l tender mee a foole.

   Ofel. I ſhall obay my lord in all I may.

   Cor. *Ofelia*, receiue none of his letters,
" For louers lines are ſnares to intrap the heart;
" Refuſe his tokens, both of them are keyes
To vnlocke Chaſtitie vnto Deſire;
Come in *Ofelia*, ſuch men often proue,
" Great in their wordes, but little in their loue.

   Ofel. I will my lord.   *exeunt.*

       Enter Hamlet, Horatio, *and* Marcellus.

   Ham. The ayre bites ſhrewd; it is an eager and
An nipping winde, what houre i'ſt?

   Hor. I think it lacks of twelue,   *Sound Trumpets.*

   Mar. No, t'is ſtrucke.

                          Hora.

Prince of Denmarke.

Hor. Indeed I heard it not,what doth this mean my lord?

Ham. O the king doth wake to night, & takes his rowse,
Keepe waſſel,and the ſwaggering vp-ſpring reeles,
And as he dreames, his draughts of reniſh downe,
The keṭṭle, drumme, and trumpet, thus bray out,
The triumphes of his pledge.

Hor. Is it a cuſtome here?

Ham. I mary iſt and though I am
Natiue here, and to the maner borne,
It is a cuſtome, more honourd in the breach,
Then in the obſeruance.

Enter the Ghoſt.

Hor. Looke my Lord, it comes.

Ham. Angels and Miniſters of grace defend vs,
Be thou a ſpirite of health, or goblin damn'd,
Bring with thee ayres from heauen, or blaſts from hell:
Be thy intents wicked or charitable,
Thou commeſt in ſuch queſtionable ſhape,
That I will ſpeake to thee,
Ile call thee *Hamlet*, King, Father, Royall Dane,
O anſwere mee, let mee not burſt in ignorance,
But ſay why thy canonizd bones hearſed in death
Haue burſt their ceremonies:why thy Sepulcher,
In which wee ſaw thee quietly interr'd,
Hath burſt his ponderous and marble Iawes,
To caſt thee vp againe: what may this meane,
That thou, dead corſe,againe in compleate ſteele,
Reuiſſets thus the glimſes of the Moone,
Making night hideous, and we fooles of nature,
So horridely to ſhake our diſpoſition,
With thoughts beyond the reaches of our ſoules?
Say,ſpeake,wherefore,what may this meane?

Hor. It beckons you,as though it had ſomething
To impart to you alone.

Mar. Looke with what courteous action,
It waues you to a more remoued ground,

The Tragedie of Hamlet

But do not go with it.

   Hor. No, by no meanes my Lord.

   Ham. It will not speake, then will I follow it.

   Hor. What if it tempt you toward the flood my Lord.
That beckles ore his bace, into the sea,
And there assume some other horrible shape,
Which might depriue your soueraigntie of reason,
And driue you into madnesse : thinke of it.

   Ham. Still am I called, go on, ile follow thee.

   Hor. My Lord, you shall not go.

   Ham. Why what should be the feare?
I do not set my life at a pinnes fee,
And for my soule, what can it do to that?
Being a thing immortall, like it selfe,
Go on, ile follow thee.

   Mar. My Lord be rulde, you shall not goe.

   Ham. My fate cries out, and makes each pety Artiue
As hardy as the Nemeon Lyons nerue,
Still am I cald; vnhand me gentlemen;
By heauen ile make a ghost of him that lets me,
Away I say, go on, ile follow thee.

   Hor. He waxeth desperate with imagination.

   Mar. Something is rotten in the state of *Denmarke*.

   Hor. Haue after; to what issue will this sort?

   Mar. Lets follow, tis not fit thus to obey him.   *exit.*

       Enter Ghost and Hamlet.

   Ham. Ile go no farther, whither wilt thou leade me?

   Ghost Marke me.

   Ham. I will.

   Ghost I am thy fathers spirit, doomd for a time
To walke the night, and all the day
Confinde in flaming fire,
Till the foule crimes done in my dayes of Nature
Are purged and burnt away.

   Ham. Alas poore Ghost.

   Ghost Nay pitty me not, but to my vnfolding

                           Lend

Prince of Denmarke.

Lend thy liftning eare, but that I am forbid
To tell the fecrets of my prifon houfe
I would a tale vnfold, whofe lighteft word
Would harrow vp thy foule, freeze thy yong blood,
Make thy two eyes like ftars ftart from their fpheres,
Thy knotted and combined locks to part,
And each particular haire to ftand on end
Like quils vpon the fretfull Porpentine,
But this fame blazon muft not be,to eares of flefh and blood
Hamlet, if euer thou didft thy deere father loue.

   Ham. O God.
   Gho. Reuenge his foule, and moft vnnaturall murder :
   Ham. Murder.
   Ghoft Yea, murder in the higheft degree,
As in the leaft tis bad,
But mine moft foule,beaftly,and vnnaturall.

   Ham. Hafte me to knowe it, that with wings as fwift as
meditation, or the thought of it,may fweepe to my reuenge.

   Ghoft O I finde thee apt , and duller fhouldft thou be
Then the fat weede which rootes it felfe in eafe
On *Lethe* wharffe : briefe let me be.
Tis giuen out, that fleeping in my orchard,
A Serpent ftung me ; fo the whole eare of *Denmarke*
Is with a forged Proffes of my death rankely abufde:
But know thou noble Youth : he that did fting
Thy fathers heart, now weares his Crowne.

   Ham. O my prophetike foule, my vncle! my vncle!

   Ghoft Yea he, that inceftuous wretch, wonne to his will
O wicked will,and gifts! that haue the power   (with gifts,
So to feduce my moft feeming vertuous Queene,
But vertne, as it neuer will be moued,
Though Lewdneffe court it in a fhape of heauen,
So Luft, though to a radiant angle linckt,
Would fate it felfe from a celeftiall bedde,
And prey on garbage : but foft, me thinkes
I fent the mornings ayre, briefe let me be,

                        Sleeping

Sleeping within my Orchard, my cuſtome alwayes
In the after noone, vpon my ſecure houre
Thy vncle came, with iuyce of Hebona
In a viall, and through the porches of my eares
Did powre the leaprous diſtilment, whoſe effect
Hold ſuch an enmitie with blood of man,
That ſwift as quickeſilner, it poſteth through
The naturall gates and allies of the body,
And turnes the thinne and wholeſome blood
Like eager dropings into milke.
And all my ſmoothe body, barked, and tetterd ouer.
Thus was I ſleeping by a brothers hand
Of Crowne, of Queene, of life, of dignitie
At once depriued, no reckoning made of,
But ſent vnto my graue,
With all my accompts and ſinnes vpon my head,
O horrible, moſt horrible!
   Ham. O God!
   ghoſt If thou haſt nature in thee, beare it not,
But howſoeuer, let not thy heart
Conſpire againſt thy mother aught,
Leaue her to heauen,
And to the burthen that her conſcience beares.
I muſt be gone, the Glo-worme ſhewes the Martin
To be neere, and gin's to pale his vneffectuall fire:
Hamlet adue, adue, adue: remember me.   *Exit*
   Ham. O all you hoſte of heauen! O earth, what elſe?
And ſhall I couple hell; remember thee?
Yes thou poore Ghoſt; from the tables
Of my memorie, ile wipe away all ſawes of Bookes,
All triuiall fond conceites
That euer youth, or elſe obſeruance noted,
And thy remembrance, all alone ſhall ſit.
Yes, yes, by heauen, a damnd pernitious villaine,
Murderons, bawdy, ſmiling damned villaine,
(My tables) meet it is I ſet it downe,

                                    That

Prince of Denmarke

That one may fmile, and fmile, and be a villayne;
At leaſt I am ſure, it may be ſo in *Denmarke*.
So vncle, there you are, there you are.
Now to the words; it is adue adue : remember me,
Soe t'is enough I haue ſworne.

    Hor. My lord, my lord.   *Enter. Horatio,*
    Mar. Lord Hamlet.   *and Marcellus.*
    Hor. Ill, lo, lo, ho, ho.
Ham.Mar. Ill, lo, lo, ſo, ho, ſo, come boy, come.
    Hor. Heauens ſecure him.
    Mar. How i'ſt my noble lord?
    Hor. What news my lord?
    Ham. O wonderfull, wonderful.
    Hor. Good my lord tel it.
    Ham. No not I, you'l reueale it.
    Hor. Not I my Lord by heauen.
    Mar. Nor I my Lord.
    Ham. How ſay you then? would hart of man
Once thinke it? but you'l be ſecret.
    Both. I by heauen, my lord.
    Ham. There's neuer a villaine dwelling in all *Denmarke*,
But hee's an arrant knaue.
    Hor. There need no Ghoſt come from the graue to tell
you this.
    Ham. Right, you are in the right, and therefore
I holde it meet without more circumſtance at all,
Wee ſhake hands and part; you as your buſines
And deſiers ſhall leade you : for looke you,
Euery man hath buſines, and deſires, ſuch
As it is, and for my owne poore parte, ile go pray.
    Hor. Theſe are but wild and wherling words, my Lord.
    Ham. I am ſory they offend you; hartely, yes faith hartily.
    Hor. Ther's no offence my Lord.
    Ham. Yes by Saint *Patrike* but there is *Horatio*,
And much offence too, touching this viſion,
It is an honeſt ghoſt, that let mee tell you,

                  D   For

For your defires to know what is betweene vs,
Or emaifter it as you may:
And now kind frends, as yon are frends,
Schollers and gentlmen,
Grant mee one poore requeft.

   Both. What i ft my Lord?

   Ham. Neuer make known what you haue feene to night

   Both. My lord, we will not.

   Ham. Nay but fweare.

   Hor. In faith my Lord not I.

   Mar. Nor I my Lord in faith.

   Ham. Nay vpon my fword, indeed vpon my fword.

   Gho. Sweare.

          The Goft vnder the ftage.

   Ham. Ha, ha, come you here, this fellow in the fellerige,
Here confent to fweare.

   Hor. Propofe the oth my Lord.

   Ham. Neuer to fpeake what you haue feene to night,
Sweare by my fword.

   Goft. Sweare.

   Ham. Hic & vbique, nay then weele fhift our ground:
Come hither Gentlemen, and lay your handes
Againe vpon this fword, neuer to fpeake
Of that which you haue feene, fweare by my fword.

   Ghoft Sweare.

   Ham. Well faid old Mole, can'ft worke in the earth?
fo faft, a worthy Pioner, once more remoue.

   Hor. Day and night, but this is wondrous ftrange.

   Ham. And therefore as a ftranger giue it welcome,
There are more things in heauen and earth *Horatio,*
Then are Dream't of, in your philofophie,
But come here, as before you neuer fhall
How ftrange or odde foere I beare my felfe,
As I perchance hereafter fhall thinke meet,
To put an Anticke difpofition on,
That you at fuch times feeing me, neuer fhall

                                With

Prince of Denmarke.

With Armes, incombred thus, or this head shake,
Or by pronouncing some vndoubtfull phrase,
As well well, wee know, or wee could and if we would,
Or there be, and if they might, or such ambiguous:
Giuing out to note, that you know aught of mee,
This not to doe, so grace, and mercie
At your most need helpe you, sweare

 Ghost. sweare.

 Ham. Rest, rest, perturbed spirit: so gentlemen,
In all my loue I do commend mee to you,
And what so poore a man as *Hamlet* may,
To pleasure you, God willing shall not want,
Nay come lett's go together,
But stil your fingers on your lippes I pray,
The time is out of ioynt, O cursed spite,
That euer I was borne to set it right,
Nay come lett's go together.   *Exeunt.*

    Enter Corambis, and Montano.

 Cor. *Montano*, here, these letters to my sonne,
And this same mony with my blessing to him,
And bid him ply his learning good *Montano*.

 Mon. I will my lord.

 Cor. You shall do very well *Montano*, to say thus,
I knew the gentleman, or know his father,
To inquire the manner of his life,
As thus; being amongst his acquaintance,
You may say, you saw him at such a time, marke you mee,
At game, or drincking, swearing, or drabbing,
You may go so farre.

 Mon. My lord, that will impeach his reputation.

 Cor. I faith not a whit, no not a whit,
Now happely hee closeth with you in the consequence,
As you may bridle it not disparage him a iote.
What was I about to say,

 Mon. He closeth with him in the consequence.

 Cor. I, you say right, he closeth with him thus,

     D 2   This

The Tragedy of Hamlet

This will hee say, let mee see what hee will say,
Mary this, I saw him yesterday, or tother day,
Or then, or at such a time, a dicing,
Or at Tennis, I or drincking drunke, or entring
Of a howse of lightnes viz. brothell,
Thus sir do wee that know the world, being men of reach,
By indirections, finde directions forth,
And so shall you my sonne; you ha me, ha you not?

    Mon. I haue my lord.
    Cor. Wel, fare you well, commend mee to him.
    Mon. I will my lord.
    Cor. And bid him ply his musicke
    Mon. My lord I wil.   *exit.*
        Enter, Ofelia.

    Cor. Farewel, how now *Ofelia*, what's the news with you?
    Ofe. O my deare father, such a change in nature,
So great an alteration in a Prince,
So pitifull to him, fearefull to mee,
A maidens eye ne're looked on.
    Cor. Why what's the matter my *Ofelia?*
    Of. O yong Prince *Hamlet*, the only floure of *Denmark*,
Hee is bereft of all the wealth he had,
The Iewell that ador'nd his feature most
Is filcht and stolne away, his wit's bereft him,
Hee found mee walking in the gallery all alone,
There comes hee to mee, with a distracted looke,
His garters lagging downe, his shooes vntide,
And fixt his eyes so stedfast on my face,
As if they had vow'd, this is their latest obiect.
Small while he stoode, but gripes me by the wrist,
And there he holdes my pulse till with a sigh
He doth vnclaspe his holde, and parts away
Silent, as is the mid time of the night:
And as he went, his eie was still on mee,
For thus his head ouer his shoulder looked,
He seemed to finde the way without his eies:

                          For

Prince of Denmarke.

For out of doores he went without their helpe,
And so did leaue me.
   Cor. Madde for thy loue,
What haue you giuen him any crosse wordes of late?
   Ofelia I did repell his letters, deny his gifts,
As you did charge me.
   Cor. Why that hath made him madde:
By heau'n t'is as proper for our age to cast
Beyond our selues, as t'is for the yonger sort
To leaue their wantonnesse, Well, I am sory
That I was so rash: but what remedy?
Lets to the King, this madnesse may prooue,
Though wilde a while, yet more true to thy loue.   *exeunt.*
   Enter King and Queene, Rossencraft, and Gilderstone.
   King Right noble friends, that our deere cosin Hamlet
Hath lost the very heart of all his sence,
It is most right, and we most sory for him:
Therefore we doe desire, euen as you tender
Our care to him, and our great loue to you,
That you will labour but to wring from him
The cause and ground of his distemperancie.
Doe this, the king of *Denmarke* shal be thankefull.
   Ros. My Lord, whatsoeuer lies within our power
Your maiestie may more commaund in wordes
Then vse perswations to your liege men, bound
By loue, by duetie, and obedience.
   Guil. What we may doe for both your Maiesties
To know the griefe troubles the Prince your sonne,
We will indeuour all the best we may,
So in all duetie doe we take our leaue.
   King Thankes Guilderstone, and gentle Rossencraft.
   Que. Thankes Rossencraft, and gentle Gilderstone.
     Enter Corambis and Ofelia.
   Cor. My Lord, the Ambassadors are ioyfully
Return'd from *Norway*.
   King Thou still hast beene the father of good news.
D 3

                                             Cor.

The Tragedie of Hamlet

Cor. Haue I my Lord? I aſſure your grace,
I holde my duetie as I holde my life,
Both to my God, and to my ſoueraigne King:
And I'beleeue, or elſe this braine of mine
Hunts not the traine of policie ſo well
As it had wont to doe, but I haue found
The very depth of Hamlets lunacie.
    Queene God graunt he hath.
            Enter the Ambaſſadors.
    King Now *Voltemar*, what from our brother *Norway*?
    Volt. Moſt faire returnes of greetings and deſires,
Vpon our firſt he ſent forth to ſuppreſſe
His nephews leuies, which to him appear'd
To be a preparation gainſt the Polacke:
But better look't into, he truely found
It was againſt your Highneſſe, whereat grieued,
That ſo his ſickeneſſe, age, and impotence,
Was falſely borne in hand, ſends out arreſts
On *Fortenbraſſe*, which he in briefe obays,
Receiues rebuke from *Norway*: and in fine,
Makes vow before his vncle, neuer more
To giue the aſſay of Armes againſt your Maieſtie,
Whereon olde *Norway* ouercome with ioy,
Giues him three thouſand crownes in annuall fee,
And his Commiſſion to employ thoſe ſouldiers,
So leuied as before, againſt the Polacke,
With an intreaty heerein further ſhewne,
That it would pleaſe you to giue quiet paſſe
Through your dominions, for that enterpriſe
On ſuch regardes of ſafety and allowances
As therein are ſet downe.
    King It likes vs well, and at fit time and leaſure
Weele reade and anſwere theſe his Articles,
Meane time we thanke you for your well
Tooke labour: go to your reſt, at night weele feaſt togither:
Right welcome home.   *exeunt Ambaſſadors.*
                                                    Cor.

Prince of Denmarke.

Cor. This busines is very well dispatched.
Now my Lord, touching the yong Prince Hamlet,
Certaine it is that hee is madde: mad let vs grant him then:
Now to know the cause of this effect,
Or else to say the cause of this defect,
For this effect defectiue comes by cause.

   Queene Good my Lord be briefe.

   Cor. Madam I will: my Lord, I haue a daughter,
Haue while shee's mine: for that we thinke
Is surest, we often loose: now to the Prince.
My Lord, but note this letter,
The which my daughter in obedience
Deliuer'd to my handes.

   King Reade it my Lord.

   Cor. Marke my Lord.
Doubt that in earth is fire,
Doubt that the starres doe moue,
Doubt trueth to be a liar,
But doe not doubt I loue.
To the beautifull *Ofelia:*
Thine euer the most vnhappy Prince *Hamlet.*
My Lord, what doe you thinke of me?
I, or what might you thinke when I sawe this?

   King As of a true friend and a most louing subiect.

   Cor. I would be glad to prooue so.
Now when I saw this letter, thus I bespake my maiden:
Lord *Hamlet* is a Prince out of your starre,
And one that is vnequall for your loue:
Therefore I did commaund her refuse his letters,
Deny his tokens, and to absent her selfe.
Shee as my childe obediently obey'd me.
Now since which time, seeing his loue thus crossd,
Which I tooke to be idle, and but sport,
He straitway grew into a melancholy,
From that vnto a fast, then vnto distraction,
Then into a sadnesse, from that vnto a madnesse,

                               And

The Tragedy of Hamlet

And so by continuance, and weakenesse of the braine
Into this frensie, which now possesseth him:
And if this be not true, take this from this.

   King Thinke you t'is so?

   Cor. How? so my Lord, I would very faine know
That thing that I haue saide t'is so, positiuely,
And it hath fallen out otherwise.
Nay, if circumstances leade me on,
Ile finde it out, if it were hid
As deepe as the centre of the earth.

   King. how should wee trie this same?

   Cor. Mary my good lord thus,
The Princes walke is here in the galery,
There let *Ofelia*, walke vntill hee comes:
Your selfe and I will stand close in the study,
There shall you heare the effect of all his hart,
And if it proue any otherwise then loue,
Then let my censure faile an other time.

   King. see where hee comes poring vppon a booke.

           Enter Hamlet.

   Cor. Madame, will it please your grace
To leaue vs here?

   Que. With all my hart.   *exit.*

   Cor. And here *Ofelia*, reade you on this booke,
And walke aloofe, the King shal be vnseene.

   Ham. To be, or not to be, I there's the point,
To Die, to sleepe, is that all? I all:
No, to sleepe, to dreame, I mary there it goes,
For in that dreame of death, when wee awake,
And borne before an euerlasting Iudge,
From whence no passenger euer retur'nd,
The vndiscouered country, at whose sight
The happy smile, and the accursed damn'd.
But for this, the ioyfull hope of this,
Whol'd beare the scornes and flattery of the world,
Scorned by the right rich, the rich cursed of the poore?

                                The

Prince of Denmarke

The widow being oppreſſed,the orphan wrong'd,
The taſte of hunger, or a tirants raigne,
And thouſand more calamities beſides,
To grunt and ſweate vnder this weary life,
When that he may his full *Quietus* make,
With a bare bodkin, who would this indure,
But for a hope of ſomething after death?
Which puſles the braine, and doth confound the ſence,
Which makes vs rather beare thoſe euilles we haue,
Than flie to others that we know not of.
I that,O this conſcience makes cowardes of vs all,
Lady in thy orizons, be all my ſinnes remembred.

    Ofel. My Lord, I haue ſought opportunitie,which now
I haue,to redeliuer to your worthy handes, a ſmall remembrance, ſuch tokens which I haue receiued of you.

    Ham. Are you faire?

    Ofel. My Lord.

    Ham. Are you honeſt?

    Ofel. What meanes my Lord?

    Ham. That if you be faire and honeſt,
Your beauty ſhould admit no diſcourſe to your honeſty.

    Ofel. My Lord, can beauty haue better priuiledge than
with honeſty?

    Ham. Yea mary may it; for Beauty may transforme
Honeſty, from what ſhe was into a bawd:
Then Honeſty can transforme Beauty:
This was ſometimes a Paradox,
But now the time giues it ſcope.
I neuer gaue you nothing.

    Ofel. My Lord, you know right well you did,
And with them ſuch earneſt vowes of loue,
As would haue moou'd the ſtonieſt breaſt aliue,
But now too true I finde,
Rich giftes waxe poore, when giuers grow vnkinde.

    Ham. I neuer loued you.

    Ofel. You made me beleeue you did.

E

Ham.

The Tragedie of Hamlet

Ham. O thou shouldst not a beleeued me!
Go to a Nunnery goe, why shouldst thou
Be a breeder of sinners? I am my selfe indifferent honest,
But I could accuse my selfe of such crimes
As It had beene better my mother had ne're borne me,
O I am very prowde, ambitious, disdainefull,
With more sinnes at my backe, then I haue thoughts
To put them in, what should such fellowes as I
Do, crawling betweene heauen and earth?
To a Nunnery goe, we are arrant knaues all,
Beleeue none of vs, to a Nunnery goe.
    Ofel. O heauens secure him!
    Ham. Wher's thy father?
    Ofel. At home my lord.
    Ham. For Gods sake let the doores be shut on him,
He may play the foole no where but in his
Owne house: to a Nunnery goe.
    Ofel. Help him good God.
    Ham. If thou dost marry, Ile giue thee
This plague to thy dowry:
Be thou as chaste as yce, as pure as snowe,
Thou shalt not scape calumny, to a Nunnery goe.
    Ofel. Alas, what change is this?
    Ham. But if thou wilt needes marry, marry a foole,
For wisemen know well enough,
What monsters you make of them, to a Nunnery goe.
    Ofel. Pray God restore him.
    Ham. Nay, I haue heard of your paintings too,
God hath giuen you one face,
And you make your selues another,
You fig, and you amble, and you nickname Gods creatures,
Making your wantonnesse, your ignorance,
A pox, t is scuruy, Ile no more of it,
It hath made me madde : Ile no more marriages,
All that are married but one, shall liue,
The rest shall keepe as they are, to a Nunnery goe,

                                                    To

[26]

Prince of Denmarke.

To a Nunnery goe.   *exit.*

Ofe. Great God of heauen, what a quicke change is this?
The Courtier, Scholler, Souldier, all in him,
All dasht and splinterd thence, O woe is me,
To a seene what I haue seene, see what I see.   *exit.*

King Loue? No, no, that's not the cause,   *Enter King and*
Some deeper thing it is that troubles him.   *Corambis.*

Cor. Wel, something it is: my Lord, content you a while,
I will my selfe goe feele him: let me worke,
Ile try him euery way : see where he comes,
Send you those Gentlemen, let me alone
To finde the depth of this, away, be gone.   *exit King.*
Now my good Lord, do you know me?   *Enter Hamlet.*

Ham. Yea very well, y'are a fishmonger.

Cor. Not I my Lord.

Ham. Then sir, I would you were so honest a man,
For to be honest, as this age goes,
Is one man to be pickt out of tenne thousand.

Cor. What doe you reade my Lord?

Ham. Wordes, wordes.

Cor. What's the matter my Lord?

Ham. Betweene who?

Cor. I meane the matter you reade my Lord.

Ham. Mary most vile heresie:
For here the Satyricall Satyre writes,
That olde men haue hollow eyes, weake backes,
Grey beardes, pittifull weake hammes, gowty legges,
All which sir, I most potently beleeue not:
For sir, your selfe shalbe olde as I am,
If like a Crabbe, you could goe backeward.

Cor. How pregnant his replies are, and full of wit:
Yet at first he tooke me for a fishmonger:
All this comes by loue, the vemencie of loue,
And when I was yong, I was very idle,
And suffered much extasie in loue, very neere this:
Will you walke out of the aire my Lord?

E 2   *Ham.*

[27]

The Tragedy of Hamlet

Ham. Into my graue.

Cor. By the masse that's out of the aire indeed,
Very shrewd answers,
My lord I will take my leaue of you.

        Enter Gilderstone, and Rossencraft.

Ham. You can take nothing from me sir,
I will more willingly part with all,
Olde doating foole.

Cor. You seeke Prince Hamlet, see, there he is.   *exit.*

Gil. Health to your Lordship.

Ham. What, Gilderstone, and Rossencraft,
Welcome kinde Schoole-fellowes to *Elsanoure.*

Gil. We thanke your Grace, and would be very glad
You were as when we were at *Wittenberg.*

Ham. I thanke you, but is this visitation free of
Your selues, or were you not sent for?
Tell me true, come, I know the good King and Queene
Sent for you, there is a kinde of confession in your eye:
Come, I know you were sent for.

Gil. What say you?

Ham. Nay then I see how the winde sits,
Come, you were sent for.

Ross. My lord, we were, and willingly if we might,
Know the cause and ground of your discontent.

Ham. Why I want preferment.

Ross. I thinke not so my lord.

Ham. Yes faith, this great world you see contents me not,
No nor the spangled heauens, nor earth, nor sea,
No nor Man that is so glorious a creature,
Contents not me, no nor woman too, though you laugh.

Gil. My lord, we laugh not at that.

Ham. Why did you laugh then,
When I said, Man did not content mee?

Gil. My Lord, we laughed, when you said, Man did not
content you.
What entertainement the Players shall haue,

                                   We

Prince of Denmarke.

We boorded them a the way : they are comming to you.

  Ham. Players, what Players be they?

  Roff. My Lord, the Tragedians of the Citty,

Thofe that you tooke delight to fee fo often.   (flie?

  Ham. How comes it that they trauell? Do they grow re-

  Gil. No my Lord, their reputation holds as it was wont.

  Ham. How then?

  Gil. Yfaith my Lord, noueltie carries it away,

For the principall publike audience that

Came to them, are turned to priuate playes,

And to the humour of children.

  Ham. I doe not greatly wonder of it,

For thofe that would make mops and moes

At my vncle, when my father liued,

Now giue a hundred, two hundred pounds

For his picture : but they fhall be welcome,

He that playes the King fhall haue tribute of me,

The ventrous Knight fhall vfe his foyle and target,

The louer fhall figh gratis,

The clowne fhall make them laugh   (for't,

That are tickled in the lungs; or the blanke verfe fhall halt

And the Lady fhall haue leaue to fpeake her minde freely.

    The Trumpets found, Enter Corambis.

Do you fee yonder great baby?

He is not yet out of his fwadling clowts.

  Gil. That may be, for they fay an olde man

Is twice a childe.   (Players,

  Ham. Ile prophecie to you, hee comes to tell mee a the

You fay true, a monday laft, t'was fo indeede.

  Cor. My lord, I haue news to tell you.

  Ham. My Lord, I haue newes to tell you:

When *Roffios* was an Actor in *Rome.*

  Cor. The Actors are come hither, my lord.

  Ham. Buz, buz.

  Cor. The beft Actors in Chriftendome,

Either for Comedy, Tragedy, Hiftorie, Paftorall,

          E 3   Paftorall

The Tragedie of Hamlet

Paſtorall, Hiſtoricall, Hiſtoricall, Comicall,
Comicall hiſtoricall, Paſtorall, Tragedy hiſtoricall:
Seneca cannot be too heauy, nor *Plato* too light:
For the law hath writ thoſe are the onely men.
   Ha, O *Iepha* Iudge of *Iſrael!* what a treaſure hadſt thou?
   Cor. Why what a treaſure had he my lord?
   Ham. Why one faire daughter, and no more,
The which he loued paſſing well.
   - *Cor.* A, ſtil harping a my daughter! well my Lord,
If you call me *Iepha*, I hane a daughter that
I loue paſſing well.
   Ham. Nay that followes not.
   Cor. What followes then my Lord?
   Ham. Why by lot, or God wot, or as it came to paſſe,
And ſo it was, the firſt verſe of the godly Ballet
Wil tel you all: for look you where my abridgement comes:
Welcome maiſters, welcome all,   *Enter players.*
What my olde friend, thy face is vallanced
Since I ſaw thee laſt, com'ſt thou to beard me in *Denmarke?*
My yong lady and miſtris, burlady but your   (you were:
Ladiſhip is growne by the altitude of a chopine higher than
Pray God ſir your voyce, like a peece of vncurrant
Golde, be not crack't in the ring: come on maiſters,
Weele euen too't, like French Falconers,
Flie at any thing we ſee, come, a taſte of your
Quallitie, a ſpeech, a paſſionate ſpeech.
   Players What ſpeech my good lord?
   Ham. I heard thee ſpeake a ſpeech once,
But it was neuer acted: or if it were,
Neuer aboue twice, for as I remember,
It pleaſed not the vulgar, it was cauiary
To the million : but to me
And others, that receiued it in the like kinde,
Cried in the toppe of their iudgements, an excellent play,
Set downe with as great modeſtie as cunning:
One ſaid there was no ſallets in the lines to make thē ſauory,
                                  But

Prince of Denmarke.

But called it an honest methode, as wholesome as sweete.
Come, a speech in it I chiefly remember
Was *Æneas* tale to *Dido*,
And then especially where he talkes of Princes slaughter,
If it liue in thy memory beginne at this line,
Let me see.
The rugged *Pyrrus*, like th'arganian beast:
No t'is not so, it begins with *Pirrus*:
O I haue it.
The rugged *Pirrus*, he whose sable armes,
Blacke as his purpose did the night resemble,
When he lay couched in the ominous horse,
Hath now his blacke and grimme complexion smeered
With Heraldry more dismall, head to foote,
Now is he totall guise, horridely tricked
With blood of fathers, mothers, daughters, sonnes,
Back't and imparched in calagulate gore,
Rifted in earth and fire, olde grandsire *Pryam* seekes:
So goe on.   (accent.
   Cor. Afore God, my Lord, well spoke, and with good
   Play. Anone he finds him striking too short at Greeks,
His antike sword rebellious to his Arme,
Lies where it falles, vnable to resist.
Pyrrus at *Pryam* driues, but all in rage,
Strikes wide, but with the whiffe and winde
Of his fell sword, th'vnnerued father falles.
   Cor. Enough my friend, t'is too long.
   Ham. It shall to the Barbers with your beard:
A pox, hee's for a Iigge, or a tale of bawdry,
Or else he sleepes, come on to *Hecuba*, come.
   Play. But who, O who had seene the mobled Queene?
   Cor. Mobled Queene is good, faith very good.
   Play. All in the alarum and feare of death rose vp,
And o're her weake and all ore-teeming loynes, a blancket
And a kercher on that head, where late the diademe stoode,
Who this had seene with tongue inuenom'd speech,
                                  Would

Would treafon haue pronounced,
For if the gods themfelues had feene her then,
When fhe faw *Pirrus* with malitious ftrokes,
Mincing her husbandes limbs,
It would haue made milch the burning eyes of heauen,
And paffion in the gods.

   Cor. Looke my lord if he hath not changde his colour,
And hath teares in his eyes: no more good heart, no more.
   Ham. T'is well, t'is very well, I pray my lord,
Will you fee the Players well beftowed,
I tell you they are the Chronicles
And briefe abftracts of the time,
After your death I can tell you,
You were better haue a bad Epiteeth,
Then their ill report while you liue.
   Cor. My lord, I will vfe them according to their deferts.
   Ham. O farre better man, vfe euery man after his deferts,
Then who fhould fcape whipping?
Vfe them after your owne honor and dignitie,
The leffe they deferue, the greater credit's yours.
   Cor. Welcome my good fellowes.   *exit.*
   Ham. Come hither maifters, can you not play the mur-
der of *Gonfago?*
   players Yes my Lord.
   Ham. And could'ft not thou for a neede ftudy me
Some dozen or fixteene lines,
Which I would fet downe and infert?
   players Yes very eafily my good Lord.
   Ham. T'is well, I thanke you: follow that lord:
And doe you heare firs? take heede you mocke him not.
Gentlemen, for your kindnes I thanke you,
And for a time I would defire you leaue me.
   Gil. Our loue and duetie is at your commaund.
          Exeunt all but Hamlet.
   Ham. Why what a dunghill idiote flaue am I?
Why thefe Players here draw water from eyes:

                                         For

Prince of Denmarke

For Hecuba, why what is Hecuba to him, or he to Hecuba?
What would he do and if he had my losse?
His father murdred, and a Crowne bereft him,
He would turne all his teares to droppes of blood,
Amaze the standers by with his laments,
Strike more then wonder in the iudiciall eares,
Confound the ignorant, and make mute the wife,
Indeede his paſſion would be generall.
Yet I like to an aſſe and Iohn a Dreames,
Hauing my father murdred by a villaine,
Stand ſtill, and let it paſſe, why ſure I am a coward:
Who pluckes me by the beard, or twites my noſe,
Giue's me the lie i'th throate downe to the lungs,
Sure I ſhould take it, or elſe I haue no gall,
Or by this I ſhould a fatted all the region kites
With this ſlaues offell, this damned villaine,
Treacherous, bawdy, murderous villaine:
Why this is braue, that I the ſonne of my deare father,
Should like a ſcalion, like a very drabbe
Thus raile in wordes. About my braine,
I haue heard that guilty creatures ſitting at a play,
Hath, by the very cunning of the ſcene, confeſt a murder
Committed long before.
This ſpirit that I haue ſeene may be the Diuell,
And out of my weakeneſſe and my melancholy,
As he is very potent with ſuch men,
Doth ſeeke to damne me, I will haue ſounder proofes,
The play's the thing,
Wherein I'le catch the conſcience of the King.   *exit.*

Enter the King, Queene, and Lordes.

King Lordes, can you by no meanes finde
The cauſe of our ſonne Hamlets lunacie?
You being ſo neere in loue, euen from his youth,
Me thinkes ſhould gaine more than a ſtranger ſhould.

                                    F   Gib

The Tragedie of Hamlet

Gil. My lord, we haue done all the best we could,
To wring from him the cause of all his griefe,
But still he puts vs off, and by no meanes
Would make an answere to that we exposde.

Ross. Yet was he something more inclin'd to mirth
Before we left him, and I take it,
He hath giuen order for a play to night,
At which he craues your highnesse company.

King With all our heart, it likes vs very well:
Gentlemen, seeke still to increase his mirth,
Spare for no cost, our coffers shall be open,
And we vnto your selues will still be thankefull.

Both In all wee can, be sure you shall commaund.

Queene Thankes gentlemen, and what the Queene of
May pleasure you, be sure you shall not want. (*Denmarke*

Gil. Weele once againe vnto the noble Prince.

King Thanks to you both: Gertred you'l see this play.

Queene My lord I will, and it ioyes me at the soule
He is inclin'd to any kinde of mirth.

Cor. Madame, I pray be ruled by me:
And my good Soueraigne, giue me leaue to speake,
We cannot yet finde out the very ground
Of his distemperance, therefore
I holde it meete, if so it please you,
Else they shall not meete, and thus it is.

King What i'st *Corambis?*　　　　　　(done,

Cor. Mary my good lord this, soone when the sports are
Madam, send you in haste to speake with him,
And I my selfe will stand behind the Arras,
There question you the cause of all his griefe,
And then in loue and nature vnto you, hee'le tell you all:
My Lord, how thinke you on't

King It likes vs well, Gerterd, what say you?

Queene With all my heart, soone will I send for him.

Cor. My selfe will be that happy messenger,
Who hopes his griefe will be reueal'd to her. *exeunt omnes.*
　　　　　　　　　　　　　　　　　　　　Enter

Prince of Denmarke.

Enter Hamlet and the Players.

Ham. Pronounce me this speech trippingly a the tongue
as I taught thee,
Mary and you mouth it, as a many of your players do
I'de rather heare a towne bull bellow,
Then such a fellow speake my lines.
Nor do not saw the aire thus with your hands,
But giue euery thing his action with temperance.   (fellow,
O it offends mee to the soule, to heare a rebustious periwig
To teare a passion in totters, into very ragges,
To split the eares of the ignoraut, who for the   (noises,
Most parte are capable of nothing but dumbe shewes and
I would haue such a fellow whipt, for o're doing, tarmagant
It out, Herodes Herod.

players My Lorde, wee haue indifferently reformed that
among vs.

Ham. The better, the better, mend it all together:
There be fellowes that I haue seene play,
And heard others commend them, and that highly too,
That hauing neither the gate of Christian, Pagan,
Nor Turke, haue so strutted and bellowed,
That you would a thought, some of Natures journeymen
Had made men, and not made them well,
They imitated humanitie, so abhominable:
Take heede, auoyde it.

players I warrant you my Lord.

Ham. And doe you heare? let not your Clowne speake
More then is set downe, there be of them I can tell you
That will laugh themselues, to set on some
Quantitie of barren spectators to laugh with them,
Albeit there is some necessary point in the Play
Then to be obserued: O t'is vile, and shewes
A pittifull ambition in the foole that vseth it.
And then you haue some agen, that keepes one sute
Of ieasts, as a man is knowne by one sute of
Apparell, and Gentlemen quotes his ieasts downe

F 2   In

The Tragedy of Hamlet

In their tables, before they come to the play, as thus:
Cannot you stay till I eate my porrige? and, you owe me
A quarters wages: and, my coate wants a cullison:
And, your beere is sowre: and, blabbering with his lips,
And thus keeping in his cinkapase of ieasts,
When, God knows, the warme Clowne cannot make a ieft
Vnlesse by chance, as the blinde man catcheth a hare:
Maisters tell him of it.

   players We will my Lord.
   Ham. Well, goe make you ready.   *exeunt players.*
   Horatio. Heere my Lord.
   Ham. *Horatio*, thou art euen as iuft a man,
As e're my conuerfation cop'd withall.
   Hor. O my lord!
   Ham. Nay why fhould I flatter thee?
Why fhould the poore be flattered?
What gaine fhould I receiue by flattering thee,
That nothing hath but thy good minde?
Let flattery fit on thofe time-pleafing tongs,
To glofe with them that loues to heare their praife,
And not with fuch as thou *Horatio.*
There is a play to night, wherein one Sceane they haue
Comes very neere the murder of my father,
When thou fhalt fee that Act afoote,
Marke thou the King, doe but obferue his lookes,
For I mine eies will riuet to his face:
And if he doe not bleach, and change at that,
It is a damned ghoft that we haue feene.
Horatio, haue a care, obferue him well.
   Hor. My lord, mine eies fhall ftill be on his face,
And not the fmalleft alteration
That fhall appeare in him, but I fhall note it.
   Ham. Harke, they come.
   Enter King, Queene, Corambis, and other Lords. (a play?
   King How now fon *Hamlet*, how fare you, fhall we haue
   Ham. Yfaith the Camelions difh, not capon cramm'd,
                                     feede

Prince of Denmarke.

feede a the ayre.

I father : My lord, you playd in the Vniuerſitie.

   Cor. That I did my L: and I was counted a good actor.

   Ham. What did you enact there?

   Cor. My lord, I did act *Iulius Caſar,* I was killèd
in the Capitoll, *Brutus* killed me.

   Ham. It was a brute parte of him,

To kill ſo capitall a calfe.

Come, be theſe Players ready?

   Queene Hamlet come ſit downe by me.

   Ham. No by my faith mother, heere's a mettle more at-
Lady will you giue me leaue, and ſo forth: (tractiue:
To lay my head in your lappe?

   Ofel. No my Lord.   (trary matters?

   Ham. Vpon your lap, what do you thinke I meant con-

Enter in a Dumbe Shew, the King and the Queene, he ſits
   downe in an Arbor, ſhe leaues him : Then enters Luci-
   anus with poyſon in a Viall, and powres it in his eares, and
   goes away : Then the Queene commeth and findes him
   dead : and goes away with the other.

   Ofel. What meanes this my Lord?   *Enter the Prologue.*

   Ham. This is myching Mallico, that meanes my chiefe.

   Ofel. What doth this meane my lord?

   Ham. you ſhall heare anone, this fellow will tell you all.

   Ofel. Will he tell vs what this ſhew meanes?

   Ham. I, or any ſhew you'le ſhew him,

Be not afeard to ſhew, hee'le not be afeard to tell:

O theſe Players cannot keepe counſell, thei'le tell all.

   Prol. For vs, and for our Tragedie,

Heere ſtowping to your clemencie,

We begge your hearing patiently.

   Ham. I'ſt a prologue, or a poeſie for a ring?

   Ofel. T'is ſhort my Lord.

   Ham. As womens loue.

     Enter the Duke and Dutcheſſe.

   Duke Full fortie yeares are paſt, their date is gone,

                          F 3   Since

The Tragedie of Hamlet

Since happy time ioyn'd both our hearts as one:
And now the blood that fill'd my youthfull veines,
Runnes weakely in their pipes, and all the straines
Of musicke, which whilome pleasde mine eare,
Is now a burthen that Age cannot beare:
And therefore sweete Nature must pay his due,
To heauen must I, and leaue the earth with you.

 Dutchesse O say not so, lest that you kill my heart,
When death takes you, let life from me depart.

 Duke Content thy selfe, when ended is my date,
Thon maist (perchance) haue a more noble mate,
More wise, more youthfull, and one.

 Dutchesse O speake no more, for then I am accurst,
None weds the second, but she kils the first:
A second time I kill my Lord that's dead,
When second husband kisses me in bed.

 Ham. O wormewood, wormewood!

 Duke I doe beleeue you sweete, what now you speake,
But what we doe determine oft we breake,
For our demises stil are ouerthrowne,
Our thoughts are ours, their end's none of our owne:
So thinke you will no second husband wed,
But die thy thoughts, when thy first Lord is dead.

 Dutchesse Both here and there pursue me lasting strife,
If once a widdow, euer I be wife.

 Ham. If she should breake now.

 Duke T'is deepely sworne, sweete leaue me here a while,
My spirites growe dull, and faine I would beguile the tedious time with sleepe.

 Dutchesse Sleepe rocke thy braine,
And neuer come mischance betweene vs twaine. *exit Lady*

 Ham. Madam, how do you like this play?

 Queene The Lady protests too much.

 Ham. O but shee'le keepe her word.

 King Haue you heard the argument, is there no offence
in it?

                Ham.

Prince of Denmarke.

Ham. No offence in the world, poyfon in ieft, poifon in
King What do you call the name of the phy?			(ieft.
Ham. Moufe-trap: mary how trapically: this play is
The image of a murder done in *guyana*, *Albertus*
Was the Dukes name, his wife *Baptifta*,
Father, it is a knauifh peece a worke: but what
A that, it toucheth not vs, you and I that haue free
Soules, let the galld iade wince, this is one
Lucianus nephew to the King.

Ofel. Ya're as good as a *Chorus* my lord.

Ham. I could interpret the loue you beare, if I fawe the
poopies dallying.

Ofel. Y'are very pleafant my lord.

Ham. Who I, your onlie jig-maker, why what fhoulde
a man do but be merry? for looke how cheerefully my mother lookes, my father died within thefe two houres.

Ofel. Nay, t'is twice two months, my Lord.

Ham. Two months, nay then let the diuell weare blacke,
For i'le haue a fute of Sables : Iefus, two months dead,
And not forgotten yet? nay then there's fome
Likelyhood, a gentlemans death may outliue memorie,
But by my faith hee muft build churches then,
Or els hee muft follow the olde Epitphe,
With hoh, with ho, the hobi-horfe is forgot.

Ofel. Your iefts are keene my Lord.

Ham. It would coft you a groning to take them off.

Ofel. Still better and worfe.

Ham. So you muft take your husband, begin. Murdred
Begin, a poxe, leaue thy damnable faces and begin,
Come, the croking rauen doth bellow for reuenge.

Murd. Thoughts blacke, hands apt, drugs fit, and time
Confederate feafon, elfe no creature feeing:		(agreeing.
Thou mixture rancke, of midnight weedes collected,
With *Hecates* bane thrife blafted, thrife infected,
Thy naturall magicke, and dire propertie,
One wholefome life vfurps immediately.			*exit.*

Ham.

The Tragedy of Hamlet

Ham. Hepoyſons him for his eſtate.
King Lights, I will to bed.
Cor. The king riſes, lights hoe.

                      Exeunt King and Lordes.

Ham. What, frighted with falſe fires?
Then let the ſtricken deere goe weepe,
The Hart vngalled play,
For ſome muſt laugh, while ſome muſt weepe,
Thus runnes the world away.

    Hor. The king is mooued my lord.
    Ham. I *Horatio*, i'le take the Ghoſts word
For more then all the coyne in *Denmarke.*

           Enter Roſſencraft and Gilderſtone.

    Roſſ. Now my lord, how i'ſt with you?
    Ham. And if the king like not the tragedy,
Why then belike he likes it not perdy.
    Roſſ. We are very glad to ſee your grace ſo pleaſant,
My good lord, let vs againe intreate   (ture
To know of you the ground and cauſe of your diſtempera-
    Gil. My lord, your mother craues to ſpeake with you.
    Ham. We ſhall obey, were ſhe ten times our mother.
    Roſſ. But my good Lord, ſhall I intreate thus much?
    Ham. I pray will you play vpon this pipe?
    Roſſ. Alas my lord I cannot.
    Ham. Pray will you.
    Gil. I haue no skill my Lord.
    Ham. why looke, it is a thing of nothing,
'T is but ſtopping of theſe holes,
And with a little breath from your lips,
It will giue moſt delicate muſick.
    Gil. But this cannot wee do my Lord.
    Ham. Pray now, pray hartily, I beſeech you.
    Ros. My lord wee cannot.   (me?
    Ham. Why how vnworthy a thing would you make of
                                         You

Prince of Denmarke

You would feeme to know my ftops, you would play vpon
You would fearch the very inward part of my hart, mee,
And diue into the fecreet of my foule.
Zownds do you thinke I am eafier to be pla'yd
On, then a pipe? call mee what Inftrument
You will, though you can frett mee, yet you can not
Play vpon mee, befides, to be demanded by a fpunge.

Rof. How a fpunge my Lord?

Ham. I fir, a fpunge, that fokes vp the kings
Countenance, fauours, and rewardes, that makes
His liberalitie your ftore houfe : but fuch as you,
Do the king, in the end, beft feruife;
For hee doth keep you as an Ape doth nuttes,
In the corner of his Iaw, firft mouthes you,
Then fwallowes you : fo when hee hath need
Of you, t'is but fqueefing of you,
And fpunge, you fhall be dry againe, you fhall.

Rof. Wel my Lord wee'le take our leaue.

Ham Farewell, farewell, God bleffe you.

Exit Roffencraft and Gilderftone.

Enter Corambis

Cor. My lord, the Queene would fpeake with you.

Ham. Do you fee yonder clowd in the fhape of a camell?

Cor. T'is like a camell in deed.

Ham. Now me thinkes it's like a weafel.

Cor. T'is back't like a weafell.

Ham. Or like a whale.

Cor. Very like a whale. *exit Coram.*

Ham. Why then tell my mother i'le come by and by.
Good night Horatio.

Hor. Good night vnto your Lordfhip. *exit Horatio.*

Ham. My mother fhe hath fent to fpeake with me:
O God, let ne're the heart of *Nero* enter
This foft bofome.
Let me be cruell, not vnnaturall.

G I

I will speake daggers, those sharpe wordes being spent,
To doe her wrong my soule shall ne're consent.   *exit.*

Enter the King.

King O that this wet that falles vpon my face
Would wash the crime cleere from my conscience!
When I looke vp to heauen, I see my trespasse,
The earth doth still crie out vpon my fact,
Pay me the murder of a brother and a king,
And the adulterous fault I haue committed:
O these are sinnes that are vnpardonable:
Why say thy sinnes were blacker then is ieat,
Yet may contrition make them as white as snowe:
I but still to perseuer in a sinne,
It is an act gainst the vniuersall power,
Most wretched man, stoope, bend thee to thy prayer,
Aske grace of heauen to keepe thee from despaire.

hee kneeles.   enters Hamlet

Ham. I so, come forth and worke thy last,
And thus hee dies: and so am I reuenged:
No, not so: he tooke my father sleeping, his sins brim full,
And how his soule stoode to the state of heauen
Who knowes, saue the immortall powres,
And shall I kill him now,
When he is purging of his soule?
Making his way for heauen, this is a benefit,
And not reuenge: no, get thee vp agen,   (drunke,
When hee's at game swaring, taking his carowse, drinking
Or in the incestuous pleasure of his bed,
Or at some act that hath no relish
Of saluation in't, then trip him
That his heeles may kicke at heauen,
And fall as lowe as hel: my mother stayes,
This phisicke but prolongs thy weary dayes.   *exit Ham.*

King My wordes fly vp, my sinnes remaine below.

No

Prince of Denmarke.

No King on earth is safe, if Gods his foe.   *exit King.*
         Enter Queene and Corambis.

Cor. Madame, I heare yong Hamlet comming,
I'le shrowde my selfe behinde the Arras.   *exit Cor.*

Queene Do so my Lord.

Ham. Mother, mother, O are you here?
How i'st with you mother?

Queene How i'st with you?

Ham. I'le tell you, but first weele make all safe.

Queene Hamlet, thou hast thy father much offended.

Ham. Mother, you haue my father much offended.

Queene How now boy?

Ham. How now mother! come here, sit downe, for you
shall heare me speake.

Queene What wilt thou doe? thou wilt not murder me :
helpe hoe.

Cor. Helpe for the Queene.

Ham. I a Rat, dead for a Duckat.
Rash intruding foole, farewell,
I tooke thee for thy better.

Queene Hamlet, what hast thou done?

Ham. Not so much harme, good mother,
As to kill a king, and marry with his brother.

Queene How! kill a king!

Ham. I a King, nay sit you downe, and ere you part,
If you be made of penitrable stuffe,
I'le make your eyes looke downe into your heart,
And see how horride there and blacke it shews.   (words?

Queene Hamlet, what mean'st thou by these killing

Ham. Why this I meane, see here, behold this picture,
It is the portraiture, of your deceased husband,
See here a face, to outface *Mars* himselfe,
An eye, at which his foes did tremble at,
A front wherin all vertues are set downe
For to adorne a king, and guild his crowne,
Whose heart went hand in hand euen with that vow,

G 2   He

The Tragedy of Hamlet

He made to you in marriage, and he is dead.
Murdred, damnably murdred, this was your husband,
Looke you now, here is your husband,
With a face like *Vulcan*.
A looke fit for a murder and a rape,
A dull dead hanging looke, and a hell-bred eie,
To affright children and amaze the world:
And this same haue you left to change with this.
What Diuell thus hath cosoned you at hob-man blinde?
A! haue you eyes and can you looke on him
That flew my father, and your deere husband,
To liue in the inceftuous pleafure of his bed?
 Queene O Hamlet, fpeake no more.
 Ham. To leaue him that bare a Monarkes minde,
For a king of clowts, of very fhreads.
 Queene Sweete Hamlet ceafe.
 Ham. Nay but ftill to perfift and dwell in finne.
To fweate vnder the yoke of infamie,
To make increafe of fhame, to feale damnation.
 Queene Hamlet, no more.
 Ham. Why appetite with you is in the waine,
Your blood runnes backeward now from whence it came,
Who'le chide hote blood within a Virgins heart,
When luft fhall dwell within a matrons breaft?
 Queene Hamlet, thou cleaues my heart in twaine.
 Ham. O throw away the worfer part of it, and keepe the
better.
   Enter the ghoft in his night gowne.

Saue me, faue me, you gratious
Powers aboue, and houer ouer mee,
With your celeftiall wings.
Doe you not come your tardy fonne to chide,
That I thus long haue let reuenge flippe by?
O do not glare with lookes fo pittifull!
Left that my heart of ftone yeelde to compaffion,
         And

Prince of Denmarke.

And euery part that should assist reuenge,
Forgoe their proper powers, and fall to pitty.

   Ghost Hamlet, I once againe appeare to thee,
To put thee in remembrance of my death:
Doe not neglect, nor long time put it off.
But I perceiue by thy distracted lookes,
Thy mother's fearefull, and she stands amazde:
Speake to her Hamlet, for her sex is weake,
Comfort thy mother, Hamlet, thinke on me

   Ham. How i'st with you Lady?

   Queene Nay, how i'st with you
That thus you bend your eyes on vacancie,
And holde discourse with nothing but with ayre?

   Ham. Why doe you nothing heare?

   Queene Not I.

   Ham. Nor doe you nothing see?

   Queene No neither.   (habite

   Ham. No, why see the king my father, my father, in the
As he liued, looke you how pale he lookes,
See how he steales away out of the Portall,
Looke, there he goes.   *exit ghost.*

   Queene Alas, it is the weakenesse of thy braine,
Which makes thy tongue to blazon thy hearts griefe:
But as I haue a soule, I sweare by heauen,
I neuer knew of this most horride murder:
But Hamlet, this is onely fantasie,
And for my loue forget these idle fits.

   Ham. Idle, no mother, my pulse doth beate like yours,
It is not madnesse that possesseth Hamlet.
O mother, if euer you did my deare father loue,
Forbeare the adulterous bed to night,
And win your selfe by little as you may,
In time it may be you wil lothe him quite:
And mother, but assist mee in reuenge,
And in his death your infamy shall die.

   Queene Hamlet, I vow by that maiesty,
                  G 3   That

The Tragicall of Hamlet

That knowes our thoughts, and lookes into our hearts,
I will conceale, confent, and doe my beft,
What ftratagem foe're thou fhalt deuife.

  Ham. It is enough, mother good night:
Come fir, I'le prouide for you a graue,
Who was in life a foolifh prating knaue.

Exit Hamlet with the dead body.

Enter the King and Lordes.

  King Now Gertred, what fayes our fonne, how doe you
finde him?

  Queene Alas my lord, as raging as the fea:
Whenas he came, I firft befpake him faire,
But then he throwes and toffes me about,
As one forgetting that I was his mother:
At laft I call'd for help : and as I cried, *Corambis*
Call'd, which Hamlet no fooner heard, but whips me
Out his rapier, and cries, a Rat, a Rat, and in his rage
The good olde man he killes.

  King Why this his madneffe will vndoe our ftate.
Lordes goe to him, inquire the body out.

  Gil. We will my Lord.   *Exeunt Lordes.*

  King Gertred, your fonne fhall prefently to England,
His fhipping is already furnifhed,
And we haue fent by *Roffencraft* and *Gilderftone,*
Our letters to our deare brother of England,
For Hamlets welfare and his happineffe:
Happly the aire and climate of the Country
May pleafe him better than his natiue home:
See where he comes.

Enter Hamlet and the Lordes.

  Gil. My lord, we can by no meanes
Know of him where the body is.

  King Now fonne Hamlet, where is this dead body?

  Ham. At fupper, not where he is eating, but

Where

Prince of Denmarke.

Where he is eaten, a certaine company of politicke wormes
are euen now at him.
Father, your fatte King, and your leane Beggar
Are but variable seruices, two dishes to one messe:
Looke you, a man may fish with that worme
That hath eaten of a King,
And a Beggar eate that fish,
Which that worme hath caught.

   King What of this?

   Ham. Nothing father, but to tell you, how a King
May go a progresse through the guttes of a Beggar.

   King But sonne *Hamlet*, where is this body?

   Ham. In heau'n, if you chance to misse him there,
Father, you had best looke in the other partes below
For him, aud if you cannot finde him there,
You may chance to nose him as you go vp the lobby.

   King Make haste and finde him out.

   Ham. Nay doe you heare? do not make too much haste,
I'le warrant you hee'le stay till you come.

   King Well sonne *Hamlet*, we in care of you: but specially
in tender preseruation of your health,
The which we price euen as our proper selfe;
It is our minde you forthwith goe for *England*,
The winde sits faire, you shall aboorde to night,
Lord *Rossencraft* and *Gilderstone* shall goe along with you.

   Ham. O with all my heart: farewel mother.

   King Your louing father, *Hamlet*.

   Ham. My mother I say : you married my mother,
My mother is your wife, man and wife is one flesh,
And so (my mother) farewel: for England hoe.

        exeunt all but the king.

   king Gertred, leaue me,
And take your leaue of *Hamlet*,
To England is he gone, ne're to returne:
Our Letters are vnto the King of England,
That on the sight of them, on his allegeance,

                                He

He prefently without demaunding why,
That *Hamlet* loofe his head, for he muft die,
There's more in him than fhallow eyes can fee:
He once being dead, why then our ftate is free.   *exit.*

Enter Fortenbraffe, Drumme and Souldiers.

Fort. Captaine, from vs goe greete
The king of Denmarke:
Tell him that *Fortenbraffe* nephew to old *Norway,*
Craues a free paffe and conduct ouer his land,
According to the Articles agreed on:
You know our Randevous, goe march away.   *exeunt all.*

enter King and Queene.

King *Hamlet* is fhip't for England, fare him well,
I hope to heare good newes from thence ere long,
If euery thing fall out to our content,
As I doe make no doubt but fo it fhall.
  Queene God grant it may, heau'ns keep my *Hamlet* fafe:
But this mifchance of olde *Corambis* death,
Hath pierfed fo the yong *Ofeliaes* heart,
That fhe, poore maide, is quite bereft her wittes.
  King Alas deere heart! And on the other fide,
We vnderftand her brother's come from *France,*
And he hath halfe the heart of all our Land,
And hardly hee'le forget his fathers death,
Vnleffe by fome meanes he be pacified.
  Qu. O fee where the yong *Ofelia* is!

Enter Ofelia playing on a Lute, and her haire
downe finging.
  Ofelia How fhould I your true loue know
From another man?
By his cockle hatte, and his ftaffe,

                                        And

And his fandall fhoone.
White his fhrowde as mountaine fnowe,
Larded with fweete flowers,
That bewept to the graue did not goe
With true louers fhowers:
He is dead and gone Lady, he is dead and gone,
At his head a graffe greene turffe,
At his heeles a ftone.
  king How i'ft with you fweete *Ofelia?*
  Ofelia. Well God yeeld you,
It grieues me to fee how they laid him in the cold ground,
I could not chufe but weepe:
And will he not come againe?
And will he not come againe?
No, no, hee's gone, and we caft away mone,
And he neuer will come againe.
His beard as white as fnowe:
All flaxen was his pole,
He is dead, he is gone,
And we caft away moane:
God a mercy on his foule.
And of all chriften foules I pray God.
God be with you Ladies, God be with you. *exit Ofelia.*
  king A pretty wretch! this is a change indeede:
O Time, how fwiftly runnes our ioyes away?
Content on earth was neuer certaine bred,
To day we laugh and liue, to morrow dead.
How now, what noyfe is that?
          A noyfe within.   enter Leartes.
  Lear. Stay there vntill I come,
O thou vilde king, giue me my father:
Speake, fay, where's my father?
  king Dead.
  Lear. Who hath murdred him? fpeake, i'le not
Be juggled with, for he is murdred.
  Queene True, but not by him.

          H   *Leartes*

Lear. By whome, by heau'n I'le be refolued.

king Let him goe *Gertred*, away, I feare him not,
There's fuch diuinitie doth wall a king,
That treafon dares not looke on.
Let him goe *Gertred*, that your father is murdred,
T'is true, and we moft fory for it,
Being the chiefeft piller of our ftate:
Therefore will you like a moft defperate gamfter,
Swoop-ftake-like, draw at friend, and foe, and all?

Lear. To his good friends thus wide I'le ope mine arms,
And locke them in my hart, but to his foes,
I will no reconcilement but by bloud.

king Why now you fpeake like a moft louing fonne:
And that in foule we forrow for for his death,
Your felfe ere long fhall be a witneffe,
Meane while be patient, and content your felfe.

Enter Ofelia as before.

Lear. Who's this, *Ofelia*? O my deere fifter!
I'ft poffible a yong maides life,
Should be as mortall as an olde mans fawe?
O heau'ns themfelues! how now *Ofelia*?

Ofel. Wel God a mercy, I a bin gathering of floures:
Here, here is rew for you,
You may call it hearb a grace a Sundayes,
Heere's fome for me too: you muft weare your rew
With a difference, there's a dazie.
Here Loue, there's rofemary for you
For remembrance: I pray Loue remember,
And there's panfey for thoughts.

Lear. A document in madnes, thoughts, remembrance:
O God, O God!

Ofelia There is fennell for you, I would a giu'n you
Some violets, but they all withered, when
My father died: alas, they fay the owle was
A Bakers daughter, we fee what we are,
But can not tell what we fhall be.

　　　　　　　　　　　　　　　　　　　　　　For

Prince of Denmarke.

For bonny sweete Robin is all my ioy.

  Lear. Thoughts & afflictions, torments worse than hell.

  Ofel. Nay Loue, I pray you make no words of this now:
I pray now, you shall sing a downe,
And you a downe a, t'is a the Kings daughter
And the false steward, and if any body
Aske you of any thing, say you this.
To morrow is saint Valentines day,
All in the morning betime,
And a maide at your window,
To be your Valentine:
The yong man rose, and dan'd his clothes,
And dupt the chamber doore,
Let in the maide, that out a maide
Neuer departed more.
Nay I pray marke now,
By gisse, and by saint Charitie,
Away, and fie for shame:
Yong men will doo't when they come too't:
By cocke they are too blame.
Quoth she, before you tumbled me,
You promised me to wed.
So would I a done, by yonder Sunne,
If thou hadst not come to my bed.
So God be with you all, God bwy Ladies.
God bwy you Loue.   *exit Ofelia.*

  Lear. Griefe vpon griefe, my father murdered,
My sister thus distracted:
Cursed be his soule that wrought this wicked act.

  king Content you good Leartes for a time,
Although I know your griefe is as a floud,
Brimme full of sorrow, but forbeare a while,
And thinke already the reuenge is done
On him that makes you such a haplesse sonne.

  Lear. You haue preuail'd my Lord, a while I'le striue,
To bury griefe within a tombe of wrath,

H 2

Which

The Tragedy of Hamlet

Which once vnhearsed, then the world shall heare
Leartes had a father he held deere.

king No more of that, ere many dayes be done,
You shall heare that you do not dreame vpon.   *exeunt om.*

Enter *Horatio* and the *Queene.*

Hor. Madame, your sonne is safe arriv'de in *Denmarke,*
This letter I euen now receiv'd of him,
Whereas he writes how he escap't the danger,
And subtle treason that the king had plotted,
Being crossed by the contention of the windes,
He found the Packet sent to the king of *England,*
Wherein he saw himselfe betray'd to death,
As at his next conuersion with your grace,
He will relate the circumstance at full.

Queene Then I perceiue there's treason in his lookes
That seem'd to sugar o're his villanie:
But I will soothe and please him for a time,
For murderous mindes are alwayes jealous,
But know not you *Horatio* where he is?

Hor. Yes Madame, and he hath appoynted me
To meete him on the east side of the Cittie
To morrow morning.

Queene O faile not, good *Horatio*, and withall, com-
A mothers care to him, bid him a while   (mend me
Be wary of his presence, lest that he
Faile in that he goes about.

Hor. Madam, neuer make doubt of that:
I thinke by this the news be come to court:
He is arriv'de, obserue the king, and you shall
Quickely finde, *Hamlet* being here,
Things fell not to his minde.

Queene But what became of *Gilderstone* and *Rossencraft?*

Hor. He being set ashore, they went for *England,*
And in the Packet there writ down that doome
To be perform'd on them poynted for him:
And by great chance he had his fathers Seale,

So

Prince of Denmarke.

So all was done without difcouerie.

Queene Thankes be to heauen for bleffing of the prince,
Horatio once againe I take my leaue,
With thowfand mothers bleffings to my fonne.

   Horat. Madam adue.

      Enter King and Leartes.

   King. Hamlet from *England!* is it poffible?
What chance is this? they are gone, and he come home.

   Lear. O he is welcome, by my foule he is:
At it my iocund heart doth leape for ioy,
That I fhall liue to tell him, thus he dies.

   king Leartes, content your felfe, be rulde by me,
And you fhall haue no let for your reuenge.

   Lear. My will, not all the world.

   King Nay but Leartes, marke the plot I haue layde,
I haue heard him often with a greedy wifh,
Vpon fome praife that he hath heard of you
Touching your weapon, which with all his heart,
He might be once tasked for to try your cunning.

   Lea. And how for this?

   King Mary Leartes thus: I'le lay a wager,
Shalbe on *Hamlets* fide, and you fhall giue the oddes,
The which will draw him with a more defire,
To try the maiftry, that in twelue venies
You gaine not three of him : now this being granted,
When you are hot in midft of all your play,
Among the foyles fhall a keene rapier lie,
Steeped in a mixture of deadly poyfon,
That if it drawes but the leaft dramme of blood,
In any part of him, he cannot liue:
This being done will free you from fufpition,
And not the deereft friend that *Hamlet* lov'de
Will euer haue Leartes in fufpect.

   Lear. My lord, I like it well:
But fay lord *Hamlet* fhould refufe this match.

   King I'le warrant you, wee'le put on you

H 3

Such

Such a report of singularitie,
Will bring him on,although againſt his will.
And leſt that all ſhould miſſe,
I'le haue a potion that ſhall ready ſtand,
In all his heate when that he calles for drinke,
Shall be his period and our happineſſe.

    Lear. Tis excellent, O would the time were come!
Here comes the Queene.   *enter the Queene.*
    king How now Gertred,why looke you heauily?
    Queene O my Lord, the yong *Ofelia*
Hauing made a garland of ſundry ſortes of floures,
Sitting vpon a willow by a brooke,
The enuious ſprig broke, into the brooke ſhe fell,
And for a while her clothes ſpread wide abroade,
Bore the yong Lady vp: and there ſhe ſate ſmiling,
Euen Mermaide-like, twixt heauen and earth,
Chaunting olde ſundry tunes vncapable
As it were of her diſtreſſe, but long it could not be,
Till that her clothes, being heauy with their drinke,
Dragg'd the ſweete wretch to death.
    Lear. So,ſhe is drownde:
Too much of water haſt thou *Ofelia,*
Therefore I will not drowne thee in my teares,
Reuenge it is muſt yeeld this heart releeſe,
For woe begets woe,and griefe hangs on griefe.   *exeunt.*
       enter Clowne and an other.
    Clowne I ſay no, ſhe ought not to be buried
In chriſtian buriall.
    2. Why ſir?
    Clowne Mary becauſe ſhee's drownd.
    2. But ſhe did not drowne her ſelfe.
    Clowne No, that's certaine,the water drown'd her.
    2. Yea but it was againſt her will.
    Clowne No, I deny that, for looke you ſir, I ſtand here,
If the water come to me, I drowne not my ſelfe:
But if I goe to the water, and am there drown'd,
                             Ergo

Ergo I am guiltie of my owne death:
Y'are gone, goe y'are gone fir.

   2. I but fee, fhe hath chriftian buriall,
Becaufe fhe is a great woman.

   Clowne Mary more's the pitty, that great folke
Should haue more authoritie to hang òr drowne
Themfelues, more than other people:
Goe fetch me a ftope of drinke, but before thou
Goeft, tell me one thing, who buildes ftrongeft,
Of a Mafon, a Shipwright, or a Carpenter?

   2. Why a Mafon, for he buildes all of ftone,
And will indure long.

   Clowne That's prety, too't agen, too't agen.

   2. Why then a Carpenter, for he buildes the gallowes,
And that brings many a one to his long home.

   Clowne Prety agen, the gallowes doth well, mary howe
dooes it well ? the gallowes dooes well to them that doe ill,
goe get thee gone:
And if any one aske thee hereafter, fay,
A Graue-maker, for the houfes he buildes
Laft till Doomef-day. Fetch me a ftope of beere, goe.

           Enter Hamlet and Horatio.

   Clowne A picke-axe and a fpade,
A fpade for and a winding fheete,
Moft fit it is, for t'will be made,   *he throwes vp a fhouel.*
For fuch a gheft moft meete.

   Ham. Hath this fellow any feeling of himfelfe,
That is thus merry in making of a graue?
See how the flaue joles their heads againft the earth,

   Hor. My lord, Cuftome hath made it in him feeme no-

   Clowne A pick-axe and a fpade, a fpade,   (thing.
For and a winding fheete,
Moft fit it is for to be made,
For fuch a gheft moft meet.

   Ham. Looke you, there's another *Horatio.*

                    Why

Why mai't not be the scull of some Lawyer?
Me thinkes he should indite that fellow
Of an action of Batterie, for knocking
Him about the pate with's shouel: now where is your
Quirkes and quillets now, your vouchers and
Double vouchers, your leases and free-holde,
And tenements? why that same boxe there will scarse
Holde the conueiance of his land, and must
The honor lie there? O pittifull transformance!
I prethee tell me *Horatio*,
Is parchment made of sheep-skinnes?

    Hor. I my Lorde, and of calues-skinnes too.

    Ham. Ifaith they prooue themselues sheepe and calues
That deale with them, or put their trust in them.
There's another, why may not that be such a ones
Scull, that praised my Lord such a ones horse,
When he meant to beg him? *Horatio*, I prethee
Lets question yonder fellow.
Now my friend, whose graue is this?

    Clowne Mine sir.

    Ham. But who must lie in it?   (sir,

    Clowne If I should say, I should, I should lie in my throat

    Ham. What man must be buried here?

    Clowne No man sir.

    Ham. What woman?

    Clowne. No woman neither sir, but indeede
One that was a woman.

    Ham. An excellent fellow by the Lord *Horatio*,
This seauen yeares haue I noted it: the toe of the pesant,
Comes so neere the heele of the courtier,
That hee gawles his kibe, I prethee tell mee one thing,
How long will a man lie in the ground before hee rots?

    Clowne I faith sir, if hee be not rotten before
He be laide in, as we haue many pocky corses,
He will last you, eight yeares, a tanner
Will last you eight yeares full out, or nine.

                                                 Ham.

Prince of Denmarke

Ham. And why a tanner?

Clowne Why his hide is so tanned with his trade,
That it will holde out water, that's a parlous
Deuourer of your dead body, a great soaker.
Looke you, heres a scull hath bin here this dozen yeare,
Let me see, I euer since our last king *Hamlet*
Slew *Fortenbrasse* in combat, yong *Hamlets* father,
Hee that's mad.

Ham. I mary, how came he madde?

Clowne Ifaith very strangely, by loosing of his wittes.

Ham. Vpon what ground?

Clowne A this ground, in *Denmarke*,

Ham. Where is he now?

Clowne Why now they sent him to *England*.

Ham. To *England*! wherefore?

Clowne Why they say he shall haue his wittes there,
Or if he haue not, t'is no great matter there,
It will not be seene there.

Ham. Why not there?

Clowne Why there they say the men are as mad as he.

Ham. Whose scull was this?

Clowne This, a plague on him, a madde rogues it was,
He powred once a whole flagon of Rhenish of my head,
Why do not you know him? this was one *Yoricke* scull.

Ham. Was this? I prethee let me see it, alas poore *Yoricke*
I knew him *Horatio*,
A fellow of infinite mirth, he hath caried mee twenty times
vpon his backe, here hung those lippes that I haue Kissed a
hundred times, and to see, now they abhorre me : Wheres
your iests now *Yoricke*? your flashes of meriment : now go
to my Ladies chamber, and bid her paint her selfe an inch
thicke, to this she must come *Yoricke*. *Horatio*, I prethee
tell me one thing, doost thou thinke that *Alexander* looked
thus?

Hor. Euen so my Lord.

Ham. And smelt thus?

                              I   *Hor.*

Hor. I my lord, no otherwife.

Ham. No, why might not imagination worke, as thus of
Alexander, Alexander died, *Alexander* was buried, *Alexander*
became earth, of earth we make clay, and *Alexander* being
but clay, why might not time bring to paffe, that he might
ftoppe the boung hole of a beere barrell?
Imperious *Cefar* dead and turnd to clay,
Might ftoppe a hole, to keepe the winde away.

    /   *Enter King and Queene, Leartes, and other lordes,*
                  with a Prieft after the coffin.

Ham. What funerall's this that all the Court laments?
It fhews to be fome noble parentage:
Stand by a while.

    Lear. What ceremony elfe? fay, what ceremony elfe?
    Prieft My Lord, we haue done all that lies in vs,
And more than well the church can tolerate,
She hath had a Dirge fung for her maiden foule:
And but for fauour of the king, and you,
She had beene buried in the open fieldes,
Where now fhe is allowed chriftian buriall.

    Lear. So, I tell thee churlifh Prieft, a miniftring Angell
fhall my fifter be, when thou lieft howling.

    Ham. The faire *Ofelia* dead!

    Queene Sweetes to the fweete, farewell:
I had thought to adorne thy bridale bed, faire maide,
And not to follow thee vnto thy graue.

    Lear. Forbeare the earth a while: fifter farewelle
        Leartes leapes into the graue.
Now powre your earth on *Olympus* hie,
And make a hill to o're top olde *Pellon*:   *Hamlet leapes*
Whats he that coniures fo?   *in after Leartes*

    Ham. Beholde tis I, *Hamlet* the Dane.

    Lear. The diuell take thy foule.

    Ham. O thou praieft not well,
    I prethee take thy hand from off my throate,
For there is fomething in me dangerous,

                               Which

Prince of Denmarke.

Which let thy wiſedome feare, holde off thy hand:
I lou'de *Ofelia* as deere as twenty brothers could:
Shew me what thou wilt doe for her:
Wilt fight, wilt faſt, wilt pray,
Wilt drinke vp veſſels, eate a crocadile? Ile doot:
Com'ſt thou here to whine?
And where thou talk'ſt of burying thee a liue,
Here let vs ſtand : and let them throw on vs,
Whole hills of earth, till with the heighth therof,
Make Ooſell as a Wart.

 King. Forbeare *Leartes*, now is hee mad, as is the ſea,
Anone as milde and gentle as a Doue:
Therfore a while giue his wilde humour ſcope.

 Ham. What is the reaſon ſir that you wrong mee thus?
I neuer gaue you cauſe : but ſtand away,
A Cat will meaw, a Dog will haue a day.
    Exit Hamlet and Horatio.

 Queene. Alas, it is his madnes makes him thus,
And not his heart, *Leartes*.

 King. My lord, t'is ſo : but wee'le no longer trifle,
This very day ſhall *Hamlet* drinke his laſt,
For preſently we meane to ſend to him,
Therfore *Leartes* be in readynes.

 Lear. My lord, till then my ſoule will not bee quiet.

 King. Come *Gertrad*, wee'l haue *Leartes*, and our ſonne,
Made friends and Louers, as befittes them both,
Euen as they tender vs, and loue their countrie.

 Queene God grant they may: *exeunt omnes.*
    Enter Hamlet and Horatio

 Ham. beleeue mee, it greeues mee much *Horatio*,
That to *Leartes* I forgot my ſelfe :
For by my ſelfe me thinkes I feele his griefe,
Though there's a difference in each others wrong.
    Enter a Bragart Gentleman.

 Horatio, but marke yon water-flie,
The Court knowes him, but hee knowes not the Court.

     I 2   *Gen.*

Gent. Now God saue thee, sweete prince *Hamlet*.

Ham. And you sir: foh, how the muske-cod smels!

Gen. I come with an embassage from his maiesty to you

Ham. I shall sir giue you attention:

By my troth me thinkes t is very colde.

Gent. It is indeede very rawish colde.

Ham. T'is hot me thinkes.

Gent. Very swoltery hote:

The King, sweete Prince, hath layd a wager on your side,

Six Barbary horse, against six french rapiers,

With all their acoutrements too, a the carriages:

In good faith they are very curiously wrought.

Ham. The cariages sir, I do not know what you meane.

Gent. The girdles, and hangers sir, and such like.

Ham. The worde had beene more cosin german to the

phrase, if he could haue carried the canon by his side,

And howe's the wager? I vnderstand you now.

Gent. Mary sir, that yong Leartes in twelue venies

At Rapier and Dagger do not get three oddes of you,

And on your side the King hath laide,

And desires you to be in readinesse.

Ham. Very well, if the King dare venture his wager,

I dare venture my skull: when must this be?

Gent. My Lord, presently, the king and het maiesty,

With the rest of the best iudgement in the Court,

Are comming downe into the outward pallace.

Ham. Goe tell his maiestie, I wil attend him.

Gent. I shall deliuer your most sweet answer. *exit.*

Ham. You may sir, none better for y'are spiced,

Else he had a bad nose could not smell a foole.

Hor. He will disclose himselfe without inquirie.

Ham. Beleeue me *Horatio*, my hart is on the sodaine

Very sore, all here about.

Hor. My lord, forbeare the challenge then.

Ham. No *Horatio*, not I, if danger be now,

Why then it is not to come, theres a predestinate prouidence,

                                                        in

in the fall of a sparrow: heere comes the King.

Enter King, Queene, Leartes, Lordes.

King Now sonne *Hamlet*, we haue laid vpon your head,
And make no question but to haue the best.

Ham. Your maiestie hath laide a the weaker side.

King We doubt it not, deliuer them the foiles.

Ham. First Leartes, heere's my hand and loue,
Protesting that I neuer wrongd *Leartes*.
If *Hamlet* in his madnesse did amisse,
That was not *Hamlet*, but his madnes did it,
And all the wrong I e're did to *Leartes*,
I here proclaime was madnes, therefore lets be at peace,
And thinke I haue shot mine arrow o're the house,
And hurt my brother.

Lear. Sir I am satisfied in nature,
But in termes of honor I'le stand aloofe,
And will no reconcilement,
Till by some elder maisters of our time
I may be satisfied.

King Giue them the foyles.

Ham. I'le be your foyle *Leartes*, these foyles,
Haue all a laught, come on sir: *a bit.*

Lear. No none.   *Heere they play.*

Ham. Iudgement.

Gent. A hit, a most palpable hit.

Lear. Well, come againe.   *They play againe.*

Ham. Another. Iudgement.

Lear. I, I grant, a tuch, a tuch.

King Here *Hamlet*, the king doth drinke a health to thee

Queene Here *Hamlet*, take my napkin, wipe thy face.

King Giue him the wine.

Ham. Set it by, I'le haue another bowt first,
I'le drinke anone.

Queene Here *Hamlet*, thy mother drinkes to thee.

Shee drinkes.

King Do not drinke *Gertred* : O t'is the poysned cup!

I 3   *Ham.*

[61]

Ham. *Leartes* come, you dally with me,
I pray you paſſe with your moſt cunningſt play.
    Lear. I! ſay you ſo? haue at you,
Ile hit you now my Lord:
And yet it goes almoſt againſt my conſcience.
    Ham. Come on ſir.

    They catch one anothers Rapiers, and both are wounded,
    Leartes falles downe, the Queene falles downe and dies.

    King Looke to the Queene.
    Queene O the drinke, the drinke, Hamlet, the drinke.
    Ham. Treaſon, ho, keepe the gates.
    Lords How iſt my Lord *Leartes?*
    Lear. Euen as a coxcombe ſhould,
Fooliſhly ſlaine with my owne weapon:
Hamlet, thou haſt not in thee halfe an houre of life,
The fatall Inſtrument is in thy hand.
Vnbated and invenomed: thy mother's poyſned
That drinke was made for thee.
    Ham. The poyſned Inſtrument within my hand?
Then venome to thy venome, die damn'd villaine:
Come drinke, here lies thy vnion here.   *The king dies.*
    Lear. O he is iuſtly ſerued:
Hamlet, before I die, here take my hand,
And withall, my loue: I doe forgiue thee.   *Leartes dies.*
    Ham. And I thee, O I am dead *Horatio*, fare thee well.
    Hor. No, I am more an antike Roman,
Then a Dane, here is ſome poiſon left.
    Ham. Vpon my loue I charge thee let it goe,
O fie *Horatio*, and if thou ſhouldſt die,
What a ſcandale wouldſt thou leaue behinde?
What tongue ſhould tell the ſtory of our deaths,
If not from thee? O my heart ſinckes *Horatio*,
Mine eyes haue loſt their ſight, my tongue his vſe:
Farewel *Horatio*, heauen receiue my ſoule.   *Ham. dies.*
                                       Enter

Prince of Denmarke.

Enter Voltemar and the Ambaſſadors from England.
enter Fortenbraſſe with his traine.

Fort. Where is this bloudy fight?

Hor. If aught of woe or wonder you'ld behold,
Then looke vpon this tragicke ſpeĉtacle.

Fort. O imperious death! how many Princes
Haſt thou at one draft bloudily ſhot to death?   (land,

Ambaſſ. Our ambaſſie that we haue brought from Eng-
Where be theſe Princes that ſhould heare vs ſpeake?
O moſt moſt vnlooked for time! vnhappy country.

Hor. Content your ſelues, Ile ſhew to all, the ground,
The firſt beginning of this Tragedy:
Let there a ſcaffold be rearde vp in the market place,
And let the State of the world be there:
Where you ſhall heare ſuch a ſad ſtory tolde,
That neuer mortall man could more vnfolde.

Fort. I haue ſome rights of memory to this kingdome,
Which now to claime my leiſure doth inuite mee:
Let foure of our chiefeſt Captaines
Beare *Hamlet* like a ſouldier to his graue:
For he was likely, had he liued,
To a prou'd moſt royall.
Take vp the bodie, ſuch a ſight as this
Becomes the fieldes, but here doth much amiſſe.

Finis

BIBLIOGRAPHY

BRENNECKE, ERNEST, ed. and trans. *Der Bestrafte Brudermord, oder Prinz Hamlet aus Dänemarck.* In *Shakespeare in Germany, 1590-1700, With Translations of Five Early Plays.* Chicago: University of Chicago Press, 1964.

ELIOT, T. S. "Hamlet and His Problems." In *Twentieth Century Interpretations of Hamlet: A Collection of Critical Essays,* edited by David Bevington. Englewood Cliffs, NJ: Prentice Hall, 1968.

FOSTER, JOHN. *A Shakespeare Word-Book.* New York: Russell and Russell, 1908, 1969.

FURNESS, HORACE HOWARD, ed. *A New Variorum Edition of Shakespeare. Hamlet,* Vols. 1 and 2. Philadelphia: J. B. Lippincott and Company, 1877; New York: Dover Publications, 1963.

GIBSON, WILLIAM. *Shakespeare's Game.* New York: Atheneum, 1978.

GOLLANCZ, SIR ISRAEL, ed. *The Sources of "Hamlet": With Essay on the Legend by Sir Israel Gollancz.* London: Oxford University Press, 1926.

GOLLANCZ, ISRAEL. Preface to *The Tragedy of Hamlet, Prince of Denmark.* Vol. 5 of *The Works of William Shakespeare,* De Luxe ed., edited by J. Ellis Burdick. New York: Bigelow, Smith and Company, 1909.

HARRISON, G. B., ed. Introduction to *The Harbinger Shakespeare: Hamlet Prince of Denmark.* New York and Burlingame: Harcourt, Brace and World, 1948, 1952.

HARTLEY, DOROTHY. *Lost Country Life.* New York: Pantheon Books, 1979.

HEMINGE, JOHN AND HENRY CONDELL, comps. *Mr. William Shakespeares Comedies, Histories, and Tragedies.* London: Isaac Jaggard and Ed. Blount, 1623. Facsimile ed. prepared by Helga Kokeritz. New Haven: Yale University Press, 1954; London: Oxford University Press, 1954.

HOTSON, LESLIE, *Mr W. H.* London: Rupert Hart-Davis, 1964.

JENKINS, HAROLD, ed. *Hamlet,* Vol. 12 of *The Arden Shakespeare.* London and New York: Methuen, 1981.

JONES, ERNEST. *Hamlet and Oedipus.* London: V. Gollancz, 1949.

KITTREDGE, GEORGE LYMAN, ed. *The Tragedy of Hamlet Prince of Denmark.* Boston and New York: Ginn and Company, 1939.

MARTIN, M. R., and R. C. HARRIER. *The Concise Encyclopedic Guide to Shakespeare.* New York: Horizon Press, 1971.

OLIVIER, SIR LAURENCE. *Laurence Olivier on Acting.* New York: Simon and Schuster, 1986.

RHYS, E., ed. *The Complete Plays of Ben Jonson.* London and Toronto: J. M. Dent and Sons, Ltd., 1925; New York: E. P. Dutton and Company, 1960.

Shakespeare's Hamlet, The First Quarto, 1603. Facsimile ed. San Marino, CA: Henry E. Huntington Library, 1931.

Shakespeare's Hamlet, The Second Quarto, 1604. Facsimile ed. San Marino, CA: Henry E. Huntington Library, 1938.

TYNAN, KENNETH. *Curtains.* New York: Atheneum, 1961.

WIMSATT, W. K., JR., ed. SAMUEL JOHNSON ON SHAKESPEARE, New York: Hill and Wang, 1960.

INDEX

Page numbers in brackets refer to our facsimile edition of Q1.

CHRONOLOGY OF THE ACTION
IN THE FIRST QUARTO

The following is a chronological index of the action in Quarto One as analyzed in Chapter Two. In addition, the page numbers in brackets locate the action in our facsimile of Q1.

ACT I: pp. 25-27, [1-19]
Scene i: first platform scene
    sentinels change watch; Horatio and Marcellus enter, 25, [1]
    Ghost appears and disappears twice, 25, [2, 4]
    Horatio explains reasons for warlike preparations, peace being threatened by young Fortenbrasse of Norway, 25, [3-4]
    watch breaks up with decision to report appearance of Ghost to Hamlet, 25-26, [5]

Scene ii: first court scene
    King sends Cornelia and Voltemar to negotiate peace with Norway; gives Leartes permission to return to France, 26, [5-6]
    King and Queen persuade Hamlet to remain in Denmark; King rebukes him for long mourning, 26, [6]
    court exits, leaving Hamlet alone on stage for soliloquy decrying his mother's second marriage, 26, [7]
    Horatio and Marcellus enter and report Ghost's appearing to them; Hamlet agrees to join them that night, 26, [7-10]

Scene iii: a room in Corambis's house
    Leartes warns Ofelia against Hamlet's suit, 26, [10-11]
    Corambis gives precepts to Leartes, 26, [11-12]
    Corambis warns Ofelia against Hamlet, forbidding any communication with him, 26, [12]

Scenes iv and v: second and third platform scenes
    Hamlet, entering with Marcellus and Horatio, is led to a place apart by Ghost who tells how he was murdered, calling on Hamlet to right the wrongs committed, but not to conspire against his mother, 27, [12-16]
    Marcellus and Horatio join Hamlet, who does not reveal what he has learned, but swears them to secrecy about that night's

events and to antic disposition he may assume, 27, [17-18]
Hamlet curses his fate, despite his expressed determination, 27, [19]

ACT II: pp. 28-39, [19-33]
Scene i: a room in Corambis's house
Corambis sends Montano to Leartes in Paris, 28, [19-20]
Ofelia describes Hamlet's frightening appearance and behavior,
28, [20-21]
Corambis concludes Hamlet's madness is due to Ofelia's rejec-
tion; he says "Lets to the King," 28, [21]

Scene ii: second court scene
King instructs Rossencraft and Gilderstone to seek cause of
Hamlet's behavior, 28, [21]
Corambis and Ofelia enter; Cornelia and Voltemar report success-
ful negotiations with Norway, 28, [21-22]
Corambis expounds his theory of cause of Hamlet's "lunacie";
Corambis proposes overheard encounter between Hamlet and
Ofelia, 28-29, [23-24]
Hamlet enters with "To be, or not to be"; encounters Ofelia,
29-34, [24-27]
King is dubious that it is love that troubles Hamlet, 34, [27]
Hamlet makes a fool of Corambis when approached by Corambis
alone, 34, [27-28]
Rossencraft and Gilderstone admit to Hamlet they were sent
for by King; they announce the approach of Players, 34,
[28-29]
Corambis announces arrival of Players, 34, [29-30]
Hamlet and Players recite passionate speech; he plans with
Players, to put on *The Murder of Gonzago,* with a dozen or
sixteen lines inserted by him, 34-37, [30-32]
Hamlet has his soliloquy, "Why what a dunghill slave am I?,"
37-39, [32-33]

ACT III: pp. 39-55, [33-46]
Scene i: third court scene
Rossencraft and Gilderstone announce the play; King and Queen
agree to attend, 39, [33-34]
King and Queen agree to Corambis's plan for Queen to interview Hamlet after the play, with Corambis eavesdropping,
39-40, [34]

Scene ii: a room in the castle

> Hamlet instructs Players on delivery of lines; castigates clowns, 40, [35-36]
>
> Hamlet alerts Horatio to watch King during the play, 40-41, [36]
>
> Hamlet , Ofelia, King, and Queen engage in byplay as Players perform, 41-48, [36-39]
>
> Players perform *The Murder of Gonzago,* including Hamlet's ten lines for the Duchess and six lines for the Murderer, 43-49, [37-39]
>
> King breaks off the performance and exits; Hamlet and Horatio agree the King is guilty, 49, [40]
>
> first Rossencraft and Gilderstone, and then Corambis, summon Hamlet to his mother, 49, [40-41]
>
> Hamlet prepares himself for the meeting with soliloquy, "My mother she hath sent to speake with me," 49-50, [41-42]

Scene iii: a room in the castle

> Hamlet comes upon King kneeling, 50-51, [42-43]
>
> Hamlet mistakes King's outward semblance of repentance for true repentance; decides against immediate revenge, 51-52, [42-43]

Scene iv: Queen's bedroom scene

> Hamlet confronts his mother, stabs the eavesdropping Corambis through the arras, suggests his mother may have killed a king and married with his brother, 52-53, [43]
>
> Hamlet specifically accuses her present husband of his father's murder, 53-54, [43-44]
>
> Ghost enters to protect Queen when Hamlet rails against the marriage, 54, [44-45]
>
> Queen vows innocence of the murder and Hamlet confides that he is sane, 55, [45]
>
> Queen promises secrecy and help with the revenge; Hamlet exits with dead body of Corambis, 55, [45-46]

Act IV: pp. 56-71, [46-54]

Scene i: a room in the castle

> King questions Hamlet about where he has hidden the body of Corambis; Hamlet continues to assume the antic disposition; Hamlet leaves for England; King, alone, reveals death-plot 58-60, [46-48]

Scene ii: a plain in Denmark
Fortenbrasse enters, dispatches Captain to request a permit over the land; all exit, 60, [48]

Scene iii: a room in the castle
King ambiguously predicts "good news" from England to Queen, 60, [48]
Queen announces Ofelia's madness and King reports Leartes's rebellious return from Paris, 61, [48]
Ofelia sings farewell song (first mad scene), 61-63, [48-49]
King reacts, 63, [49]
Leartes enters and threatens King, with Queen intervening, 64-65, [49-50]
Ofelia distributes flowers (second mad scene) and sings valentine song, 65-67, [50-51]
King quiets Leartes by prophesying that he will be revenged, 67-68, [51-52]

Scene iv: a room in the castle
Horatio brings Queen news of Hamlet's escape from King's treasonous plan, 68-69, [52-53]
Queen is shown as an ally to Hamlet while continuing her role as wife of King, 68-69, [52]
Horatio discloses the fate of Rossencraft and Gilderstone to Queen, 69, [52-53]

Scene v: a room in the castle
King, having heard of Hamlet's escape, persuades Leartes to plan a fatal duel between himself and Hamlet, 69-71, [53-54]
Queen describes Ofelia's death by drowning, 71, [54]

ACT V: pp. 71-86, [54-63]
Scene i: the graveyard scene
two Clowns discuss suicide and their profession of grave-digging, 71-72, [54-55]
Clown 1 remains on stage as Hamlet and Horatio enter, 72, [55]
Hamlet philosophizes as he observes the matter-of-fact Clown; Clown turns up a skull and identifies it as a "madde rogue"'s, 72-74, [56-57]
Hamlet learns the skull was Yoricke's; reflects on the universal ignominy of the dead, 74-75, [57-58]

a funeral procession enters revealing Ofelia's death to Hamlet; he announces himself as royal *("Hamlet* the Dane") and confronts Leartes in Ofelia's grave, 75-77, [58-59]

Hamlet indirectly accuses Leartes of being a rebel; Hamlet and Horatio exit, 77-78, [59]

King promises Leartes that Hamlet will die that night, but tells Queen the duel will reconcile her son and Leartes, 78-79, [59]

Scene ii: a hall in the castle

Hamlet confides to Horatio that he forgot himself to Leartes, 79, [59]

terms of the duel are announced to Hamlet by braggart Gentleman, 79-80, [59-60]

Hamlet accepts the duel, 80, [60]

Hamlet has premonition of danger, but when Horatio suggests that he forebear the duel, he rejects the suggestion and leaves all to "predestinate providence," 80, [60-61]

court assembles for the duel, 81, [61]

Hamlet begins duel scene with an apology to Leartes, who partially accepts it, 81, [61]

the duel begins, the first two hits, 82-83, [61]

divine intervention upsets King's plot: Queen unexpectedly drinks from the poisoned cup; and the foils are exchanged so that the poisoned sword, after wounding Hamlet, wounds Leartes, 83, [61-62]

Queen gives her redeeming cry; Leartes reveals plot of the poisoned foil; Hamlet takes command and kills King with King's own weapons; Leartes and Hamlet exchange forgiveness; Leartes dies, 84, [62]

Hamlet forestalls Horatio's suicide to request that Horatio tell Hamlet's story so that his name may be cleared of scandal, 85-86, [62]

Hamlet dies, 86, [62]

Fortenbrasse enters; ambassadors return from England; Horatio orders a scaffold reared in the marketplace where the sad story will be told; Fortenbrasse lays claim to the kingdom and orders Hamlet to be carried like a soldier to his grave, 86, [63]

COLOPHON

*The text of this edition has been prepared by Maxwell E. Foster
and edited by Anne Shiras. Typography and printing by
Davis & Warde, Inc., Pittsburgh, under the supervision of
James J. Sommer. Text is set in Century Old Style.
Printed on Warren seventy pound Patina matte.
Bound by Steadfast Bookbinding, Pittsburgh.*